New Horizons in Journalism

Howard Rusk Long, *General Editor*

News from the Capital

The Story of Washington Reporting

By **F. B. MARBUT**

Foreword by Howard Rusk Long

Southern Illinois University Press   *Carbondale and Edwardsville*

Feffer & Simons, Inc.   London and Amsterdam

Contents

List of Illustrations

Authority attempts to keep its own counsel. Legislators, magistrates, bureaucrats, and managers of great enterprises prefer fog to sunlight. Those who govern would remain forever behind closed doors except for the necessity, from time to time, to rationalize their actions to the governed. In contrast the people whose fortunes rest upon the decisions of their rulers, political, economic or spiritual, search the wind for every straw of enlightenment. For the most part it has been an unequal contest. Chinese emperors removed the heads of servants who gossiped in the tea houses. English history is filled with the names of men punished at the hands of king or Parliament for daring to tell what they believed others should know.

But the democratic institutions cherished in Britain and America finally came into being because brave men won the right to report the news of government and to comment freely upon the actions of public officials. In his reference to the Fourth Estate, Macaulay, in 1828, simply acknowledged the truism that representative government cannot exist without a press to enlighten the people. In the American struggle for freedom and unity the people were well served by a vigorous press, which by the time the new nation had made Washington its capital, had fully established its role in the governing process.

Professor Marbut picks up this story in the administration of Thomas Jefferson and, with the rare, ripe scholarship so frequently idealized to his students by the late Frank Luther Mott, carries it forward from the first official report of the successful Lewis and Clark expedition to the part played by the press in the Bay of Pigs fiasco. This work, however, is more than a catalog of journalists covering the news in Washington and their relationships with those at the source of news.

If journalists participate in the political process the history of journalism can best be understood as only a few threads in a complete fabric. And this is the method of Professor Marbut. The act of the journalist thus becomes more significant in the light of his association with the event or series of events. These events likewise assume new perspectives when related to the part played by the journalist. Thus the struggle of some reporters for access to information, the willingness of others to serve as pawns of their sources, and the resulting punishment or rewards, are a part of the action which made the history of our nation what it is.

From Jefferson to Kennedy journalists had supporting roles in all the great events. On obscure occasions theirs were the leading parts. They made their mistake no more and no less than the politicians and the statesmen. The important thing is that they were there. Looking ahead, it is even more important to the future that in Washington and at whatever place in the universe the influence of Washington is felt, representatives of the press continue their presence among the great, the near great and the functionaries. For the sake of our nation it is important that the press, in the name of the people, continue to observe and report, to analyze, to criticize and to antagonize, in the future, as in the past, those at the pressure points of power.

Howard Rusk Long

Carbondale, Illinois
December 10, 1970

The son of a government scientist, I lived in Washington through most of my childhood and I earned my undergraduate degree at George Washington University. I worked as a copy reader on the *Evening Star* and as a rewrite man on the Washington *Times,* holding each job for several months, and I was a reporter in the Washington bureau of the Associated Press for more than four years between 1933 and 1937. Thus I was a member of the congressional press galleries and of the White House Correspondents Association. I also worked on some Middle Western newspapers and for the Associated Press in Connecticut.

In 1938 I entered the Harvard Graduate School. I earned the degree of doctor of philosophy in history partially by writing a dissertation on the "History of Washington Newspaper Correspondence to 1861." From 1950 to 1955 I carried on research to bring the study up to date and to rewrite the whole as a book. Then various problems forced me to turn away from it. I found it possible to turn my attention to this study again in 1967.

My adviser when I wrote my doctoral dissertation was Dr. Arthur M. Schlesinger. In a letter to me shortly before he died he expressed surprise that he had not seen my thesis in print. I regret that he did not live to see it come out. But I take this opportunity to join the ranks of his doctoral candidates who are deeply indebted for his guidance.

Another who, I am very sorry to say, did not live to see between covers the book to which he contributed a great deal and to whom my most heartfelt thanks are due is James D. Preston. Jim's father was Washington correspondent for the New York *Herald* in the closing decades of the last Century. Jim was a newspaperman, superintendent of the Senate press gallery, an employee of the Secretary of the Senate, at one time consultant to Hollywood in making a motion picture revolving around that body, and a lifetime student of the Washington press and its history. He told me much that came from his own memory and research and he directed me to source material which I would not otherwise have uncovered. And he read an earlier draft of the book. He died on January 31, 1959, at the age of eighty-three.

David Rankin Barbee, a former Washington correspondent who devoted his retirement to research on the Civil War period, likewise occupies a high place on the list of those to whom I am indebted. He directed me to material, principally in manuscript sources and newspaper files in the Library of Congress, which has been invaluable. Dr. Elizabeth Gregory McPherson of the Manuscript Division of the Library of Congress was helpful through her knowledge of that collection and through her own research on a field closely related to mine.

Mrs. Beth Campbell Short and former President Truman opened the way for me to use a then unpublished report on the Office of War Information. It came about originally through Lloyd A. Lehrbas. He, like both Mrs. Short and her husband, Joseph H. Short, Truman's press secretary, were coworkers of my own in the Associated Press. In 1952 Mr. Lehrbas, then attached to the State Department, started wheels moving which resulted in my being allowed to examine the department's typescript copy of the report which Elmer Davis submitted to the president when the OWI ceased to operate in 1945. I asked Mr. Davis for permission to quote from the document. He replied that he was willing but that since it was a report to the White House, clearance must come from there. While this correspondence was being carried on, Mr. Short died suddenly, to the sorrow of his former fellow workers who, like myself, regarded him with affection for his personal qualities and respect for his professional ability. Soon thereafter President Truman appointed Mrs. Short to the White House staff. I wrote to her, and she secured the desired permission from the president. Thus President Truman, Mr. Davis, Mrs. Short and Mr. Lehrbas all have claims on my gratitude.

Dr. Milton S. Eisenhower read an earlier draft of the chapters on the history of government information services and of the OWI and made suggestions which were incorporated. Others who read those chapters and offered corrections were: Mr. Davis; Theodore F. Koop, formerly with the Office of Censorship and now a vice

president of the Columbia Broadcasting System; Michael J. Mc-
Dermott, former special assistant to the secretary of state for press
relations, and C. Herschel Schooley, former Department of Defense director of information. Mr. Schooley also laid the copy
which I sent to him before some of the veteran Pentagon correspondents. My thanks are due to Mr. Koop not only for help on
these chapters but also for providing me with certain information
about the National Press Club, of which he was president in 1953.

There were others who helped, in 1953 and 1954, with the
chapters on the information services. I wish in particular to express my appreciation to Lt. Col. Frederick D. Blanchard of the
Office of Information, Department of the Army; Commander
James C. Shaw, Office of Information, Department of the Navy;
Captain Walter Karig, former special assistant to the secretary of
the Navy; Miss Helene Philibert, who worked for several years in
the information section of the Office of Naval Intelligence, and
Robinson McIlvaine, former assistant to the assistant secretary of
state for public affairs.

Paul Wooton, correspondent for the New Orleans *Times-
Picayune* and some trade journals, provided me in personal inter-
views with information about the White House Correspondents'
Association. Mr. Short and E. B. Vaccaro, president of the association in 1952, arranged for me to copy its charter in the White
House press room. Katherine Brooks of the *Evening Star*, Marie
Sauer of the *Post* and Margaret A. Kilgore of United Press International gave me material on the women's press clubs. Clayton
Knowles of the New York *Times,* chairman of the Standing Committee of Correspondents in 1952, secured the committee's permission to examine its records. Harold R. Beckley, then superintendent of the Senate press gallery and custodian of the records,
provided them and allowed me to work at his own desk to take
notes.

The Radio and Television Correspondents' Association gave
me the same privilege, by order of Richard Harkness of the National Broadcasting Company, its president in 1954. D. Harold
McGrath, then superintendent of the Senate radio and television
gallery, gave me the records from his files and a place to work as
Mr. Beckley had done. Mr. McGrath and Robert M. Menaugh,
superintendent of the House radio and television gallery, discussed with me many phases of the history of the radio and tele-

vision facilities. In 1968 Menaugh brought me up to date on later developments. Although I called on them in June 1954, when the hearings before a Senate investigations subcommittee on the dispute between Senator Joseph R. McCarthy and the army were forcing them to work for exhausting hours, several radio correspondents took the time to grant me interviews and give me the benefit of their memory of events in which they took part. They were Fulton Lewis, Jr. of the Mutual Broadcasting System, Bryson Rash of the American Broadcasting Company, Lewis B. Shollenberger of the Columbia Broadcasting System, and Fred Morrison of the National Broadcasting Company. William M. Perry, superintendent of the Senate periodical press gallery, and George Cullen, another Associated Press coworker of mine and president of the Periodical Correspondents' Association in 1954, gave me data on that organization. Frank McNaughton, former correspondent of *Time*, later associated with Senator Paul H. Douglas of Illinois, wrote to me an extended letter on the history of the magazine's Washington bureau.

I called on several other Washington newsmen for answers to specific questions as they arose. Among those who responded with personal letters are: David Lawrence, publisher of *U.S. News & World Report;* Frederick A. Emery, a Washington newspaperman for more than fifty years; John Russell Young, for many years White House reporter for the *Evening Star* and later a District of Columbia commissioner; Mrs. Elisabeth May Craig, correspondent for the Guy Gannett chain of Maine newspapers, and columnist William S. White. White had been another of my fellow workers in Associated Press days. The Honorable Joseph W. Martin, Speaker of the House of Representatives in the Eighty-third Congress, answered my query to straighten me out on the application of a rule. Frank Cormier and Douglas B. Cornell, Associated Press correspondents at the White House, filled me in during two different telephone interviews on some points regarding Nixon's relations with the press. Cornell, a longtime staff member, was another fellow worker of my own in my days on the Associated Press staff. When I resumed work on the book after 1967 among those who helped me were: Robert J. McCloskey, deputy assistant secretary of state for public affairs; William E. Odom, special assistant to the assistant secretary of defense for public affairs; Ernest K. Lindley, special assistant to the secretary of state, and

Jack Matteson of the staff of the Government Information Sub-committee of the House Committee on Government Operations.

Most of my research was done in the Library of Congress and the National Archives. I have also examined newspaper files, manuscripts, or other documents in the libraries of the University of Illinois, the University of Pennsylvania, the Pennsylvania State University, and the Historical Society of Pennsylvania. Photostats were provided at my request by the New York Historical Society and the John Carter Brown Library of Brown University. My thanks go out to the staffs of all of these institutions.

It is customary in such acknowledgments as this for the writer to add his own wife to those to whom he extends appreciation. It is peculiarly appropriate for me to do so. Novelist Ann Marbut, author of *A Bill of Particulars* and *The Tarnished Tower*, is a valuable and helpful critic of the literary structure of my own writing. More than that, however, I am indebted to her for the patience she displayed when I disappeared for long periods in Washington leaving her alone to handle the problems of growing children and other complications.

F. B. Marbut

Pennsylvania Furnace, Pennsylvania
January 1, 1971

1. News in Washington: 1806 and 1969

Captains Meriwether Lewis and William Clark, at the head of an exploring expedition of forty-two men, reached the Mandan Indian villages on the Missouri River in the autumn of 1804 and passed the winter there. From that point they sent part of their force back with a report to President Thomas Jefferson. Then they disappeared. Their president and fellow citizens in the settled parts of the country heard nothing more from them until after they reached the west coast and then returned to St. Louis. They arrived in that city on September 23, 1806.

Jefferson must have been excited and relieved as he sat at his desk in the executive mansion to tell the country that they were back and safe. He wrote the following note to Samuel Harrison Smith, who published the *National Intelligencer* in a small building on the broad, unpaved thoroughfare called Pennsylvania Avenue.

ThJ to mr. Smith
Mr. Smith may notify in his paper that I have received a letter from Capt. Lewis dated at St. Louis Sep. 23 at that place. himself capt. Clarke & their party arrived that day. they had past the preceding winter at a place which he calls Fort Clatsop near the mouth of the Columbia river. They set out thence on the 27th of March last, and arrived at the foot of the Rocky Mountains May 10, where they were detained until June 24, by the snows which rendered the passage over those mountains impracticable until then. he found it 2575 miles from the mouth of the Missouri to the great falls of that river, thence by

*land passing the Rocky Mountains to a navigable part of the Koos-
kooske 340 miles of which 200 would admit good road and 140 miles
over tremendous mountains which for 60 miles are covered with eternal snows. then 73 miles down the Kooskooske into a South Eastwardly
branch of the Columbia, and then 413 miles to the Pacific in all 3555
miles from the mouth of the Missouri to the mouth of the Columbia.
In this last river the tide flows 183 miles, to within 7 miles of it's great
rapids, and so far would admit large periaugurs. he speaks of this
whole line furnishing the most valuable furs in the world and a short
and direct course for them to the Eastern coast of China; but that the
greatest part of these would be from the head of the Missouri. he says
it is fortunate he did not send back from the head of the Missouri any
part of his force, consisting of 31. men, as more than once they owed
their lives & the fate of the expedition to their numbers. one man of
his party, had died when he reached fort Mandan in 1804. every other
one is returned in good health.*

*Capt. Lewis expected to remain at St. Louis some days to settle
with and discharge his men, and would then set out for Washington,
by the way of Vincennes, Louisville, Abington, Fincastle, Staunton and
Charlottesville. he is accompanied by the great Mandan chief, who is
on a visit to Washington. Capt. Lewis speaks of his colleague, Capt.
Clarke, in the most affectionate terms, and declares his equal title to
whatever merit may be ascribed to the success of that enterprise.*

The *National Intelligencer* of October 27, thirty-four days
after the explorers reached St. Louis, announced their safe return. Its account opened:

> It is with the sincerest pleasure, that we announce to our
> fellow citizens, the arrival of CAPTAIN LEWIS, with his
> exploring party at St. Lewis.
> The President of the United States has received a letter
> from him, dated at St. Louis, September 23, at which place
> himself, Captain Clarke and their party arrived that day.

Maybe editor Smith was excited, to have spelled the name
of the city "St. Lewis" in the first paragraph and to have corrected
it farther down. The rest of the account was in the exact language
of the president's letter. Smith had, however, corrected Jefferson's
capitalization, punctuation and spelling and had substituted
spelled-out numbers for figures.

Philadelphians heard the news two days later. The *Aurora
and General Advertiser* announced the explorers' return by printing parts of letters which the editor had received from St. Louis.

On October 31 it used the *National Intelligencer* account in full, acknowledging its debt to its Washington colleague with a line in italic type above the story. *Poulsen's American Daily Advertiser*, in the same city, published the *National Intelligencer* account on the 30th, also giving due credit to its source. The New York *American Citizen* of the 30th printed a letter which it received, it said, "From our Correspondent," dated from Baltimore on October 25. The writer gave a little information which he had received from a friend in "St. Louis, Upper Louisiana." The next day it used the *National Intelligencer*'s more detailed account, duly credited to that paper. It took until November 6 for Bostonians to learn that the explorers were back. The *Courier* used the *National Intelligencer* story on that date, without giving credit. It carried no other account of the expedition. This was how Americans received news from the White House in 1806. This was the ancestor of today's presidential news conference.

The *National Intelligencer* was regarded then as an official paper, similar to Napoleon's *Moniteur* or the *London Gazette* of the English royal family. To use a twentieth-century term, although it is not a perfect parallel, Smith was Jefferson's press secretary. The two met around 1797 when the former bought the *Independent Gazetteer*, a Republican (that is, Jeffersonian) paper in Philadelphia, and the latter was vice-president. As the year 1800 advanced, with Jefferson's election as President soon to take place and with the government preparing to move from Philadelphia to the new capital on the Potomac, Jefferson suggested that Smith set up his press in the new city. The first issue of the *National Intelligencer* appeared in Washington on October 31, 1800.

During the eight years in which Jefferson directed the young nation's affairs he kept in close touch with Smith. Whether he were in the "President's House" or in Monticello, the chief executive penned for the editor bits of information, requests for help, or suggestions for editorial support of the administration or the party. Mrs. Smith (née Bayard, of a prominent Philadelphia family) also received chatty notes. From his Virginia mountain-top home the president sent her gardening suggestions, seeds, and plants.

Let us look at some of Jefferson's notes and the way the editor used them. On one occasion the scientifically minded chief executive sent a description which he had received from Europe of a new type of lifeboat. The paper described the craft. Mr. and Mrs. Smith received a printed invitation to dine at the "President's House" on April 23, 1804. There were doubtless many others, but this one has been preserved. The invitation contained an added line in Jefferson's handwriting telling the guests to bring "any friends who may be with them." The president also used the *Intelligencer* for information which he wished to place before the public unofficially. He wrote on October 23, 1802: "The enclosed paper seems intended for the legislative as well as Executive eye; but certainly not to be laid before the former in the regular way. The only irregular one would be in the newspapers, but this must depend on it's merit and your opinion of it. There are a few just ideas in it, but they are a few grains of wheat in a bushel of chaff." The enclosed paper has not been preserved, but the *Intelligencer*'s issues of the next several days published several articles any one of which might have originated with this note.

In one note Jefferson asked Smith whether or not it was "worth while to contradict the barefaced falsehoods of Coleman in the 2d page 5th column of the enclosed paper." The president, obviously angry at some aspersions on his conduct as a member of the Continental Congress during the War of Independence which had been printed in the Federalist New York *Evening Post,* underlined certain phrases of his letter. The *Intelligencer* of July 23, 1804, without mentioning the fact that the editor had received a personal note, replied sharply to the *Evening Post* attack. That *Intelligencer* editorial and another a few days later were in the language of the president's letters. Those sentences which Jefferson had underlined were printed in italics.[1]

Smith's paper was practically the only channel available for the country to learn of the president's official acts. The personal details in the life of the chief executive and his family, which occupy so much space in today's press, were not then regarded as news, unless they could be made a basis for political attack in the opposition journals. Editors everywhere reprinted what they found in the *National Intelligencer* or the several less informed and less authoritative papers which were published in the capital. They secured from those papers, too, news of proceedings in the two separate sandstone buildings which crowned the hill at the other end of Pennsylvania Avenue.

The *National Intelligencer* of October 27, 1807, may be taken as a typical example. On the second page there was found the word CONGRESS and below that, *House of Representatives.* The text followed:

> This being the day fixed by the proclamation of the President of the U.S. for the meeting of Congress, a majority of the members of both houses convened at the Capitol.
>
> The assistant clerk of the House of Representatives having called the names of the members, announced 117 members and one delegate to be present.
>
> He then enquired if it were the pleasure of the House to proceed with the election of a Speaker, which being determined in the affirmative, the members proceeded to ballot for that officer, Messrs. Cutts. Helms and John Campbell being named tellers.
>
> The tellers, after examining the votes, reported that 117 were received and that James B. Varnum, a representative from the state of Massachusetts, having 59 of them, was declared to be elected.

The account went on to give, in parliamentary language, the rest of the votes, a description of the ceremony by which the new Speaker was conducted to the chair, his acceptance speech in full, and the proceedings in the election of a Clerk. It ended by saying that a committee was named to join a similar Senate committee to wait upon the president and tell him that the two houses were organized and ready to receive any communications which he might have to make to them. Continuing down the same column of the same issue, we read on:

> TUESDAY, OCTOBER 27
>
> *Mr. Bassett,* from the committee appointed yesterday to wait upon the President of the U. States, to inform him Congress was formed and ready to receive any communication he might have to make to them, reported, that he would make a communication to the two Houses by message at 12 o'clock this day.
>
> Accordingly at 12 o'clock the message of the President was delivered by his Secretary (a copy of which is inserted

in today's paper) which, after being read, was committed to the committee of the whole house on the state of the union, and 1,000 copies ordered to be printed.

It went on in this fashion, but that is enough to show how it was done. The same literary form can be found today in the *Congressional Record,* but not in today's newspapers. The text of the president's message on the state of the Union was on page 3. Like the *Intelligencer's* accounts from the executive mansion, these proceedings were copied in the press of the rest of the country. The horse-drawn mail coaches took three days to carry the papers to Philadelphia. The New York papers published items selected from the Washington journals three or four days late and another two days passed before they appeared in Boston. This is how the country and the world received the news when Washington was a small, muddy, artificial community being carved out of the woods along Tiber Creek and the Potomac River.

On January 17, 1969, Eric Sevareid, news commentator of the Columbia Broadcasting System, referred to news as "the other industry" in Washington. On other broadcasts he has said that politics and news were the capital city's two businesses. His remarks reflect the fact that news and its related fields of public relations and lobbying have grown to mammoth proportions. No other national capital has anything comparable. A very large force serves the newspapers, magazines, radio, television, specialized journals and commercial news letters. The *Congressional Directory* lists about a thousand newspaper correspondents, nearly five hundred for radio and television, and about the same for magazines. There are nearly one hundred and fifty names in the photographers' press gallery. Included in these totals are about a hundred who report for foreign newspapers, press services, radio and television.

The *Congressional Directory* listing does not give all of the news force in Washington. Any effort to carry out the impossible task of totalling the journalistic corps has to take into consideration the government public information employees. From the press secretary to the president, including aides on the office staffs of many members of Congress, and down to the large numbers in the public information offices of the government departments, this group runs into the thousands. The public relations forces of the national political party committees and of the lobby groups, labor unions and trade associations further swell the numbers of the news force.

These men and women guide themselves by their own practical experience, by theories, and by inherited customs and facilities that have been developing over many years. They follow traditions whose evolution will be described in this book. But they scrap those inherited traditions as changing conditions make that necessary. This has been especially true within the last quarter of a century. The new position of the United States as international leader and as the defender of the Free World has placed strains on the news structure for which experience has not entirely prepared either government officials or newsmen. That this is true has been pointed up with peculiar force by the controversy between the press and government officials resulting from the U-2 incident, the Bay of Pigs, the Cuban missile crisis and the Vietnam war. And the disputes over the Columbia Broadcasting System documentary, "The Selling of the Pentagon," and over newspaper publication of secret Pentagon documents saw the government actually try, unsuccessfully, to move legally against the press.

Samuel Harrison Smith, a newspaper proprietor and the owner of a printshop, was also a close personal friend of the president. He was admittedly a partisan spokesman. He was the only contact which the nation's press had with the Executive. Opposition papers copied news from Smith's journal and did not try to approach Jefferson in person. At the same time they criticized the president viciously without trying to separate news from editorial opinion or to maintain objectivity in the news columns. There was no separate editorial column in the earliest years of Smith's newspaper experience. It did not occur to editors to report the news objectively. It was not then part of the press tradition. As the federal government approaches the end of its second century of existence the White House staff includes a press secretary. He has at least one assistant and a substantial clerical and office force. The president from time to time holds news conferences at which several hundred correspondents question him. Occasionally the president sees individual reporters or small groups of them.

The press and the president assume that news written by

the reporters will be objective and as accurate as it is possible for the reporters to make it. Whether or not the news stories they write or deliver orally by radio or television are entirely accurate is sometimes a matter of dispute, due to the varying emphasis that may be given under conditions in which the possible implications of complex groups of facts are hard to assess. The president is sensitive to stories that, in spite of the tradition of objectivity, seem to reflect discredit on himself personally or on his administration. He is sensitive to stories about him or his acts which have not been given out through approved channels and which, on being laid before the public, affect his acts. He is sensitive to the publication of news which he feels it is in the public interest to withhold. Reporters, on the other hand, are sensitive about what they regard as arbitrary concealment on the part of the president and his aides. And even reporters whose journals opposed his election and criticize him on the editorial page are sensitive if they suspect that he is showing favoritism in giving out news to other selected newsmen.

The telegraphic press associations, the broadcasting chains, and many of the largest newspapers maintain reporters who spend all of their working hours at the White House watching as far as possible every act of the president and of his staff. Whenever he travels, either within the United States or abroad, they follow him in special planes or trains. A press room is maintained at the White House for their convenience. Furthermore, in addition to those who devote their full-time attention to the Executive, several hundred others appear at the news conferences. Many of those conferences are televised live, bringing the radio listening and television viewing audience into the State Department auditorium or the White House East Room.

Smith covered not only the president for his own journal and for the rest of the country's press. He also provided the country with news of the floor proceedings of the two houses of Congress. News from the Capitol consisted of the step-by-step proceedings on the floor of the two houses. Committees were ignored. Speeches were summarized through the peculiar use of both the first and the third person which marked the imperfect stenography of the time. In view of the fact that the official journals of the two houses recorded only parliamentary steps and did not give speeches, the press accounts were the only record of what was said on the floor and are the only sources available to-day to historians. The press accounts were later compiled and published. Today's *Congressional Record* was not established until 1873.

In addition to reporting proceedings, Smith was printer to Congress and to the executive departments, doing the work that is today carried on by the Government Printing Office. That is, committee reports and other congressional documents were done in his shop, with the name "S. H. Smith" given as the printer on the title page. The rates paid him for this work did much to make him a well-to-do man.

Today the press pays little attention to speeches made on the floor of either house. Several hundred reporters swarm through the Capitol and the House and Senate Office Buildings every day when Congress is in session. But most of the time the press gallery itself, which looks down from above the rostrum on the legislators debating below, is practically empty. Each telegraphic press association is careful to keep one man there at all times. Most of the time he watches idly, bored and inattentive, his presence necessitated only by the unlikely possibility that some dramatic occurrence might take place, such as a legislator dropping dead or a disturbance in the galleries. Normally if other journalists are present they merely sit idly, resting before they go off somewhere else in search of news. Routine recording of the proceedings and speeches is left to the clerks and to the stenographers for the *Congressional Record*.

This is not true at all times. There are days on which the floor is jammed with excited, clamoring members. The presiding officer's gavel bangs repeatedly as he tries to enforce order. There is noisy confusion as members try to offer amendments to the legislation under consideration, as they try to offer substitute bills, as they "move to strike out the enacting clause," as they address parliamentary inquiries and demand unanimous consent for certain action. On such days the press galleries, too, are jammed. It has become necessary to order "Special Card Days" to limit the number admitted by each newspaper and each press association. And on those days the reporters watch for significant speeches and carefully keep track of the complicated parliamentary maneuvers. But their attention is directed far more to analyzing the power plays and legislative steps and to writing stories which reflect the forces behind the moves than merely to recording proceedings. This is one of the major changes in practice in more than a hundred years of relations between the press and Congress.

Smith, no doubt, had informal and very friendly relationships with members of Congress, especially with those of his own and the president's political views. He published nothing from any such conversations, however. The interview had not been thought of. If the press now pays little attention to routine debate, members nevertheless get their views before the country through the press to a far greater degree than they did through the speeches carried in the press of Smith's day. Reporters who spend little time listening to floor proceedings devote hours to talking to members of the two houses in their offices, their homes, in bars or restaurants, or in special areas off the floor of each house which are reserved for that purpose. These expressed views are worked into the stories which develop all aspects of any political or legislative situation. Furthermore, members regularly appear before the microphones in the radio and television galleries to have their voices and images recorded for broadcast news shows.

The preoccupation of Smith and his readers with floor speeches also reflected the fact that they paid no attention to committees. But at that time the committee system had not developed into the important thing it has since become. Today they are major sources of news. Since the last years of the last century the press has more and more come to look at committee testimony as one of its major interests. The appearance of cabinet members and other leaders of the executive departments, of well-known leaders of business organizations, of labor, and of social, professional and lobby groups is described at length in news stories. And selected parts of such testimony appear on television screens.

As Douglass Cater has pointed out, congressmen and senators regard such appearances as important to their political advancement. In many cases the publicity thus derived becomes the major purpose of committee investigation.[2] These proceedings are supposed to be carried on in order to secure the information necessary for intelligent consideration of legislation or to ascertain how administrative offices have used the funds which Congress has appropriated or how they have carried out congressional mandates. But members argue that these ends are at times achieved when extensive publicity is secured through the hearings. And the hearings are often staged more for that purpose—and to put the committee chairman onto the nation's television screens and strengthen his position as national party conventions approach—than for the traditional reasons. After such hearings the final committee report may be pointless and receive little attention from the press.

When legislators, especially those in the English Parliament, established their practices and fought for their powers between the thirteenth and the eighteenth centuries, they had little means for the exchange of views except through floor debate. Speeches delivered on those occasions were extensive and to the point. And when newspapers, in the eighteenth century, first began printing legislative proceedings they did so because public interest in those speeches reflected their significance. Changes in both the press and Congress have brought about the situation today in which floor speeches are relatively unimportant. The House of Representatives has been forced to adopt rules limiting debate simply to get through the vast volume of business which requires its attention. The Senate clings to the tradition of unlimited debate. But it often gets bogged down in so doing.

The function which floor debate had prior to 1800 has been transferred to the public media. The interviews which members of the two houses give to the press, their appearances before the microphones and the television cameras, the letters which they receive as a result, all combine vastly to broaden the information available to members as they consider their votes or the drafting of their legislative proposals. And the give-and-take through the public media strengthens or weakens as the case may be the pressures put upon members by their party or by the leadership. This has been one of the major changes to be brought about in the period which we will consider.

Smith had a quarrel with the Speaker over his right to be present in the House chamber and to take notes. Quarrels between the press and one or the other house of Congress were characteristic of the early years. The last took place in 1929. Today each house provides extensive facilities to the information media. The words *press gallery* need definition. On the one hand these words refer to the actual gallery, not very large, located on the gallery level in back of the rostrum in each chamber. From there, reporters may look down on the proceedings below. The words are also customarily used to refer to the rooms onto which those galleries open. Here are lounge areas with couches, cards, checkers and chessmen. There are also telephones, typewriters, stationery, telegraph offices, and washrooms. Lady correspondents secured their washrooms in the press galleries in 1938 only after a battle with the all-male Standing Committee of Correspondents. A separate gallery permits radio and television reporters to observe proceedings. And that, in each legislative hall, gives access to the radio and television gallery where there are studios for broadcasting or for filming or taping speeches or interviews, as well as the typewriters, telephones and rest areas comparable to those in the press galleries. A periodical press gallery provides similar facilities in each chamber and a workroom in each end of the Capitol for magazine writers. A photographers press gallery gives the cameramen a place to hang their hats, store equipment and receive messages as they move around Capitol Hill in the course of their duties.

In each case the gallery is administered under the rules of each house although the immediate control is exercised by an elected committee of the correspondents. Each gallery has a superintendent and several assistants who are named by the correspondents' governing group although they are paid out of public funds appropriated by Congress. This book will tell the background of these developments. It will set out the evolving press-governmental relationship from the time of Samuel Harrison Smith to that of Eric Sevareid.

2. Parliament and Congress: 1600–1815

The newspaper is a product of the epoch and of the conditions that made England's parliament dominant in England's governmental structure and made Parliament the model for our own legislative bodies. Historically, the newspaper and legislative government grew together.

Before 1600 several printed publications had appeared in some of the German, Dutch and Italian commercial cities giving military, political and commercial information of value to merchants. These normally were not periodical. They were published once in book form and then ceased. The regular emission of periodical news publication did not become a regular feature of the European literary scene until after 1600. In 1620 some English printers began to reprint Dutch publications that gave continental news. These so-called corantos struggled along for a few years in the face of official suspicion. But the real origin of periodical journalism, and the situation that gave the newspaper its traditional characteristic both as a source of news and as a weapon in political controversy, is to be found in the struggle between Parliament and Charles I.

As a result of a series of laws and edicts dating back more than a century English printers were subject to censorship which was enforced through the arbitrary judicial procedures of the Court of Star Chamber. A quarrel over the respective constitutional powers of the king and of Parliament had been building up ever since James I came to the throne in 1602. Because of that quarrel, James's son, Charles I, ruled without calling Parliament from 1629 to 1640.

Some readers will quarrel with the statement in the first paragraph of this chapter that the newspaper and Parliament grew together. Of course some sort of council or legislative body in nearly all European states is much older than the newspaper. In England, from 1485 to 1600 the monarch rather than the legislature occupied the power center. It is correct to say that the establishment of the newspaper coincided with the seventeenth-century struggles that saw Parliament establish its dominant position. The newspaper grew in England as a part of that struggle and gained a stature far ahead of the more slowly evolving press on the continent.

In 1640 the turn of politics put Charles in a position in which he simply could proceed no further. He called into session a Parliament which he knew would be hostile. The members of the House of Commons who gathered that November had gained their seats by inheritance, by enjoyment of certain local rights, or by purchase, rather than by the support of a mass electorate who might demand the right to influence members' stands on public problems. Among the parliamentary traditions which members enjoyed was that of privilege. Under that principle they were exempt from certain provisions of the criminal law, including liability for words spoken in debate. Furthermore, they were suspicious of any outside effort to bring pressure upon them and they felt that their debates were not of public concern. Privilege gave them the legal power to punish those who sought to bring pressure upon them. (Imagine being jailed for writing your congressman!) This they came in time to apply to publication of their proceedings. They met in secret, although many of them talked fairly freely outside and the gossip of the taverns and public meeting places meant that informed persons were able to learn a good deal of what took place on the floor. One of their first acts, in 1641, was to abolish the hated Court of Star Chamber. Although that was not their purpose, by so doing they abolished the legal machinery by which the press had been censored. For two years English printers enjoyed unchecked freedom. But that freedom was simply an accident and was not backed up by any theoretical belief in such a doctrine. Almost no one then gave any thought to freedom of the press.

In the House of Commons were some of the greatest political and legal minds and deepest thinkers on theological questions to be found in an age in which religion and government, as well as physics and geography, were the subjects of extensive philosophic discussion. The debates in the House constituted serious and well-informed consideration of the questions of the day. Taking advantage of the abolition of the Court of Star Chamber, taking advantage of the political excitement of the time when news was eagerly sought, and taking advantage of the fact that some members of Parliament wanted their views laid before the country, English printers began to produce a flood of publications which summarized the proceedings of one or both houses and in some cases provided fairly extensive reports of speeches.

At first, these publications, brought out with a page size equal to that of a book, were known variously as diurnals or newsbooks. About twenty-five years later the word *newspaper* came into the language. Publication became more regular, and some of the practices which had developed in hit-or-miss fashion at the time of the Long Parliament became more systematic. As it gained ascendancy in the English constitutional structure, however, Parliament became suspicious. Members raised the question whether or not periodical publication of speeches and proceedings did not constitute a violation of parliamentary privilege. Legislation intended to restrict the press was passed in 1643. For another 128 years an intermittent running battle was waged between Parliament and those papers which tried to print accounts of floor proceedings and anonymous articles on public matters.

After 1700 both the newspaper press and the party-parliamentary-cabinet system of government developed rapidly. Parliament failed to renew the old license and censorship acts in 1694, leaving English printers free to enjoy what they now hailed as "liberty of the press," although there were still many restrictions. And more and more the existing Whig and Tory parties subsidized the newspapers and bribed writers. By the time George III ascended the throne in 1760, these practices were well established. Parliamentary membership, however, still did not represent a mass of voters who held members subject to their wishes. Furthermore the prevailing concept of privilege held that members had a right and duty similar to that which is supposed to prevail today in a courtroom.

The legislators felt that no pressure was to be brought upon them from outside for much the same reason that judicial theory today insists that a jury is to consider only testimony presented within the courtroom and receive no information or pressure from any other source. The lawmakers reached their decisions on the basis of debate on the floor. (Of course there were party discipline, bribery, and various other pressures applied, but what is written here was at least the theory.) And that debate was not to be heard by those outside. Better informed than outsiders, members believed, they were duty-bound to guide their proceedings on the basis of action within the chamber. And their concept of privilege gave either house the power to punish for contempt any effort to influence them or any effort to inform the general public of their proceedings.

Under these circumstances, as the growing newspaper and magazine press indicated interest in publishing parliamentary proceedings, members felt that privilege authorized them to punish that publication. From 1724 on, newspaper and magazine proprietors found that their readers wanted parliamentary accounts. Readers, who were then limited to an educated upper class who were interested and informed regarding public affairs, were well aware that parliamentary debates constituted significant discussions.

Therefore, in spite of frequent punishment, from 1724 to 1771 newspapers and magazines, using various expedients to secure the debates from behind the closed parliamentary doors and using various expedients to avoid punishment, published what their readers understood to be the debates. From time to time a printer was seized on a Speaker's warrant, brought into the House by the sergeant-at-arms, forced to bow before the Speaker in the presence of members, and imprisoned, fined, or placed under bonds for future good behavior. The accounts were written by a corps of literary adventurers. They were probably fairly accurate in presenting the essential content of speeches. Certainly in some cases their reports, prepared by skilled writers from sketchy notes or secondhand oral accounts, were probably better than the speech as originally given. Dr. Samuel Johnson is said to have written the published accounts of the speeches of the elder William Pitt for which that great statesman has been praised.

The practice of punishing the publication of proceedings

ended in 1771 as a result of a rather silly incident. Speaker's warrants were issued for the arrest of several printers who had published material offensive to some members. They were thereupon seized by messengers of the sergeant-at-arms. But the messengers were arrested on orders of John Wilkes, a city alderman, and the printers were freed. Wilkes was looking for a fight. He was a born troublemaker, a popular leader to whom the king once referred as "that devil Wilkes." In both Britain and her North American colonies voluble supporters in mass meetings and in the streets shouted the slogan, "Wilkes and Liberty." A few years earlier he had served a prison term for material which he had printed in the paper, the *North Briton,* of which he was then proprietor. In the uproar that followed the arrest of the officers of the House of Commons, with angry recriminations in the House and with controlled and organized mobs (used by political leaders in both London and Boston at the time) running the streets, the House failed to secure the arrest of the offending printers. No such attempt has been made since then.

Wilkes was himself a member of the House, where he was looked upon with aversion by many of his fellows. Here he took certain steps to inform his London constituents of House proceedings and to lead some of the London members to respect their backers' wishes. Herein he was moving in what was a novel direction but which is customary in modern legislative bodies. No English scholar has carried through details of the relationship between the press and Parliament in this period and the provision of space for reporters. In time it became customary for both houses to meet with the doors open. And when the legislative halls were rebuilt in 1834, press galleries were provided. It seems probable that American precedent was at least partially responsible for this.[1]

Throughout the colonial period the legislative body in each colony normally met in secret, respecting the tradition of the mother country. During the controversy which preceded the outbreak in 1775, the Massachusetts General Court at times allowed its proceedings to be observed, but newspapers did not publish them. Hugh Gaine, a New York printer, was once arrested by order of the colony's assembly in a manner reminiscent of the practice in England. After newspapers appeared in North America—the first in Boston in 1704—the clerks of the legislative bodies occasionally, on instruction by the members, made public acts or resolutions, but not speeches or debate. In that case, the complete text, without commentary or supplementary information, appeared in the newspaper. For example, note the publication in the *Pennsylvania Evening Post* of July 6, 1776, of the complete text of a notable statement which had been adopted in closed session by the Continental Congress two days earlier.

The Congress met in secret during the War of Independence and afterwards. So did the Constitutional Convention of 1787. As the latter meeting organized and debated its rules, there was some sentiment for opening the doors, reflecting what was by then a growing practice. But a majority of members opposed it. By the time the new government was established in 1789 the English press was regularly publishing the proceedings of the House of Commons. By now, too, some of the state legislatures in this country were sitting with the doors open and the press and public allowed to observe their proceedings.

The House of Representatives of the First Congress went along with the new way of things practically from the start. Called for March 4, 1789, in New York, it collected a quorum and organized on April 6. That first session followed time-honored practice and met in secret. On the 8th, however, the doors were opened, with the public admitted to an area which would not interfere with proceedings. By tacit consent stenographers recording the debates for the press were allowed seats in front of the Speaker's table.[2] A few months later there flared up the first dispute of a type that occasionally marked contacts between the press and Congress down to 1929. Representative Aedanus Burke of South Carolina introduced a resolution on September 26, 1789, which charged that inaccurate reporting violated the privileges of the House. The stenographers did not await final action on his move but fled to the public galleries.[3] They were back at the beginning of the next session, however. When Congress moved to Philadelphia in 1790 four seats on the windowsills were provided for them. The Senate was more conservative. It clung to secret sessions for five years. In 1794 it was decided that the doors would be opened as soon as suitable galleries could be built. They were installed in the summer of 1795, so when Congress convened the next December the public was admitted. Reporters here were not given the special privileges which they received in the House. They had to work in the public galleries.[4] On Monday, December 1, 1800, Congress met for the first time in the present United States Capitol. Then it was still two separate buildings with an open space where the Rotunda is today. The House met in what is now Statuary Hall. Smith appeared to report proceedings as he had done in Philadelphia. In the new quarters, however, he could not hear. So on Thursday he asked better accommodations. The *House of Representatives Journal* records that "A memorial of Samuel H. Smith and Thomas Carpenter, Stenographers, of the city of Washington, was presented to the House and read, stating the impossibility of their taking, with accuracy, the debates of the House from the station at present allotted them; and praying that they may be admitted to places within the bar, more convenient for that purpose."[5]

The memorial was referred to a special committee. That group reported on December 8 recommending that the petition not be granted. The legislators voted the next day forty-five to forty-five on whether or not to accept the report. Federalist Speaker Theodore Sedgwick broke the tie by voting with the committee. Thus he forced Smith to stay out with the public where he found it hard to hear.[6] He was driven out of there a month later. On January 12, 1801, when he took his usual seat, the sergeant-at-arms ordered him to leave. He moved to another position, and was again ordered out. Three days later he had a talk with the Speaker which he reported in the paper. The Speaker told him that because "either through incompetency, or intentionally, you grossly misrepresented my conduct as well as that of the House," he would be barred if he came to report. He would, however, be allowed to publish such papers as the Clerk might consent to let him have. In giving such an order the Speaker was reverting to colonial practice.

The Federalists lost the election of 1800. Therefore, when Congress convened in December, 1801, Jefferson, Smith's political patron, was in the executive mansion, the editor's political partisans dominated Congress, and the hostile Sedgwick had been replaced in the chair by Representative Nathaniel Macon of North Carolina. Smith must have felt triumphant satisfaction when Macon invited him to a better spot on the floor. The House not only watched its Speaker informally admit the editor-reporter-stenographer within the sacred area of the chamber. On January

2, 1802, it adopted an addition to its Standing Rules and Orders which directed the Speaker to assign to stenographers such places "as shall not interfere with the convenience of the House." Thus the legislators protected the press's right to report their proceedings by a specific provision of the rules.[7]

The Senate had already moved in the same direction. Two days earlier, as the year 1801 ended, the president of the Senate laid before it a letter from Smith asking to be allowed to sit "in the lower area of the Senate Chamber for the purpose of taking with correctness the debates and proceedings of that body." The solons promptly adopted a resolution authorizing the presiding officer to admit stenographers to any point that he saw fit.[8] It was, however, only a resolution and not an addition to the rules such as the House had provided.

The House Rules Committee proposed slight changes in the wording of the rule on December 22, 1811, and the change was adopted.[9] In June, 1813, the lower body ordered that two hundred dollars be spent to provide suitable accommodations in the galleries and resolved that as soon as the changes were made the reporters would not be admitted to the floor.[10] Two years later they were back. They seem to have convinced the lawmakers that they could not hear well enough in the gallery. On December 31, 1815, the House repealed the clause in the rules which limited them to the gallery and authorized the Speaker "to assign them such station in the House as he shall deem convenient and proper."[11]

These stenographers or reporters presented start-to-finish accounts of floor proceedings which were modeled after those which had already been developed by the English press. Floor speeches were paraphrased. Sometimes they were reported at length; sometimes they were short. Sometimes they were fairly accurate; sometimes they were cut or distorted deliberately. That occurred when the speaking member represented a political stand contrary to that of the reporter or his paper. Smith himself was probably never guilty of that, but it seems that some other stenographers who appeared in the early years may have been. Sometimes members wrote out their speeches and the journals printed them as written. Deliberate distortion for political purposes, or errors due to imperfect stenography or imperfect hearing angered the members. What could they do about it? The point where the ancient

concept of privilege surrendered to new American ideas of freedom of the press was not clear. There was a conflict of principle
which experience had yet to work out. A series of investigations
resulted. Several times reporters were arrested by the sergeant-
at-arms.

The first such detention took place while Congress still met
in Philadelphia. On February 19, 1800, the *Aurora and General
Advertiser*, the Democrats' most vigorous organ, rapped a bill
which the Federalists had introduced in the Senate. The bill
would authorize a special congressional committee to examine
the electoral votes when cast and to reject those which did not
qualify under regulations which would be laid down in the proposed measure. The article said, and it was correct, that the bill
was intended to make it possible for the Federalists to steal the
coming presidential election in case Jefferson were to win a
majority. (He won that majority, but the bill had been defeated.
Jefferson took office a year later in spite of this Federalist move.)

After a four-day debate over procedure and powers the
Senate ordered the Committee on Privileges to consider possible
action. On March 18 the committee reported out a resolution
ordering William Duane, the editor, to appear on the 24th "to
make any proper defense for his conduct in publishing the aforesaid false, defamatory, scandalous and malicious assertions and
pretended information on the subject." The Senate adopted the
resolution. Duane appeared on the appointed day. The charges
against him were read and he asked to be allowed to secure
counsel. The Senate released him, ordering him to return two
days later. On the 26th he failed to appear. He wrote to the
president of the Senate saying that his intended counsel had
refused to serve. "I therefore think myself bound by the most
sacred duties to decline any further voluntary appearance upon
that body," his note said, "and leave them to pursue such measures in this case as in their vision they may deem meet." Jefferson,
then vice-president, was forced by the opposition Senate majority
to sign a warrant for the arrest of his party's leading editor. On
May 14 the Senate asked President John Adams to have Duane
prosecuted in the civil courts. The editor was sentenced to thirty
days in jail and ordered to pay costs.[12]

Twelve years later another editor was arrested. The incident
brought up such debatable issues as the propriety of secret ses-

sions, the power of the House to arrest a citizen or a newspaper-man, its power to compel testimony, and even its power to punish its own members for violation of its rules. It ended in a draw with none of the questions settled.

By April 1812, the "war hawks" in both houses had almost succeeded in forcing the United States into war against England. On the first of that month the House of Representatives went into executive session to receive and debate a secret special message from President James Madison. Actually it was an open secret. It was widely known that the president asked Congress to enact an embargo to prevent American merchant ships from sailing before the expected declaration of war.

According to the rules members were pledged to secrecy, under threat of punishment. While secrecy was still in force the Alexandria *Herald* and the *Spirit of 'Seventy-six*, a short-lived Washington paper, each published a paragraph giving the substance of the message. Having passed the embargo in closed session, the House kept the doors shut to debate whether or not to punish the offending editors or to see if any of its own members should be cited for revealing confidential House business. It named a select committee to investigate.

The committee examined the editors of the *Spirit of 'Seventy-six*. Those editors got the facts from Nathaniel Rounsavell, editor of the Alexandria *Herald,* they said. Rounsavell, brought before the committee, said he learned them "from the conversation of members of the House, with whom he accidentally fell in company." But when the committee demanded the names of the members, where the conversation took place, and whether or not he had seen the members again afterwards, Rounsavell refused to answer. The committee ordered the sergeant-at-arms to hold him and reported the matter to the House. The House ordered the sergeant-at-arms to bring Rounsavell in. The Speaker repeated the first question which had been asked by the committee. "I refused to answer that question when before the committee, and I continue steadfast in that refusal," he answered. He was taken away under guard. The next day the Speaker laid before the House a letter from him saying that he disclaimed "any intention to have violated the respect due to the House" and that the conversation of members which he had overheard was entirely inadvertent on their part. His only motive in refusing to answer the question, he wrote, was fear that it might result in "criminating those who had committed no crime."

The debate that followed brought out the fact that several members had refused to be bound by the House secrecy order. Indeed, Representative Josiah Quincy of Massachusetts, a Federalist and a bitter foe of the war plans, had sent a special express to Boston to warn his shipowner constituents to rush their vessels to sea ahead of the restrictive legislation. The British consul at Baltimore had been told what was happening and had notified his home office. It was brought out, too, that one member, feeling ill, had returned to his boarding house. Later in the day a fellow member sought him out in his bedroom and told him what was in the president's message. While they talked they looked up and found that Rounsavell was standing in the door, listening. The editor was brought before the Speaker again and agreed to answer any questions. The House, however, decided to drop the matter and ordered him discharged. The House also failed to punish the several members who admitted that they had refused to be bound by the secrecy order.[13]

Thus Congress and the president, during the first twenty years in which the young government felt its way, developed new procedures in press relationships or adapted those inherited from the mother country. Thus, too, Congress clung to some of the traditional powers of the legislative body. Thus the *National Intelligencer*, as the authoritative newspaper close to the administration, and several lesser papers in the new capital made themselves the central sources of information for the press of the country. Some papers in the older commercial cities, however, experimented with other means.

Look at some Washington news in the New York *Evening Post*. This paper was established in 1801 by William T. Coleman, backed by Alexander Hamilton and other New Yorkers who were eager to rejuvenate the dying Federalist party. It continues today as the tabloid *Post*. On February 26, 1805, it said:

> CONGRESS—Letters received by the mail of this morning, give us many interesting particulars from Washington.
> The Yazoo Bill seems to have called up all the worst passions of the human heart. Randolph absolutely foams with rage because his party have not implicitly obeyed his nod on this occasion; . . .

The following extracts from our Correspondent's letter, are given as we receive them.

Washington, February 20
"The High Court of Impeachments have been in session, on the trial of Judge Chase, every day (Sundays excepted) since the 4th inst., five-sixths of the time have been taken up in the examination of witnesses. . . .

Extract of Another
"In the letter which I wrote to you this day, I had intended to mention that after the examination of witnesses ended at eleven o'clock, Mr. Early, of Georgia, on the part of the Managers, rose and addressed the Court. . . ."

This was the way New Yorkers were kept posted five or six days late as the Senate sat as a Court of Impeachment on federal Judge Samuel Chase and as the House debated the administration's compromise effort to protect those investors who were threatened with loss in Georgia's corrupt Yazoo land sales. These were not the major source of Washington news, however. The *Evening Post* relied principally on clipped and properly acknowledged accounts from the *National Intelligencer* in spite of the political enmity between the two papers.

Here is Washington news in a paper outside the capital late in Jefferson's administration. There were no paid correspondents. On the other hand, although editors relied principally on the Washington journals they had supplementary information from informal letters. Much obviously came from members of Congress, although the names of the writers were never revealed. Private citizens, lobbyists, visiting office-seekers, or merely curious travellers, writing either to the editors or to friends who in turn made their letters available for publication, swelled the material. On the other hand, as Jefferson and his party tried first an embargo and then the Non-Intercourse Act to defend neutral rights against Europe's deadlocked belligerents, certain press leaders in Philadelphia and New York tried more direct coverage.

The Embargo Act passed Congress on December 22, 1807. On January 1, 1808, the Federalist *United States Gazette* of Philadelphia announced that it would "republish every article which appears in the National Intelligencer on the subject of the embargo, for the purpose of letting the people see what is the best thing the government can say in vindication of that measure." Three days later it said:

> We congratulate the readers of the UNITED STATES GAZETTE upon an arrangement by which the editor is enabled to obtain *earlier,* and he trusts *more full and correct* information of the proceedings of congress and the measures of government, than can be had from the Washington papers. We have hitherto been obliged to depend primarily upon the National Intelligencer for reports of the proceedings of Congress; a paper which is conducted with very considerable ability, but with very little candour, inasmuch as the wishes of the president and his particular friends must be consulted in whatever representations are there made. At such a time as this it is important to the nation to know, not only what is done by government and legislature of the union, but in what manner. To accomplish this object a gentleman of superiour talents and a liberal education has been engaged to spend a winter at Washington, and make reports for this Gazette, as well of the proceedings of congress as of whatever else may be interesting to the publick at this crisis.

This seems to have been the first time that a paper outside of Washington arranged for regular transmission of news from that city. It is impossible to learn who the *Gazette's* correspondent was although he was probably an editor of the Washington *Federalist.* The routine beginning-to-end congressional accounts were now marked, in roman type, "Reported for the United States Gazette" while other types of editorial articles from the capital were credited in italics, *"Communications from Washington, to the Editor of the U. States Gazette."* They continued until Congress adjourned, the last on April 28, 1808. The *Freeman's Journal* of Philadelphia, meanwhile, copied the *Gazette's* congressional reports, properly giving credit to the source, and the New York *Evening Post* clipped both of these papers as well as the *National Intelligencer* and the Washington *Federalist.*

The *Gazette* must have found a Washington correspondent too expensive a luxury. When Congress reconvened the next November the paper printed the accounts of the opening days' proceedings credited "FROM OUR CORRESPONDENT AT WASHINGTON," but ran under each a line acknowledging the Washington *Federalist* as its source. Now the *Freeman's Journal* took up the burden. In December 1808 it started printing almost daily accounts of congressional proceedings under a standing two-line headline of type that was quite large for that time. The first line, in roman type, read "From our Correspondent," and the second, in all-capital italics, "*AT WASHINGTON*."

We know who the *Freeman's Journal's* correspondent was. He was James Elliot, a Vermont member of the House, who entered into partnership with William M'Corkle, editor, in November 1808.[14] The *Evening Post*, although it clipped the *Federalist* early in the session, relied increasingly on the *Freeman's Journal* as the administration's mercantile foes pounded for a modification of the embargo.

During that tense winter of 1808–9, Elliot mailed news practically every day which normally appeared in Philadelphia two days after the event occurred in the capital. That was fairly fast in an age of horse-drawn postal service. On December 13 the New York *Evening Post* said that the *Freeman's Journal* had sent a proof sheet in advance of publication of Elliot's Washington material. Through the rest of the winter, the Federalist organ in New York was able to publish Elliot's material three days after the news broke in Washington, thanks to the cooperation it got through speedy relay from Philadelphia. Elliot reported the repeal of the embargo and the passage of the Non-Intercourse Act a few days before Jefferson's administration expired on March 4, 1809.

Elliot retired from Congress at that time. Nevertheless, when the legislators reconvened on May 22, called into special session by the new president, James Madison, the *Freeman's Journal* and the *Evening Post* continued to run letters which seem to have been his. They continued to use special Washington correspondence through the session which began in December 1809. On April 5, 1810, however, the *Freeman's Journal* announced that ill health had forced Elliot to withdraw from the partnership, although it said arrangements had been made for him to "devote a considerable portion of his time and talents" to the paper. The Philadelphia and New York papers printed letters which were apparently his for two more years. The last appeared in the *Freeman's Journal* of April 25, 1812. Then, in spite of the approaching war and presidential campaign, the letters stopped.

In June, with the Senate debating behind closed doors

whether or not to enact the declaration of war already approved by the House, the *Evening Post* tried again. On the 12th it said that "we thought proper, once more, to despatch our Ariel to Washington to see what discoveries he could make." "Ariel," if it were Elliot, fumbled. He reported that war would not be declared and that the embargo then in force would be continued. The *Freeman's Journal* had no such letter, but on June 18 it published in very large italic type an "Extract of a way letter (written in extreme haste after the mail was closed) from a Gentleman in Washington, to another in this city, dated June 16." The letter said that the war bill had just passed the Senate 19 to 13. The next day the paper said its account had been erroneous, but on the 22nd it gave the text of the bill and the president's proclamation. It copied them from the *National Intelligencer*.

The *Evening Post* of June 19 clipped the *Freeman's Journal's* excited statement of the previous day, including it in a column of speculation taken from several papers. On June 20 it said positively that war had been declared, quoting orders received by the commander of federal troops in New York. Two days later it copied from the *National Intelligencer* the text of the war bill and Madison's proclamation. During the war and for some years afterwards, however, the major daily newspapers in the nation's commercial cities again depended on the Washington journals and informal letters. The establishment of the capital press corps had to wait another dozen years.

3. Correspondents Appear at the Capital

Benjamin Perley Poore—or Ben: Perley Poore, for his writings were published with the author's first name and the colon used in this fashion—was the first chronicler of the Washington press corps. His name will appear frequently in these pages. Descended from a well-to-do Newburyport, Massachusetts, family, he was born there on November 2. 1802. He learned the printing trade at Worcester and for a short time edited the *Southern Whig* at Athens, Georgia. He traveled in Europe from 1841 to 1848 and in 1854 became the Washington correspondent for the Boston *Journal*. When Millard Fillmore ran a poor third in the 1856 presidential race, Poore good-naturedly paid an election bet by pushing a wheelbarrow from his Newburyport farm to the State House in Boston, a distance of about thirty-five miles. For the next thirty years he made his home in Washington, where he was popular in press and political circles. In addition to his newspaper correspondence he wrote a series of biographies of public figures, contributed to magazines, compiled three lists of government publications, edited the *Congressional Directory* and served as clerk to a Senate committee. He died on May 29, 1887, in the Ebbitt Hotel, which stood on the site now occupied by the National Press Building.

His two-volume *Perley's Reminiscences of Sixty Years in the National Metropolis,* which was published in 1886 and outlines Washington events from the Administration of John Quincy Adams to that of Grover Cleveland, includes frequent references to the press. He discussed the early correspondents in more detail in an article in 1874 in *Harper's New Monthly Magazine.*[1] That article is the best available source from which to start a study of the correspondents who began to appear after 1820, although what Poore says clashes in several details with the findings of present-day research. He credited James Cheetham, editor of the New York *Citizen* during Jefferson's administration, James Duane of the *Aurora* of Philadelphia and Joseph Gales of the *National Intelligencer* with having written Washington letters for their own or other papers outside the capital. There is, however, no indication that any of them corresponded very much, if at all, for the outside press. It is possible that Cheetham and Duane visited Washington briefly and sent back material which was published anonymously, but their files show nothing clearly identifiable as such.

The article goes on to list, with a brief description of each, John Agg, Lund Washington (a distant relative of the first president), James Montague, Joseph L. Buckingham, Eliab Kingman, Samuel L. Knapp, Nathaniel Carter, and Daniel Lee Child, all of whom, he wrote, appeared in the administration of John Quincy Adams or earlier. He describes Kingman as the first professional news-gatherer, saying he came from Rhode Island in 1822. The trail of James Montague has disappeared, leaving nothing more on him than this reference. Agg and Washington were stenographers who reported routine congressional proceedings for the Washington papers. Agg became a particular friend of Daniel Webster and dabbled in writing poetry. The frequent references to them in the records of capital journalism, however, contain no indication that Washington ever wrote for outside papers, although Agg may have contributed to Whig journals after 1836. David Lee Child, to whom Poore apparently referred when he said Daniel Lee Child, practiced law in Boston, edited the *Massachusetts Journal* in 1830, and from 1841 to 1849, working with his famous wife, Lydia Maria Child, put out the *Anti-Slavery Standard* in New York. Poore said he corresponded for the Boston *Advertiser.* But its files for the 1820s show no Washington letters, and there is no indication that he wrote for any others.

Knapp, Buckingham, and James Gordon Bennett turned up in 1827. Since the session which began in December of that year, every Congress has had its proceedings reported in some paper, somewhere in the country, by its own correspondent. That year saw the beginning of the Washington press corps as a continuing institution. The founders probably were hardly aware that they were starting something new. As is usual when new tools appear, at the time it seemed only a step in advance of existing practice.

Letters giving news, exchanged between merchants and politicians, predated printed periodicals. When newspapers first appeared, in the middle of the seventeenth century, their proprietors formed the habit of publishing such of these letters as came to their hands. It was the easiest form of early news-gathering. When the press became tied up with political parties or with certain business groups, its political or mercantile patrons wrote, presenting their contributions in the form of letters, with a greeting and a signature. As the eighteenth century advanced and the English political party structure and cabinet system developed, the press became a major weapon in political infighting. The same became true in America when the colonial press matured, especially after 1765. The English law of seditious libel made it desirable to conceal, or to pretend to conceal, the identity of newspaper contributors. Furthermore, those political figures who wrote for the press and the writers whose pens the politicians bought felt that they could better secure information if it were not generally known that they were writers.

The word *correspondent* came early to be applied to the non-journalist, either a merchant or a politician, who sent a letter to the newspaper proprietor for publication. Such letters might give news, or they might be polemic arguments on a public problem. They might be literary essays. The use of the word today, applying to a salaried reporter who files up-to-the-minute news by telegraph or broadcasts by radio or television, has come directly from a letter-writing ancestor, just as the word *reporter* has come from the early stenographers who appeared in the legislative halls. By 1820 seditious libel was no longer a problem. Nevertheless, the tradition of signed letters, with the signatures designed to conceal the identity of the writer, was strong. It made it possible to write highly controversial material without accepting the responsibility for that material. The practice continued until after the Civil War, and was used by war correspondents who followed the armies during that struggle. In actual fact, the identity of those Washington correspondents who used regular signatures became generally known.

Thus it was that when newspapers began to demand something more from Washington than merely to clip the capital journals or to accept occasional letters from supporting politicians they had only to adapt what was already a fairly well-established practice. After 1820, and particularly after 1828, there was a rapid increase in the country's press of Washington letters bearing fictitious signatures. Some may have been faked in the home offices. Much, however, was the work of editors who went to Washington during the sessions of Congress or of others who lived in the capital and used this means to develop a supplementary income. At the beginning, none supported themselves on the earnings as letter writers. Some held political office and wrote anonymously to support their party positions or to forward their own political ambitions. Some, like Kingman, who worked in the office of the Clerk of the House during the early years of his newspaper writing, eventually made correspondence their sole occupation.

Of those whom Poore named, Carter was the first whose work can be identified in the newspaper files. He started in 1822. A native of New Hampshire, he worked on a newspaper in Albany and was one of the partners when the New York *Statesman and Evening Advertiser* was founded on January 2, 1822, as a protectionist organ. Nearly a year later, on December 11, 1822, it said:

> The Editors of the New York Statesman and Evening Advertiser beg leave to inform their friends and the public, that they intend giving in their paper a concise and accurate original abstract of the proceedings and debates of Congress during the present session, together with an abridgment of reports and public documents of all kinds, sketches of distinguished individuals, notices of political transactions, and generally, the latest intelligence of every description, which can be obtained at the seat of government. For this purpose, the senior editor of the Statesman (Mr. Carter) departed this morning for Washington where he will remain the greater part of the winter.

To reveal the name of the writer, as this notice did, was unusual. Carter's first letter was dated from Washington on December 16 and appeared in the issue of the 19th. Like his later ones, it was printed under an all-capital heading, "FROM ONE OF THE EDITORS." Written in the first person, it discussed the steamboat and stage journey and first impressions of the city. The letters were run, with a few exceptions, every day until February 15, 1823. A three-day lag normally existed between the date on the article and the date of publication. The last, for this session, was written in Lancaster, Pennsylvania, on the 12th and said that the writer was on his way home. In December 1823 when Congress convened, Carter returned to Washington. His first letter, dated the 1st and appearing on the 4th, discussed the organization of Congress. But it was not from its Washington correspondent that the *Statesman* got the news, which was printed in that issue, of a milestone in American history and a cornerstone in foreign policy.

An adjoining column said, "An express from Washington arrived this forenoon, with copies of the National Intelligencer Extra, containing the Message of the President, delivered on Tuesday, which we hasten to lay before our readers, to the exclusion of all other articles in preparation." The text of President Monroe's message on the state of the Union followed. It was from the *Intelligencer*, therefore, and not from its own Washington correspondent, that the *Statesman* got the news of the Monroe Doctrine. The document, in which the hands-off policy was set out near the end after other matters were discussed, was printed in full, as was the custom, with no indication that particular significance attached to those paragraphs. Two days later the *Statesman* printed a letter from Carter dated the 2d, the day the message was delivered. Commenting on the several issues which the president raised, it said he had incurred some responsibility "in speaking so freely of the machinations and probable intentions of the Holy Alliance." But it expressed the belief the country would "very cheerfully assume" it.

From the beginning of the session, Carter's column had been headed daily, "EDITORIAL CORRESPONDENCE." On January 3, 1824, however, that was changed to "WASHINGTON CORRESPONDENCE." The letter, dated "Monday, 29th Dec. 1823," explained that by changing the heading the writer opened the column to contributors in the capital other than himself. "If anything should appear, which it would be improper for a reporter to say, but which either a member or gallery spectator might," he wrote, "the presumption would be that it came from one of my correspondents. . . . Our readers will not hereafter be obliged to consider all which may appear under the Washington head as my own."

This was the first use of the phrase "Washington Correspondence" as applied to a regular newspaper feature. It appeared until March 12, 1824, and then the letters disappeared without explanation. Carter never returned to the capital. Later he spent several years wandering in Europe, writing letters to his paper. Those letters were subsequently republished in book form. He died in Marseilles on January 2, 1830.

Poore was incorrect in giving "L" as Buckingham's middle initial. Born in Connecticut, Joseph Tinker Buckingham served out a printing apprenticeship in that state, worked as a journeyman in several other New England shops and established the *New England Galaxy,* a literary repository with comparatively little interest in politics, in Boston in 1817. In 1824 he started the Boston *Courier,* a daily newspaper, to argue the protectionist side in the debate then going forward between the free-trade heirs of New England's shipping tradition and the rising manufacturing interests.

His two-volume memoirs, published in 1852, explained that his winter in Washington was a move in the protectionist fight.[2] He went to the capital in December 1827, he said, at the instance of tariff supporters. They succeeded, in May 1828, in putting through Congress the bill with very high rates which came to be known as the "Tariff of Abominations." Buckingham wrote for the *Courier* routine reports of congressional proceedings as well as long expository arguments in favor of protection. He sent his last letter for the issue of March 11, 1828, and returned to Boston, so he was not on the scene when the bill was passed. His experience must have made him feel that Washington correspondence was worth while. There was a year's lapse, but when Congress reconvened in December 1829 the *Courier* featured letters from the capital which were signed "E," "Moth," "N," "E. B.," and "W." Who they were cannot be established now, but it is possible that one was Samuel L. Knapp.

His name turns up here and there among the records of Washington journalism in ways that make it hard to piece together a consistent story. It is clear, however, that he was a capital contemporary of Bennett and of Buckingham. A graduate of Dartmouth, he practiced law for a short time in Newburyport, Massachusetts, and then moved to Boston. In 1817 he wrote articles on freemasonry for Buckingham's *Galaxy* and served as counsel when his editor was prosecuted for criminal libel on the complaint of the Russian consul. From 1825 to July 1826 he edited a monthly magazine in Boston. Washington city directories of 1827 and 1830 list him, and in 1828 he published an address on DeWitt Clinton which he delivered before District of Columbia masons.

Aaron Smith Willington, who had edited the Charleston (S.C.) *Courier* since 1804, was a former resident of Massachusetts, so it is possible that he had contacts in his former home through which he and Knapp got in touch with each other. The *Courier* started regular Washington letters in December 1828 and Poore's reference points to Knapp as the probable author. Although Buckingham's memoirs refer to Knapp's writings on freemasonry in 1817, they do not again refer to him or to any Washington correspondent other than himself. There is nothing to prove whether or not Knapp was the writer or one of the writers when letters began to appear in the Boston *Courier* in 1829. His name was missing from the 1834 Washington city directory. For a time in 1835 he edited a magazine in New York devoted to articles on American history. His name does not reappear in Washington.

The third of the 1827 founders of Washington correspondence was the vigorous, brilliant, ambitious Scot who was then relatively unknown. A graduate of Blair College in Aberdeen, Scotland, James Gordon Bennett taught school in Nova Scotia and worked as a proof reader in a commercial printing plant in Boston. He was introduced to Journalism on the Charleston *Courier*. In 1827 Mordecai M. Noah of the New York *Enquirer*, who disliked Bennett's vigor but who needed competent assistance, took him on. They did not get along well. Therefore, when the time approached for Congress to convene in December 1827 and Bennett suggested that he go to Washington, Noah was glad to ship him off.[3]

A story which Bennett told on himself is that he drew the inspiration for the literary tone of his Washington correspondence from the letters of Horace Walpole about the court of George II, a volume of which Bennett found in the Library of Congress. Deciding to apply the same spirit to "the court of John Quincy Adams," Bennett wrote several years later, "all the political, gay, fashionable, witty beautiful characters that appeared in Washington during that winter, were sketched off at random." [4] Any one reading his correspondence is particularly struck by the extent to which he was concerned with "the ladies," although he avoided mentioning the names of particular ladies. There was a lightness, wit and vigor about his style that was far from the heavier argumentation of other newspaper writers of the time. He remained through each session of Congress, although he often wandered elsewhere during recess, until 1831. Of him, more later.

Kingman was the man whom Poore credited with having been the first "professional newsgatherer" in the capital. Poore says that he came in 1822, but other material, which seems more reliable, gives 1824 as the date of his arrival in Washington, so he was behind Carter. He was in the city ahead of those who came in 1827, but newspaper files reveal little that could have come from his pen until after 1830. Later his name was to stand out among the leaders of the correspondents. He was born in Bridgewater, Massachusetts, on May 24, 1797, and graduated from Brown University in 1816. Soon thereafter he became a tutor in the home of Governor Henry S. Foote of Virginia and was placed in touch with other Virginians in Washington. He moved to that city after he married a Washington girl, daughter of a Virginian who had relocated in the capital. For a time he worked in the Office of the Clerk of the House. In 1829 he moved to Boston and bought the *New England Palladium,* a weekly which he converted to a daily. During his editorship it carried letters from Washington correspondents using different signatures. In 1830 he sold the paper and returned to the capital. He devoted the rest of a long life to newspaper writing, to several different jobs at the Capitol, and to managing real estate holdings. His home on Fourteenth Street near Thomas Circle became a favorite gathering place for a selected elite of congressional leaders and cabinet officers. He retired from newspaper work in 1861 and died in 1883.[5] A short street located where his home stood now bears his name.

When James Brooks was a member of Congress from New York, between 1866 and 1875, he was sometimes informally referred to as the originator of Washington correspondence. Actually he did not come to Washington until 1832, and was the last to arrive of those for whom precedence is claimed. He was born in Portland, Maine, on November 10, 1810, and worked for a storekeeper in Lewiston when he was eleven. Later he studied in an academy in Monmouth, Maine, taught school, and graduated from Waterville College. In Portland he read law and wrote anonymously for the *Advertiser*. At twenty-one he was elected to the Maine legislature and continued to write for the press. The next year he went to Washington and sent letters to the Portland *Advertiser*. After Congress adjourned he traveled in the South and continued to write. In 1836 he founded the New York *Express* as a Whig organ. He did not return to Washington as a correspondent although we shall hear later from his younger brother, Erastus.[6]

While these pioneers laid the foundations for the corps of correspondents for the outside press, presidents still gave their confidence to the editor of a selected Washington paper. The *National Intelligencer*, however, was shouldered aside. Smith remained at the helm as long as Jefferson was in the White House. Soon thereafter he abandoned journalism in favor of banking. In 1807, Joseph Gales, Jr., joined the staff, bringing skills both as a stenographer and as a printer. Three years later Smith sold out to him. In October 1812 Gales was joined by his brother-in-law, William Winston Seaton, to found the firm of Gales and Seaton. They remained powers in the political and journalistic scene until the Civil War. Gales died on July 21, 1860, and Seaton on June 16, 1866. The venerable paper gave up soon thereafter.

They enjoyed the confidence of both Madison and Monroe. But as the campaign of 1824 approached, they bet on the wrong horse. Looking to William H. Crawford of Georgia as the probable winner, they backed him and thus alienated the final victor, John Quincy Adams. At least Adams said in his diary that that was the reason they opposed him.[7] Even before Monroe left the White House Adams, then secretary of state, gave his confidence to the *National Journal*. That paper had been founded in 1822 but was taken over in July 1824 by Peter Force, who used it actively to support the Massachusetts statesman.

Adams's inauguration, therefore, gave Force the rail position in the race for White House news and the printing from the Executive departments although Gales and Seaton continued to hold office for both houses of Congress. Force or some of his staff were admitted to seats in each house adjoining those of the *National Intelligencer* reporter-stenographers.

Supporters of Andrew Jackson, who had received a larger popular vote than any of his competitors in the four-way 1824 presidential race although the office slipped from his grasp, now went to work to elect their idol in 1828 without any slip-ups. They backed Duff Green, a Missouri lawyer, newspaper editor and former member of that state's legislature, in establishing the *United States Telegraph* in 1826. For the next two years he was the journalistic spark plug of the Tennessean's campaign and was recognized as editor of the official paper after March 4, 1829. He succeeded, also, in pushing aside Gales and Seaton as printers to Congress.

4. Jacksonian Democracy and the Press

Andrew Jackson entered the executive mansion on March 4, 1829, to become the first president who was neither a landed Virginian nor a Massachusetts Adams. The jubilant celebrants who followed their idol into the White House that day, destroying upholstery, drapery and furnishings with their muddy boots and tobacco juice, actually crowded in with such force as to threaten bodily injury to the aging Tennesseean. To them his election was a revolution, the triumph of true democracy. And the society of which they were a part, bringing about changes some of which were already under way and some of which were brought about through the aggressive policies of Jackson and his political associates, has been stamped by historians with his name. Jacksonian Democracy saw a new alignment of political parties. It saw an enormous growth in the country's transportation system. It saw marked industrial development, reorganization of the nation's currency and credit system, and a dramatic upswing in the rate of population growth. Cities, in particular, grew rapidly.

These years saw new departures in journalism and a new importance given to Washington correspondence as a part of those new departures. Although correspondents started to appear before 1828, the press corps owes its establishment on a firm basis to the developments in politics and the press while Old Hickory occupied the White House. Until 1833 American newspapers had been content to play to a small circulation group among the educated and well-to-do. Farmers and laborers read them, or had them read to them, in the taverns. The New York *Sun*, established on September 3, 1833, was the first successful paper to have copies hawked on the streets for a penny per copy and to print material appealing to a wider reader market. Sales multiplied many times over and imitators soon appeared.

The typical American newspaper of those years was closely allied to a political party, and often to a particular clique within the party. It supported the party wholeheartedly and without reserve. In the first flush of their new constitutionally-protected freedom of the press, the Federalist and Republican papers reporting the lusty political wars from 1789 to 1812 had in many cases thrown reserve and good taste to the winds, exploring the depths of vituperation, raking up vicious scandals, frankly spreading and repeating malicious tales about their political opponents. Editorials as well as correspondents' contributions were political weapons and objective, responsible reporting was rare. There were a few exceptions, notably the greater dignity of the *National Intelligencer*. Although the press became slightly less venal as federalism died out after 1816, leaving a breathing space before the nation's party structure squared away for new battles, the journalistic precedent of vitriol was there.

Jackson's two terms saw two-fisted, no-holds-barred political and journalistic wars resumed. The paper which marched in front of the Democratic party's mobilized press warriors and gave the commands was Francis Preston Blair's Washington *Globe*. When Jackson was inaugurated, Duff Green and the *United States Telegraph* enjoyed the monopoly on news from the Which House as well as the profitable printing from Congress and the executive departments. A close personal and political associate of Vice-President John C. Calhoun, Green was a willing lieutenant as the South Carolinian sought the presidency in 1832. Events of Jackson's first administration led to enmity between the president and vice-president. They led, therefore, to Green's fall from favor. Consequently Blair, a Virginian whose contributions to a party paper in Frankfort, Kentucky, had attracted the attention of some of the Kitchen Cabinet, was encouraged to come to Washington. He brought out the first issue of his Washington *Globe* on December 7, 1830. After John C. Rives of Nashville arrived in 1832 to take over the business management of the paper the firm name of Blair and Rives attained a prominence equal to that of Gales and Seaton in Washington's political, social and press circles.

Originally the *Globe* pretended to be an associate and supporter of the official *United States Telegraph*. But as word went out to the cabinet that Blair was eligible for departmental printing Green swung into opposition, although he held on as printer to Congress. Blair entered into a personal relationship with the president which was probably more intimate than any occurring at any point in American history between a chief executive and a newspaperman. The *Globe* became the channel through which Jackson announced his moves and mobilized public support in the fights revolving around nullification, the Bank war, the withdrawal of the deposits and the censure and expunging resolutions. Its editor's caustic pen, skilled in the journalistic political battling of the day, set the pace for the party's press throughout the country.

Blair's conduct of the official editorship marked the high point in the history of administration presses. When Martin Van Buren came into the White House in 1837 as Jackson's designated heir, he, Blair, and Senator Thomas Hart Benton of Missouri continued to cooperate, a triumvirate carrying on Old Hickory's policies. After the Whig victory of 1840, however, no paper held the mantle for as long a period, or with as much influence, as had Blair's *Globe*. The profitable official editorship and public printing provided Blair, who had been $40,000 in debt before he came to Washington, with funds to buy a farm where the District of Columbia boundary crossed the Seventh Street Pike, the road that was later named Georgia Avenue. The name he gave the property, Silver Spring, is borne now by a populous suburb. He also bought a city mansion on Pennsylvania Avenue across from the White House and in the adjoining block. He and his sons continued to play leading roles through the Civil War. Although a slaveholder, he was a staunch adherent of Jackson's nationalism and went over to the Republican party when disunion threatened. One son was Lincoln's postmaster general and another served the Union cause in the army, in Congress, and in Missouri politics. In 1942 a descendant sold the "Blair House" on Pennsylvania Avenue to the United States government to be used as a guest residence for distinguished foreign visitors. Kings and visiting presidents have slept there in the last twenty-five years. It became the executive mansion when the White House underwent repairs between 1950 and 1952.[1]

If the political wars tightened press and party affiliations in many cases, there were already indications of journalistic independence. Such papers as the New York *Sun,* the Philadelphia *Public Ledger,* and the New Orleans *Picayune* played down party loyalty. The great supporter of political nonpartisanship, however, was James Gordon Bennett's New York *Herald,* established on May 6, 1835. The editor, who had believed in 1832 that party support was necessary if a paper were to survive, now trumpeted his independence in blatant editorials. Actually the *Herald* and its Washington correspondents tended to praise officials who cooperated in giving exclusive information and to blast harshly those who remained aloof. There are indications that *Herald* Washington correspondents came and went in some cases as it became necessary to shift the personal associations which they had developed in the capital to conform to shifts in support of or opposition to cooperative or stubborn public officials.

Not only did political realignments cause press habits to change and Washington correspondents to rise to new importance. Until 1827 the typical American newspaper had been content to wait for the mails to bring the correspondence and exchanges with which it filled its columns. In that year, however, both the New York *Journal of Commerce* and the *Enquirer* engaged fast-sailing small boats to meet incoming ships outside New York harbor and rush their European news back to the city. With this beginning a new interest developed in quicker and competitive news communication, especially from Washington. For several years the New York papers had been in the habit of cooperating to meet the cost of expresses to rush ahead of the mail such news as the annual message on the state of the Union. Expresses were relays of galloping horses ridden by skilled riders and set up by the livery stables, stage lines or companies engaged in wagon transport. They could be hired when fast messenger service was wanted, either by businessmen or by the press.

In 1833 the *Journal of Commerce* bore the cost alone of an express bringing the president's message, as well as special letters which were probably the work of Eliab Kingman. The message and letters, printed on December 4, were brought from the capital in fourteen hours. The message, sent up as Congress convened early in each December, was the normal occasion for hiring expresses, and for several years continued to be the news break that called forth expenditure, enterprise and competition for fast transmission. By December 1834 there was steamboat and rail connection between New York and Philadelphia. In that year the *Courier and Enquirer* offered the Camden and Amboy Railroad $200 to send ahead of the mail the president's message. Negotiation failed, however, for the paper used horses for the whole distance. For the next two years it led the race. An article in the issue of December 16, 1834, told how it was done. Printed copies were given the first rider at the *Globe* office. He did not leave the Capitol until the clerks had started reading the message. It had passed Baltimore, thirty-six miles away, before the reading was finished. The horses were kept at a full gallop and changed every four or five miles. Each rider rode about thirty miles.

When Congress next convened, in December 1835, the *Courier and Enquirer* arranged to run an express with Washington news every day instead of only on the day the president's message was sent. That document was brought by horseback in twelve and one-half hours. In 1836 Congress authorized the postmaster general to establish an editor's express mail, a special service at an increased rate, to rush newspapers and proof sheets ahead of the regular mail. The government bought the *Courier and Enquirer*'s line. Meanwhile the railroads appeared, making it possible for the private expresses or the government express mail to use locomotives in place of horses on parts of the journey. The Camden and Amboy line stretched across New Jersey through the winter of 1834–35. As fast as parts were finished service was opened on those links. By spring the line and its steamboat connections offered through service between New York and Philadelphia. The first train ran between Baltimore and Washington on August 25, 1835, and construction was started between the Pennsylvania and Maryland cities. In 1842 it became possible to travel between Washington and New York by rail, although the Susquehanna, Delaware, and Hudson rivers still had to be ferried.

As we have seen, James Gordon Bennett started writing Washington letters for Noah's New York *Enquirer* in 1827. Two years later Noah sold the paper to James Watson Webb, owner and editor of the *Morning Courier*. The combined *Courier and Enquirer* led the New York newspaper field with a circulation of 4,000 and at first adhered loyally to the Jackson standard. It went along with the president's early moves against the Bank of the United States. As the Battle of the Bank grew heated, Webb developed doubts although he printed Bennett's Washington letters which went all the way with Jackson. Investigation later brought out that Webb secured loans, directly or through third parties, totaling $52,975 from the institution, although he insisted before a congressional committee that he had applied only after financial houses in New York refused accommodation. In April 1831 the paper came out in support of a limited recharter, contrary to the president's position. In other respects it continued to support Jackson.

Bennett left. The paper had no Washington correspondent when Jackson vetoed the Bank recharter bill on July 10, 1832. In August it trumpeted its opposition to the president's reelection with an ostentatious "Manifesto" in its regular edition and in a special edition of 20,000 copies. On November 30, after Jackson had been triumphantly reelected in spite of the paper's opposition, the *Courier and Enquirer* printed the first letter from "The Spy in Washington." The paper characteristically made the gesture of concealing "The Spy's" identity. On January 28 it went so far as to deny that the letters were the work of the solicitor of the treasury, as had been rumored. The Spy was Matthew L. Davis. Poore described him as "probably the most influential of Washington correspondents." A former New York printer, he had entered politics as early as 1790 and was an intimate, and later the official biographer, of Aaron Burr. He turned to journalism after some business ventures failed. From 1832 to about 1840 he wrote from Washington both to the *Courier and Enquirer* and to the London *Times*. His contributions to the English paper appeared over the signature, "A Genevese Traveler."

After he left the *Courier and Enquirer* Bennett tried to join Blair. But loyal party men distrusted him, seeming to feel that he was incapable of subjecting himself to the necessary discipline. He established papers in New York and later in Philadelphia hoping to secure Jacksonian support. Both failed when political backing was not forthcoming. So he founded his *Herald* free from political ties. Here he found the formula for success—sensational success. Himself a claimant to the title of first Washington correspondent, Bennett naturally saw that he was covered in the capital when he had his own paper. The issue of November 30, 1835, coming out as Congress prepared to convene for the first time after the *Herald* was established, said a competent writer had been engaged. "Our correspondent is a gentleman of high character and good attainments, having access to the movements of all parties in the capital," the paper said. "He is not a politician—he is as we are, independent in thought and action, and one who will tell the truth of all parties, men and measures." Who the correspondent was cannot now be ascertained. "Private Correspondence No. I," which appeared in the column below the notice, was written in a mild style which lacked the light, often satiric, touch with which Bennett in his Washington days had described the city's political and social scene.

This year the still young, financially insecure *Herald* did not burden itself with the cost of expresses to compete with the galloping riders hired by the *Journal of Commerce* and *Courier and Enquirer*. But James Gordon Bennett was not the man to admit defeat. In using the name of Richard Adams Locke as his butt, Bennett referred to an actually existing man who was vulnerable. The previous August the New York *Sun* had printed seven articles written in an interesting though ostentatiously scientific manner which the paper said it had copied from the *Edinburgh Journal of Science*. The articles set out the supposed findings of Sir John Herschell, who actually was an eminent astronomer, in which he claimed to have discovered living beings on the moon. Sir John, the articles said, made his observations through a powerful telescope set up in South Africa. The articles brought a very great spurt in the *Sun's* circulation and were widely reprinted before Locke had a few drinks one night and let slip the fact that he had faked them. *Sun* readers then accepted the situation as a good joke and the paper's circulation remained high.

The *Herald* of December 7, 1835, said, "Sir Richard Adams Locke, L.L.D., A.S.S., the moon hoax man, has turned a red herring abolitionist." On the 9th, while the rest of New York's press and business community awaited Jackson's annual presentation of his views before Congress, the *Herald* printed:

By Express—Twelve Hours From Washington
Original Draft of the President's Message

We have the pleasure of presenting our readers this morning with the *Original Draft of the President's Message,* as read by that venerable and distinguished Patriot to the "Cabinets proper and improper," on Saturday last. The paper usually read to Congress, and called the Message, is a document prepared by the Secretaries, Vice President and Post Master General from the original itself. In the present instance, the document which may be published by our contemporaries this morning has been diluted and expanded by those windy men to thirteen columns brevier, while the spirit-stirring original only fills two columns and a half of the Herald. As to the spirit, the substance, the fire, the natural energy of expression, the unstudied beauty and brevity of phrase, there is no comparison between the original and the dilution.

We have the pleasure also of announcing to our readers that our Express beat the famous one of the Courier and Enquirer and the Journal of Commerce exactly *two hours and forty-six minutes.* It was entirely organised and set in operation by that wonderful genius Sir Richard Adams Locke, L.L.D. The apparatus is of the most novel construction—a magnificent improvement on the Vilocepede, invented a few years ago.—Sir Richard rode the express himself, all the way.—Through his great influence with the Kitchen Cabinet, he procured a copy of the Original, the only copy we believe now in existence.

We have, in addition, the pleasure to state, that we are now in treaty with the same great genius to run a other daily express calculated to beat the other daily express from Washington by at least three hours every day. Sir Richard says, by a few more screws and a little sweet Kitchen grease on the wheels, he can easily beat any express ever attempted in this country or in the world.

As to the Sun and Transcript express, it is almost too contemptible to notice. Sir Richard assures us that it was hobbling along on the other side of Baltimore, at the rate of four miles an hour, when he past it. It may arrive probably tomorrow or next day—not sooner.

The "Original Message" in the column below was a friendly take-off on Jackson's manner of speech and writing, interspersed with frequent interjections of "By the Eternal," the president's favorite expletive, and reference to how "I" licked the red coats at New Orleans on December 8, 1815. Its last paragraph was a witty reference to Bennett's past support of the party and a promotion piece for the *Herald*. Finally there came the printed signature, "ANDREW JACKSON."

Bennett pulled another obvious fake a month later when the country awaited the president's special message on our critical relations with France. The national temper was roused when the French Chamber refused to appropriate funds to pay claims pressed by American shipowners which had been accepted by French diplomats as just. A Washington letter in the *Herald* of January 3, 1836, said that the special message was expected the next day. Another column of the same issue was headed by an engraving of two galloping horses, one black and one white, ridden by jockeys. Under it appeared:

Express From Washington

We have the felicity this morning of presenting exclusively to our *thirty thousand* readers and subscribers one of the most important documents that ever was sent to an American Congress—the SPECIAL MESSAGE OF THE PRESIDENT OF THE UNITED STATES, delivered to both Cabinets on Saturday evening last. It was received last evening by express, exclusively run for the Herald, by the greatest Lunar Astronomer of the age, Sir Richard Adams Locke, L.L.D.A.S.S. Sir Richard tells us that our Friday evening final despatches from France were received by the President—that he took the pipe instantly from his mouth—looked over the packet—started up with a sublime energy—strode across the East Room—smashed his pipe in a thousand pieces—sat down with a patriot's fury and wrote the annexed document, which for profoundness, beauty, energy and point, yet outstrips any thing that has come from that source.

Knowing the extreme anxiety of the public mind to learn the actual state of our relations with France, we have incurred the enormous expence of establishing this express exclusively for the Herald; and we are happy to say that thus far, it leaves immeasurably behind the spavined and broken down hacks of the Courier and Enquirer, which bring nothing from the capital but the merest twaddle and long winded nonsense so frequently alluded to by our venerable President. At the very jump our black pony took the lead, as will appear by the above accurate engraving. At the end of the first ten miles, the Courier express was left at least a mile behind.

The half-column "Message" was a friendly skit by a clever humorist taking off the president's presumed anger over the French situation. A few selected excerpts follow:

Original Special Message

Fellow citizens of the Senate
and House of Representatives

At the opening of the present session, I sent you a pretty long Message, treating on the affairs of the nation, and explaining to you your duty—what I and the people want you to do, but as yet you have done not a thing but make speeches, leave cards, eat my dinners, and talk with the ladies. I gave my last blow out at the White House on New Year's Day. You all attended but the Nullifiers, and some of you did not behave remarkably well, yet it was as much as I expected. . . .

I advise you to lay aside all idling and flirting with the ladies in the library, galleries and dark passages about the Capitol. We have already quite enough of foundlings in the Poor House. . . .

Don't be afraid of them. Remember, Andrew Jackson is your President. . . . Louis-Phillippe is a mere stock jobber like Nick Biddle and knows nothing of fighting. He may have been in a brush or two, but he never *fit* the Battle of New Orleans.

The suggestive reference was characteristic of some of his other references during his Washington correspondence days as he sometimes skirted broad meanings while writing about "the ladies." There was nothing of this spirit, however, when the actual message arrived. Submitted to Congress on January 15, it was printed in full in the *Herald* of the 21st. A short editorial merely described it as a "dignified, just, and proper document." When the Post Office Department established its express mail for editors, the *Herald,* of course, benefited with the others. After 1840 its Washington service became one of the best, if not definitely the best, in the country.

Two years later another newspaperman was seized by the sergeant-at-arms and examined before the House. The writer was Davis, "The Spy in Washington." The incident resulted in the death of a congressman in a duel. When the House convened on February 12, 1838, Representative Henry A. Wise, a Virginia Whig, rose to a question of privilege and called attention to a *Courier and Enquirer* Washington letter printed over the "Spy's" signature. Written in inflammatory language it charged that a member of one of the two houses had sought payment to use his influence with a department in favor of a constituent who wanted to sell to the government a device which he had patented. Wise introduced a resolution for the appointment of a select committee to find out who the offending member was. The issue as stated in the proposed resolution did not involve an attack on Davis or the press.

With the resolution up for debate, Representative Jonathan Cilley, a Maine Democrat, was the first to get the floor. His words cost him his life. Pointing out that the editor of the paper which had printed the charges was the one who had come out in support of the Bank of the United States after receiving $52,000 in loans, he said he did "not think his charges were entitled to much credit in an American Congress." During the parts of two days devoted to debate, no member defended Davis or the letter writers. Several denounced the group in general and spoke particularly of Davis, who was known in spite of his surface pretense that he was not the author of the "Spy" letters. The discussion showed that he was aging, bald, and bespectacled, and was in the gallery listening. Several protested that to adopt the resolution was such a recognition of a newspaper article as to be beneath the dignity of the House. One declared that "let one of these letter-writers dare to apply their false charges to myself personally, and I will settle the matter by applying my fist to his spectacles."

The resolution was amended to provide for examination at the bar of the House instead of by select committee and to instruct the Speaker to subpoena the writer. Thus modified it was approved. The next day, while the sergeant-at-arms held Davis in the lobby, the House approved a series of questions. The writer would be asked if he were the author of the letter. Then he would be asked if he knew who was the member alluded to as corrupt, whether or not he were a member of the House, and if so, what was his name. It was agreed that if it turned out that the offending legislator were not a representative the examination was to end.

Davis was brought before the Speaker and the first question put. Instead of answering, he asked the right to give his reasons for refusing. Ordering him withdrawn, the House went into a long debate while he waited under guard in the lobby. It finally voted to grant his request. The sergeant-at-arms brought him back in and, the first question being repeated, he denied that the House had a right to ask. He knew the "Spy," however, he said, and he knew the member to whom the article referred. The second question was then put. Davis replied that the legislator involved was not a representative. The House thereupon ordered him discharged and defeated a proposal that the proceedings be sent to the Senate.[2]

Nine days after the House examined Davis, Webb came to Washington and took a room at Gadsby's Hotel. He penned a note to Cilley asking if the Washington *Globe* account of his language in the debate were accurate, pointing out that the writer was editor of the *Courier and Enquirer,* and adding that "the object of this communication is to inquire of you whether I am the editor to whom you alluded, and, if so, to ask the explanation which the character of your remarks renders necessary." Representative William J. Graves of Kentucky agreed to act as courier and delivered Webb's note to Cilley on the House floor while the body was in session. Cilley refused to accept it although he insisted that his refusal meant no disrespect to the Kentuckian. Nevertheless, in a further exchange of notes which was carried on while the House continued with its regular proceedings, Graves took the attitude that he was insulted and himself challenged Cilley. They went out the road toward Marlboro, Maryland, on the afternoon of February 24 and fought with rifles at eighty yards. On the third exchange Cilley was shot through the body and died in a few minutes.

Webb and two supporters, meanwhile, were seeking the duelists. Earlier that day they had agreed to arm themselves, go to Cilley's room, and try to force him to fight the editor on the spot or to agree to meet him before meeting Graves. If the congressman refused to do either, Webb planned to fire a bullet to shatter his enemy's right arm, thus preventing the scheduled fight. Failing to find Cilley in his room, the three sought the duelists at three favorite spots in the Washington area for such affairs. If they found them, Webb planned to claim the fight as his own. If any one raised a weapon to interfere, it was agreed that Webb should shoot Cilley and that he and his friends would then defend themselves as best they could. Webb's party, however, failed to find Graves and Cilley and their party. A select committee later found that Graves and two members who had served as seconds were guilty of a breach of the privileges of the House. It recommended that the first be expelled and the other censured.[3] The House, however, failed to act.

Ten months later the angry Washington correspondent of the rabidly Democratic Baltimore *Republican* described the incident which led to the corruption charge and the duel. Davis, he wrote, was "not only a 'Spy' but a 'Pimp' in Washington." In a letter published in the issue of December 17, 1839, he told the story of a man who had invented a mailbag lock and had to come to Washington to seek a patent. He got in touch with Senator John Ruggles of Maine, chairman of the Committee on Patents. The senator bought an interest. The Baltimore *Republican* writer saw nothing wrong in that. The visitor later came to believe that he had sold his interest too cheaply, sought a way to break the contract, and spoke to a Whig congressman about it. The Whig congressman, the paper said, in turn told Davis who made it into a story of bribery and corruption which led to Wise's resolution. The Senate appointed a select committee at Ruggles's request and absolved him of any wrongdoing.[4] As the *Republican* correspondent saw it, "Ruggles was acquitted honorably, and the Spy in Washington stood before the world branded with falsehood."

This Democratic party supporter was probably the one who gave the Whigs their rallying cry for their successful presidential race in 1840. The letter about Davis was part of a series in Baltimore's Jacksonian journal appearing over the signature of "John DeZiska" or "Z." As was true of much Washington correspondence in these years, the identity of the author or authors cannot today be ascertained. John DeZiska may actually have been his name, but that is unlikely. The Whig National Convention met in Harrisburg in November 1839. At the time most followers of politics in the country assumed that Henry Clay of Kentucky would be the nominee. Instead, due to some inside maneuvering the delegates chose William Henry Harrison of Ohio. Clay's supporters were stunned by the rejection of their hero. The day the news reached Washington, "Z" wrote the following letter, which appeared in the *Republican* of December 11:

FROM OUR CORRESPONDENT

Washington, Dec. 10th, 1839

I believe the maxim of Shakespeare, or the truism of that great lord, call it what you will, which asserts, that "the stream of true love, never did run smooth," has never been disputed by Philosopher, Poet, or Divine; and if it should ever be written down that the stream of politics ever runs over beds of flinty rocks, and affords little else than sorrow, I hope that there is not a man in this world of ours who will attempt to gainsay the apothesis.

The political friends of Mr. Clay are in agonies, and well they may be, for what grosser insult could their idol and chief have received, than to have been wrapped up in a "buttoned rug" and laid away in lavender, to make way for that indiscribable lump of lead or living mass of ruined matter, the "HERO" of the North Bend.

This morning, at an early hour, as I was traversing The Avenue, I met one of the "original" friends of Mr. Clay, a man, who had stood by the "farmer" of Ashland, for upwards of thirty years.

As I approached him, he hastily threw on his specs and pulling a wet copy of the National Intelligencer from his pocket, he hastily tore it open, and striking his cane across the editorial head of it exclaimed, "see that, sir, see that; by St. Paul, is it not too much for flesh and blood to bear!"

I cast my eye over the part of the paper he had designated, and saw, in capitals, William Henry Harrison, announced a candidate for the Presidency.

"For my own part, my friend," I replied, "this matter of your Presidential candidate, is one that belongs to your own family exclusively, and I have no disposition to interfere with your domestic griefs. If, however, my opinion should be wanting on the subject, I do not think I should hesitate to say, that the Convention at Harrisburg, by nominating Mr. Harrison offered a most gross insult to Mr. Clay and Gen. Scott, and besides degrading themselves, absolutely insulted the country. Many a man of intelligence, and worth, and of high and noble principles, might indeed vote for Mr. Clay, or for Gen. Scott, without blushing for the deed, but I am very sure that the salvy or the remark, could not be applied to the man who should vote for Mr. Harrison."

"May the old bug-a-boo be———."

"Tut, tut," said I, interrupting the anticipated result and profanity of my venerable friend, "do not swear about it. Get rid of the 'hero' of the North Bend on the best terms you can. Drop him, and take up Clay or Scott, as you will." "Get rid of him," ejaculated the aged friend, "get rid of him! and pray tell me how we are to do it?"

"Give him a barrel of hard cider, and settle a pension of two thousand a year on him," I replied, "and my word for it, he will sit the remainder of his days in his log cabin by the side of a 'sea coal' fire and study moral philosophy."

"Settle a pension on him!" screamed the old gentleman; "cut my nose off if I would not sooner send him to the Alms House!"

The feeling felt, and yet to be expressed by all the friends of Mr. Clay and Gen. Scott, in relation to the nomination, is I doubt not, precisely of the quality uttered by my venerable friend this morning.

The letter continued with a discussion of Clay's probable reaction, and then discussed the difficulty the House faced in organizing because of the contested election of a New Jersey member.

Hard Cider! The Log Cabin! A Washington correspondent's derisive remark lent itself to the Whig party's effort to invest its nominee with the interests and presumably simple personal habits of the mass of rural and laboring voters. In Harrisburg Thomas Elder, a bank president, and Richard S. Elliott, a Whig editor, saw in the letter the catchwords they needed.[5] To the disgust of the *Republican's* editors, log cabins and hard cider barrels sprang up across the nation as the totems of a campaign that became a shouting, parading songfest. "Z" in letter after letter tried to undo his work by hinting that Harrison was a drunkard, saying that hard cider, used to excess, was a peculiarly revolting beverage, and by calling the nominee "a dotard, who can be used like a nose of wax, and who will be, by the black-legs that are to surround him." It was useless. Harrison swept to victory.

5. The New York Herald: 1838–1841

James Gordon Bennett's caustic editorials—often harsh and critical, often witty and sarcastic, but capable of suddenly switching to fulsome praise when he found occasion to support a public figure—were part of the aggressive character of the *Herald* which caused its circulation to boom. By 1841 it was near the top of the field in New York and was widely regarded at home and abroad as the best informed journal in the country. In that year it staged two coups. First, it quarreled with the Senate and forced it to change its rules. Secondly, it, alone, accurately predicted the outcome of President John Tyler's battle with the Whig leaders in Congress. It shared, therefore, in the angry recriminations which followed. But its circulation climbed dramatically.

The background of the Senate quarrel lay in the rules for the admission of reporters. The resolution of 1802 gave the presiding officer power to admit them where he saw fit. In 1827, when the upper house engaged in a short debate about press facilities they occupied reserved gallery seats. On December 17 of that year Senator William Henry Harrison protested that they should be placed in a position to avoid errors which he blamed on inability to hear clearly. He offered a resolution directing that they be placed on the floor. After the Senate officers asked more leeway in locating them the resolution was amended and passed in a form which merely directed the Secretary, under the direction of the president, to provide seats. Later developments show that then or later they were placed in the eastern gallery, presumably, however, in a position from which they could hear more clearly.[1]

Up to now the Senate had provided for the reporters merely by resolution. Their admission was not governed by a section of the rules as was the case in the House. In 1835, however, the upper chamber, too, writing a provision governing the galleries, ordered by rule that the reporters "be removed from the eastern gallery, and placed on the floor of the Senate, under the direction of the Secretary." [2]

Three years later both houses again juggled their provisions for the press. The House action was minor and involved no debate. On March 1, 1838, a resolution was offered ordering that no person "shall be allowed the privilege of the Hall, under the character of stenographer, without written permission from the Speaker, specifying the part of the Hall assigned to him." It was amended by adding a provision that no stenographer or reporter be admitted unless he state in writing "for what paper or papers he is employed to report." In this form it was adopted.[3]

The House action was quiet enough. But that in the Senate produced fireworks. Through actions on March 24 and 26 and April 24 it considered a special committee's proposal that the 47th rule, which listed the persons who might be admitted to the Senate floor, be amended. Most of the rule, under the proposed change, was the same as that adopted in 1835. But buried in its text, among the verbiage listing those having the floor privilege, was a new clause limiting admission to the press facilities to "two reporters for each of the daily papers, and one reporter for each tri-weekly paper published in the City of Washington, whose names shall be communicated in writing by the editors of those papers to the Secretary of the Senate, and who shall confine themselves to the seats now provided for them." That is, specific provision was made for the Washington newspaper stenographers. All others could appear only in the public galleries. They enjoyed no special access to reserved seats. The committee report lay without action until the closing night, July 9, when it was adopted in the usual end-of-the-session rush.[4]

The reason the Senate decided to admit only reporters for the Washington papers is not clear. They were still being clipped by much of the country's press. There seems, however, to be basis for the charges voiced at the time that the rule was changed at the instance of Vice-President Richard M. Johnson and Senator

John M. Niles of Connecticut who wanted to bar certain journalistic critics. Niles's target, in particular, was Erastus Brooks. He was the younger brother of James Brooks who corresponded briefly six years earlier for the Portland *Advertiser.* James was now publisher of the New York *Express* and Erastus was its Washington correspondent.

Reporters felt the rule's force the next time Congress met. The *Congressional Globe* reports that on December 22 Senator John Norvell of Michigan laid before the Senate a petition signed by six newspaper correspondents writing for eight newspapers outside of Washington. The petitioners protested the rule. They begged "that the Senate may assign them such seats on the floor, or in the galleries, as may enable them to discharge their duties to those whose agents they are." The papers they represented cut across both sides of the political fence. The *Express* was the only New York paper whose correspondent was included among the petitioners although the *Herald, Courier and Enquirer,* and *Journal of Commerce* had reporters in the capital. The petition was referred to the Committee on the Contingent Fund.[5]

On January 5, 1839, the committee proposed that the front seats of the eastern gallery to the right of the Chair be set apart for the reporters for the outside papers. The report precipitated a debate that runs through almost four pages of the *Congressional Globe* and found the Democrats, in general, opposing the reporters and the Whigs supporting them. The *Express* was a Whig organ. Some of the remarks of Senator Niles, while more violent than was typical, nevertheless show the attitude of some of his colleagues toward the reporters. He said in part, according to the peculiar style of congressional reporting of that day:

> He was somewhat surprised at a proposition that the body should sanction, and in some manner endorse, the vile slanders that issue daily from these letter writers by assigning them seats within the chamber. Who were these persons who styled themselves reporters? Why miserable slanderers, hirelings hanging on to the skirts of literature, earning a miserable subsistence from their vile and dirty misrepresentations of the proceedings here, and many of them writing for both sides. . . . Perhaps no member of that body had been more grossly misrepresented and caricatured than himself by those venal and profligate scribblers, who were

sent here to earn a disreputable living by catering to the depraved appetite of the papers they work for. . . . Was he not unwilling to do any act that might be supposed to interfere in the slightest degree with the freedom of the press, he would move some resolution to prevent their coming within the walls of that body at all. As it was, let them take their seats in the galleries and write what they pleased, without asking for the sanction of the Senate; for he would not consent for their accommodation, to exclude the honest and respectable citizens who came there as spectators.

Those senators who supported the committee's proposal agreed that much of the letter writers' work was vicious. But Senator Norvell stated their case when he said: "It would enable them to perform, with greater facility and accuracy, their engagements to the newspaper press and the reading public." Niles moved to table. The Senate supported him, twenty to seventeen. Thus the reporters lost.[6] The *Express,* for Erastus Brooks was the leader of the movement, reacted violently. On January 8 it ran an editorial part of which said:

Rights of Reporters

We see that a majority of the members of the United States Senate, 20 ayes and 17 nays, have shut out the Newspaper Reporters (for Newspapers out of the City of Washington) from the Senate, by indefinitely postponing a Resolution that seats be provided for their accommodation in the gallery. We also learn that Senators Niles, Strange and Buchanan accompanied their votes, particularly the two first, with very abusive remarks of the reporters and the Press in General.

The bitter hostility of such men as Niles to a Free Press is easily accounted for as it tears the Lion's Skin from the Jackass, and distinguishes the braying of that stupid beast from the roar of the Noble Monarch of the Wood. Nor is it remarkable, perhaps, that such a man as Strange, the cockloft hero, perhaps of some social circle, six feet by eight feet in length and breadth, should be chagrined that the Press does not discover him to be so great a man as he fancied he should be, before he trod the arena of the United States Senate. Mr. Buchanan's hostility, however, we cannot account for, as he really is a man of talent, unless he be what the Democracy of the days of Madison charged him with being—an enemy of a Free Press.

After another long paragraph the editorial was followed by a Washington letter signed by "E. B.," the initials used by Erastus Brooks. Dated "Washington, Jan. 5—Saturday Evening," it said, in part:

> Editors, Publishers and Readers you should have been in the Senate-Chamber to-day between the hours of twelve and two. You would have seen in that legislative hall, where meet a part of the assembled wisdom of the land, a sight which perhaps you have imagined although you may never have laid eyes upon the reality of the picture. You would have seen the manner of conducting a trial by some of our "most potent, grave and reverend seignoirs—our very noble and approved good masters," you would have been subdued by their arguments and have been charmed by their eloquence.

The article gave the history of the exclusive rule and described the reporters' petition. It continued:

> You have the story, and now for the actors who upon one side—favoring the report of the committee—were Messrs. Preston and Knight. Upon the other side, the speaking characters were Messrs. Niles, Buchanan, King and Strange. Let me introduce to you the characters propria persona. First then for Doctor NILES of Connecticut. Nature made him an ostler. Chance, and his own roguery made him an United States Senator. The worst part of nature, therefore has been despoiled of some of her best proportions. Never was fellow meaner than this same Niles who with the fancies of a dolt makes pretensions to the intellect of the most talented man in the country. His manners are bad, and his breeding worse.

The letter raked the other opponents, but treated none of them so harshly as it did Niles. The *Express* continued to belabor the Senate in editorials and Washington letters for a month before it gave up. The *Herald*, meanwhile, limited itself to a single sarcastic Washington letter published in the issue of January 12 and signed "Horace." The writer poked fun at both the senators and the press, making Niles a particular target. The last paragraph, written to make Vice-President Johnson seem as ridiculous as possible, ended: "But the Vice President's thoughts, when reflecting on his family, are apt to be *dark* and gloomy and confused." The word "dark" was italicized. That Johnson was the father of a Negro girl's children was a notorious morsel of Washington gossip.

During the next three years some reporters, principally those for Whig journals, managed to evade the rule. The Baltimore *Republican* of January 31, 1840, and a letter to President Pro Tem Samuel Southard of the Senate, printed in the New York *Herald* of July 2, 1841, said that the *National Intelligencer*, which was now in the Whig camp, claimed seats for reporters both for its daily and its triweekly editions. Since the congressional reports in the triweekly were printed from the type that had been used in the daily editions, one reporter's seat served for both. Therefore, the paper was able to give its extra seats to colleagues from favored outside papers.

The Whig party victory of 1840 and President William Henry Harrison's call for a special session to convene at the end of May, 1841, spurred the country's interest in capital news. Inaugurated on March 4, Harrison died on April 6. His successor, John Tyler, allowed the special session call to stand. Since the Washington papers had found complete and detailed stenographic reports of congressional proceedings an expensive burden and often abbreviated them at the expense of accuracy, and since the *Herald* was now financially strong enough to undertake a costly enterprise, it prepared to seize the prestige and circulation to be gained from the most careful and accurate reports possible of the proceedings of the two houses.

On May 24 it announced that "we have now organised, at vast expense, an efficient *corps* of the ablest reporters that this country can afford, who will furnish, at the close of every day's proceedings, a report of the debates." The reports were to be forwarded by express mail to appear in the second edition of the *Herald* on the second day after the Senate action. The announcement referred to the restrictive Senate rule, but expressed confidence that it would not be applied. The House admitted correspondents for the outside papers and therefore was not involved in the controversy that followed. The stenographic service which the *Herald* was preparing to offer would be an improvement on the type of start-to-finish proceedings that had always been reported. It would be in addition to the contributions of "correspondents" or "letter-writers" whose comments on the capital background appeared over fictitious signatures. The staff to supply the accounts was headed by an English stenographer named Robert Sutton.

The *Herald* of June 2 said that Bennett's plans had struck a snag. A Washington account dated Monday, May 31 gave a routine report on the opening day of the special session. At the end, it added that at the close of business that day Senator Southard had told Sutton that *Herald* stenographers would not be admitted to the reporters' desks. The account, which Sutton presumably wrote, discussed the Senate rule in mild language. But the editorial in the next day's paper was characteristic of Bennett.

> We have to record this day one of the most outrageous, high-handed, unconstitutional acts ever perpetrated by any legislative assembly in a free land—an act of despotism, tyranny and usurpation against the liberty of the press which the House of Lords of England, at this day, would not attempt against any newspaper in England.
>
> The reporters of the New York Herald were, on Monday last, excluded from the usual seats and facilities appropriated to such a purpose, by the Hon SAM. SOUTHARD, President, pro tem., of the U.S. Senate.

The rule, the article continued, limited press accommodations in the upper house to "the pauper and mendicant prints of Washington" and readers were promised that, since the paper had organized "a superb *corps* of Reporters at Washington, at an expense of nearly $200 per week," they would receive accounts in spite of the restriction.

Nearly every issue of the *Herald* during the next week found occasion, in connection with almost any news that was printed, to take another rap at the Senate. An editorial on June 10 included a letter which Bennett sent to Senator Clay. It pointed out that the editor intended to give the reports "without asking any of the printing or indirect remuneration of that body." This was a dig at the fact that the Washington papers which printed the congressional reports expected the profitable government printing contracts. Clay's reply was printed on the 12th. The senator said he would see if the rule could not be modified "as it would give me pleasure to be instrumental in rendering that accommodation to you."

The *Express*, which had surrendered unwillingly three years earlier when the Democrats dominated the Senate, did not support the *Herald's* fight on a chamber led by its own political patrons. Erastus Brooks was no longer its Washington correspondent but it had long accounts of floor proceedings of the two houses which must have been provided by its own staff. Only on June 23 did it comment on Bennett's dilemma, and then it extended its embattled fellow-journal no comfort.

On July 2 Senator Richard Henry Bayard of Delaware, a Whig, moved that the part of the 47th rule dealing with the admission of reporters be referred to a select committee. The resolution was adopted and Bayard made chairman of the committee.[7] On the 8th the committee reported out and the Senate adopted a resolution providing that the part of the 47th rule which admitted reporters be rescinded. It directed the Secretary to "cause suitable accommodations to be prepared in the eastern gallery for such reporters as may be admitted by the rules of the Senate."[8] On the 24th, Senator Southard issued an order which took care of the correspondents. Its provisions included: 1) None were to be admitted within the reporters' rail except *bona fide* reporters, so certified by their editors. 2) Washington daily papers were to be allowed two reporters and triweeklies one. But if a daily paper issued a triweekly it was not entitled to an additional seat. 3) No paper out of Washington was to be entitled to more than one reporter. 4) The desks were numbered from one to ten, and would be drawn for. Each seat was to be held in the name of a newspaper, not a reporter, so that occupants could be changed if desirable.[9] Thus Bennett won the fight which the *Express* had lost three years earlier.

Meanwhile, the internal stresses of the Whig party were causing tempers to shorten. Those party leaders who hoped to reestablish a central banking system similar to that which Jackson had destroyed and to force through certain other legislation in the interest of the business groups which dominated the party thought that Harrison's election had paved the way to their goal. Tyler, however, was not of their way of thinking. He was a Virginian of the states' rights school. He had joined the Whig party only as a protest against the way Jackson smothered nullification in 1832. Now, although allied with the Whigs politically, he supported neither their bank plans nor the protective tariff program of Henry Clay. Economically he was closer to the Democrats than to the party whose banner he carried.

Before he died, Harrison accepted the *National Intelligencer* as his organ. The special session of the Senate which was called immediately after inauguration to consider executive nominations dismissed Blair and Rives as its printers. Tyler, for the time being at least, continued to favor the *Intelligencer*. Gales and Seaton printed his message when the special session convened on May 31. That summer was one of intense political excitement. Tyler and the Whig leaders bickered over legislation and the president and the cabinet appointed by his predecessor found themselves increasingly uncongenial. One bill for a "fiscal corporation" passed Congress and was vetoed. Whig leaders at the Capitol went to work on another, and finally put through a measure which they thought would meet the president's objections.

Meanwhile the *Herald* eyed the situation. Bennett seems to have toyed with the idea that he could make his paper the administration spokesman even though it was not published in Washington, and thereby enjoy the benefits to be derived by being the first to get official announcements and perhaps doing some of the government printing. As the political climax built up in September the paper praised Tyler extravagantly. When the blowup came, in the form of a veto of the second fiscal corporation bill and the resignation of the cabinet, the *Herald* alone presented accurate predictions. Angry Whigs in Congress and the cabinet included in their denunciations the charge that the president revealed his intentions to the New York paper before he announced them to his political associates.

The issue of September 6 said in an editorial that the *National Intelligencer*, theoretically the president's spokesman, predicted that Tyler would sign the second fiscal corporation bill. Bennett predicted a veto. A Washington letter written on the same day and printed on the 8th denounced the cabinet opposition, said the president would object to the bill, and praised him with almost maudlin extravagance. The veto message went to Congress on the 9th. The *Herald* printed it on the 11th. The editorial column gave in tabular form the time necessary to run its special express with the veto message. A copy of the document was carried from Washington to Baltimore and from Camden to Jersey City by specially hired locomotives. Horses, however, had to be used between Baltimore and Philadelphia where the railroad was still incomplete. The whole trip required fifteen hours, which was slower than some expresses which had used horses the entire distance. The message reached the *Herald* office at 5:00 A.M.

The next Monday a Washington letter dated, as they normally were, two days earlier said the cabinet had resigned, except for Secretary of State Daniel Webster, and that Tyler had sent new nominations to the Senate. The president's veto message showed that the *Herald*'s story which had been mailed from Washington on the 6th had been accurate. The paper and the president were lumped together in some of the bad-tempered recriminations that followed. In submitting his resignation as secretary of the treasury, Thomas Ewing said that "the very secrets of your cabinet councils made their appearance in an infamous paper printed in a neighboring city, the columns of which were daily charged with flattery of yourself and foul abuse of your cabinet." Nathan Sargent, a devoted Whig, a former editor of the *United States Gazette* in Philadelphia, now combined the duties of sergeant-at-arms of the House with Washington correspondence for that journal. In a book which he wrote twenty years later he said that cabinet members and Whig congressional leaders formed the habit of reading the *Herald* to learn administration plans. Sargent did not write in complimentary terms of Bennett or his paper. He added that the paper had a correspondent, whom he did not name "who had access to the president at all times, to whom were revealed matters known only to the president and his cabinet, and intentions as to the future confided of which the members of the cabinet were profoundly ignorant." [10] The *Herald* denied improper access to the White House. It outran its competitors, Bennett wrote, only because its six reporters covered the city thoroughly.

How did the *Herald* learn the president's intentions? There are indications that its correspondents may have had a "pipeline" through Tyler's sons, with or without their father's knowledge. John Quincy Adams wrote in his diary a year later that Robert Tyler and John Tyler, Jr., "divulged all his Cabinet secrets to a man named Parmelee and John Howard Payne, hired reporters for Bennett's *Herald* newspaper at New York, who, by their intimacy with these upstart princes, crept into the familiarity of domestic inmates at the President's House." [11] Tyler named Payne as consul to Tunis, but biographers of the composer of "Home, Sweet Home" do not show that he ever corresponded for the *Herald*. Philip Hone, New York's famous diarist, referred to "a person named Parmly" as the *Herald's* Washington correspondent, said he was the president's confidential adviser.[12] No other indication that a correspondent by that name worked in Washington can be found although a series of articles entitled "Recollections of an Old Stager," published anonymously in *Harper's New Monthly Magazine* thirty years later has been credited to a T. N. Parmelee. They show the author well informed as to Washington affairs of this time.[13]

One result of the breakup of Tyler and the Whig leaders in Congress was that the *Intelligencer* was pushed aside as the president's spokesman. Gales and Seaton gave their first loyalty in these years to Daniel Webster. In their place Tyler gave his confidence to the *Madisonian,* which had been established a year earlier by Thomas Allen and John Jones. This paper, however, never achieved significant stature in the capital journalistic scene.

6. Democrats and Whigs: 1844–1846

As the date for the 1844 Democratic National Convention neared, the slavery controversy was beginning to tear the party apart. Blair had continued to publish his Washington *Globe* during the Whig administration although he did not enjoy the profitable public printing. He was a slaveowner with antecedents in the border slave states. But he was, above all, a patriotic nationalist in the Jackson tradition and feared the Southern extremists. In this he was allied with former President Martin Van Buren and with Senator Thomas Hart Benton of Missouri. At the Hermitage the unwell and aging Jackson kept in touch with events and with his friend and former editor.

By 1844 Texas had maintained an independent existence for eight years. During that time there had been repeated moves for annexation to the United States. All had been defeated by the antislavery elements. Although a nationalist, a slaveholder, and an opponent of the disunionist proslavery forces, Jackson favored annexation. Elderly Thomas Ritchie, who had edited the Richmond *Enquirer* since 1804, made his paper the spokesman for those who wished to expand to the Southwest. As a result of these pressures the convention rejected Van Buren, the 1840 standard-bearer whose renomination had been expected, in favor of James K. Polk, a relatively unknown annexationist from Tennessee. And it drew a platform calling for the acquisition of Texas and Oregon. In November the voters approved. Without waiting for the triumphant Democrats to take over in March, Congress adopted a joint resolution adding Texas to the national domain. Although a Tennesseean and a political disciple of Jackson, Polk saw his election as a triumph of the expansionists. Blair assumed that he would again become the administration editor. But as one of the Van Buren faction he was unpalatable to the element which had seized control of the party. Polk had his inaugural address printed by the *Globe*, but he made it clear that he wanted another editor.

It was arranged in April that Ritchie direct the paper, with John P. Heiss of the Nashville *Union*, an old political crony of the new president, as business manager. Unwillingly and under pressure, Blair was persuaded to sell the *Globe* for $35,000, although Blair and Rives continued to publish the *Congressional Globe*, the compilation of debates which they had founded a few years earlier. But Ritchie did not have the money. Therefore (this was the story which Senator Benton angrily told later) federal funds were provided. Robert J. Walker, the secretary of the treasury, arranged to deposit $40,000 in a small bank in Middletown, Pennsylvania. The bank was partially controlled by Senator Simon Cameron of Pennsylvania, a party stalwart and political manipulator, who in turn loaned the necessary money to Ritchie. The name of the paper was changed to the *Union*, and it came out under its new flag on May 1, 1845.

While the negotiations were being carried on Jackson bombarded Polk with letter after letter pleading with him to retain Blair. Several of the letters referred to the writer's increasing illness. Some said that he was so weak that it was hard for him to write, but that he forced himself to do so because he felt so strongly about the situation. He died on June 8.[1]

Ritchie thus guided the paper which ostensibly spoke for the administration although the party had been badly split. During the congressional recess of the summer and fall of 1845 he tried to placate the anti-Texas northern Democrats. But many came to Washington in December unwilling to help him if he ran into trouble. The Whigs were glad to make the most of the division in their foes' ranks. Supported by dissident Democrats, they struck Ritchie two heavy blows. First they pushed through a bill repealing the law of 1819 by which the two houses of Congress elected their printers. In its place they enacted legislation directing the Clerk of the House and the Secretary of the Senate to contract for the printing with the lowest bidder. Ritchie and Heiss submitted the lowest bid and thereby held on as printers to Congress. But the rates were so low that this formerly profitable source of income as a political reward brought them small return.[2] Secondly, the Whigs denied Ritchie the privilege of the Senate floor, a privilege which he normally enjoyed because as printer he was a Senate officer. Early in 1847, as the Mexican War was in progress, the Senate refused to adopt a conference report on a bill to authorize ten regiments of regular troops. On February 9 the *Union* printed an article signed "VINDICATOR" which grouped the opposing solons with the Mexicans as this country's enemies. Actually an amended conference report was accepted and the bill passed a few days later.

This time a Southern Democrat led the attack on Ritchie. David L. Yulee of Florida proposed two resolutions. The first, which would bar the editors of the *Union* from the floor, was passed after a two-day debate. This was a personal slap at Ritchie, and did not bar his reporters from the galleries. The second, stigmatizing as unfair the *Union's* report of Senate proceedings during debate on an army appropriation bill, would bar its reporters from the gallery. The motion protested that the report was one-sided, giving too little of the speeches of some senators and undue prominence to that of Lewis Cass of Michigan. This one was dropped on its sponsor's motion, however, after the vice-president read a letter from James A. Houston, one of the *Union's* Senate stenographers, explaining that the one-sidedness of the account was inadvertent. Houston explained that one of his assistants was pressed for time and therefore limited his summaries of speakers' remarks. Cass sent the complete text of his own to the printshop where a foreman inserted it without consulting the reporters. Senator Stephen A. Douglas offered a resolution expelling Houston but it was defeated.[3]

The sale of the *Globe* and the blows dealt to Ritchie marked, for all practical purposes, the end of the official paper as a significant weapon in politics or as an important medium for transmitting news to the country. The next four presidents kept up the tradition. Nevertheless, the development of Washington correspondents, the telegraph, the Associated Press, growing contempt for the system, scandals in the public printing and internal party stresses that always put the official editor in an impossible position finally brought the practice to an end.

We won't record here the papers and editors of the administrations from 1846 to 1860.[4] But we will look ahead at this point to 1860 to tell how official journalism finally died. The new Republican party did not start an organ in Washington to help its cause in the 1856 and the 1860 campaigns as had been the custom in launching presidential booms twenty and thirty years earlier. During the winter of 1860–61, Abraham Lincoln waited in Springfield for the date of his inauguration. He probably saw a letter which James E. Harvey, a Washington correspondent for the New York *Tribune,* wrote to John G. Nicolay, the President-elect's young secretary, on November 25, 1860. The letter said that S. P. Hanscom, a *Herald* correspondent whom Harvey described as "one of the most unscrupulous & notorious of all the corrupt gang who infest this Capital" was planning to start a new paper in Washington. "The attempt will be made to impress the public that it is [Lincoln's] organ & to impress the pockets of his friends for the support of adventurers," Harvey wrote.[5]

Hanscom was a *Herald* correspondent and had a reputation for corrupt intrigue.[6] And he did start a paper, the Washington *Republican.* It was only one of several mentioned as possible official journals for the incoming administration. John W. Forney, editor of the Philadelphia *Press* and one of the former editors of President James Buchanan's organ, had now turned to the Republican party and started the Washington *Chronicle.* Since Forney was also Secretary of the Senate and strong in certain party circles, and since the *Chronicle* was awarded a good deal of advertising by the executive departments, some in political circles felt that it bore the administration mantle. On March 6, 1861, the Washington correspondent of the Charleston *Mercury* (he was still active in what his editors now regarded as the capital of a foreign nation) wrote that the editors of the *National Intelligencer* hoped to regain the position they had held forty years earlier. Lincoln confounded them all. He gave no paper his exclusive confidence in the way Jackson had given his to Blair. Thus died the official press.

Turn back to 1841. In that year there appeared a new paper which was destined to become one of the most influential in the country. Horace Greeley, a loyal Whig and in particular a devotee of Henry Clay's protective tariff program, launched his New York *Tribune* on April 10. In 1846 the session that saw the Whigs deprive Ritchie of his profitable printing also saw the House quarrel with a *Tribune* correspondent. William E. Robinson, a native of Ireland and a leader of Irish-American groups in New York, became the paper's Washington correspondent in 1843. His regular letters, signed "Richelieu," appeared daily. They were comparatively restrained, dignified expressions of Whig doctrine. They followed normal party practice in calling the Democrats "locofocos."

On February 3, 1846, the *Tribune* introduced a new Washington feature. Under a small headline: "Rumors and Humors in Washington . . . No. 1," appeared the first article over the signature of "Persimmon." He was much more critical and sarcastic than "Richelieu." Robinson refused to admit that he was "Persimmon." It is possible that some other writer contributed those letters, but Capitol hangers-on believed they were Robinson's. He may have used this signature to cover letters of a harsher literary tone than he preferred to write as "Richelieu." On February 27 appeared "Rumors and Humors at Washington . . . No. II." This high tariff writer discussed humorously the opposition of an Alabama congressman to protection. Then, adding that "Every Congress brings along some strange geniuses to this city," he discussed personal idiosyncracies of other members. Part of this letter said:

> But there is one still more remarkable than the others, and that is *Hon.* W. SAWYER of Ohio.—Though his name would indicate as much, yet he is not a woodsawyer; he is I believe a blacksmith, not that I consider the trade would disgrace him. The reputation of the trade probably is the greatest suferer.
> Every day about 2 o'clock he feeds. About that hour he is seen leaving his seat, and taking a position in the window back of the Speaker's Chair, to the left. He unfolds a greasy paper in which there is contained a chunk of bread and a sausage or some other unctuous substance. These he disposes of quite rapidly, wipes his hands with the greasy paper for a napkin, and then throws it out of the window.—What

little grease is left on his hands he wipes on his almost bald head which saves any outlay for Pomatum. His mouth sometimes serves as a finger glass, his coat sleeves and pantaloons being called into requisition as a napkin. He uses a jackknife for a toothpick, and then he goes on the floor again to abuse the Whigs as the British Party, and claims the whole of Oregon as necessary for the spread of Civilizaiton. I believe he goes, like Chipman, against all seductive acts of Education —some suspect that he has a store of vegetables in his drawer. But enough of the habits of an Ohio Loco Foco.

On March 4 Sawyer had the paragraphs read by the Clerk and said that he had been unable to ascertain who wrote the letter. He would not call for any action by the House, he said, admitting that he ate his luncheon from a package in the room. He wished only to give notice that when attacked in this way he would take the matter into his own hands. Representative Jacob Brinkerhoff, from the same state and party as Sawyer, moved that *Tribune* reporters be expelled from the House. Whigs protested. Democrats backed Sawyer and Brinkerhoff and adopted the resolution.[7] The *Congressional Globe,* which was still published by Blair and Rives, did not carry the debate. "The reporter does not go into explanation," it said, "further than necessary to render intelligible the subsequent action of the House." It gave only the vote.

"Richelieu" told the story as he saw it in a letter which was published in the *Tribune* two days later. He protested that his own writings avoided the abuse which was characteristic of Washington correspondence. He avoided identifying himself or any one else as "Persimmon," saying that "The remarks made in that letter are such as I would not use in my letters, yet there is nothing in it so bad as is habitually given in other papers, and particularly in Loco-Foco papers, with respect to political opponents." An editorial on the same day said that the *Tribune* would continue to carry reports on House proceedings in spite of its reporters being barred.

Helped by the Whigs, Robinson continued to enter the House and report. He worked from the ladies' gallery, or from members' galleries into which he could be introduced by a congressman. John Quincy Adams is said to have personally escorted him to a seat and to have ordered the doorkeeper to allow him to remain.[8]

"There are fifty members," he wrote, "to introduce me to their gallery, and even the ladies have volunteered their services not only to accompany me to the gallery but to help me report, if necessary." When Congress reconvened the next December the House quietly restored the *Tribune's* privileges.[9]

7. The Telegraph

On May 24, 1844, Samuel Finley Breese Morse, the professor of portraiture at New York University whose interest had turned from art to electricity, sat at his experimental instruments in the Capitol and sent the first message to move over the electric telegraph. On March 1, 1845, President Tyler signed the congressional joint resolution annexing Texas. On March 28, 1846, United States troops under the command of Zachary Taylor reached the north bank of the Rio Grande in territory which Mexico claimed was hers. She had refused to recognize either Texan independence or annexation to this country, so she saw the presence of American troops as a violation of her territory. On April 25 a patrol from Taylor's force was destroyed when it met a Mexican column which had crossed to the north bank of the river. This series of events had a revolutionary impact on the press.

For nearly a year the original experimental telegraph line between Washington and Baltimore remained a curiosity while Morse and his associates waited for Congress to pass the legislation necessary for the government to operate it as part of the postal system. But Congress did not act. Therefore, in 1845 Morse associated himself with a group of businessmen to build a commercial line to New York. Furthermore, Morse and his partners contracted for the use of his patents in lines to be built by other companies in other areas. In 1846 and 1847 crews set poles and stretched wires in all directions from New York, from Boston up the coast toward New Brunswick, south from Washington and west from Philadelphia and Albany.

The papers of New York, together with such leaders in journalistic enterprise as the Philadelphia *Public Ledger* and Baltimore *Sun*, watched the new developments with interest. William M. Swain of the *Public Ledger*, in particular, was active. He was one of the directors of the Magnetic Telegraph Company, which Morse and his partners organized to build the line from Washington to New York. On June 13, 1845, the *Public Ledger* described optimistically the telegraph construction which Henry O'Reilly, a grantee under the Morse patents, was pushing westward from Philadelphia. "It is understood that much of the work will be finished with despatch for transmitting to Harrisburg (if not to Wheeling via Pittsburg or even to Columbus in Ohio) an abstract of the President's Message at the commencement of the next session of Congress," it said. Nevertheless, when the lawmakers gathered in December horseflesh and steam still carried Washington news. The press of the country's two largest cities still used congressional accounts two days after the events they described took place.

In January 1846 the telegraph line between Philadelphia and Newark was complete. So was the original experimental line between Washington and Baltimore. Only the gap between the Pennsylvania and Maryland cities remained to link the capital and the nation's greatest seaport. In April and May crews pushed construction from both ends of that opening. And President Polk and the country wondered what was happening to the troops occupying the disputed territory in southwest Texas.

On April 11 the *Public Ledger* instituted a new service. A train left Baltimore at 3:00 P.M. The paper's Washington correspondents recorded the routine proceedings in the two houses and telegraphed them to Baltimore up to shortly before that hour. There a messenger picked them up and took them by train to Philadelphia. He arrived during the evening after the presses had started. Therefore the copies which were printed early in the evening lacked the new material from Washington. It was quickly set in type, the presses stopped, and the later copies made over to include those congressional proceedings to 3:00 P.M. The paper boasted proudly at having yesterday's news from the legislative floor in this morning's paper. This service continued until the wire between Baltimore and Philadelphia was opened.

Two weeks later the New York papers used telegraphed congressional proceedings from Washington. The telegraph company must have forwarded from Philadelphia the material which the *Public Ledger* received by rail from Baltimore. The *Tribune's* first was on April 25. In its customary column headed, "THE SOUTH-ERN MAIL," it printed, "Proceedings in Congress Yesterday, Reported for the Tribune . . . by Magnetic Telegraph." On the 29th both the *Tribune* and the *Herald* used them. The latter, which was always blatant with self-praise when it instituted a new service, introduced this innovation this time without comment.

The day the *Tribune* introduced its first telegraphic congressional proceedings General Taylor sent a mounted patrol under Captain S. B. Thornton to investigate a report that Mexican troops had crossed to the north bank of the Rio Grande. The patrol moved up the river about twenty-five miles from Taylor's camp opposite Matamoros and collided with a large Mexican force. The captain was wounded and all in his command were killed or captured. Before Washington could learn of the incident Taylor had to send messengers by horseback to his base at Point Isabel. Steamers took the reports to New Orleans, and from there couriers traveled to Washington partly by steam and partly by horseback or horse-drawn coach. Once Washington received the news, correspondents, who were beginning to experiment with the telegraph line, were able to forward it by that means as far as Baltimore and from Philadelphia north. The gap between those cities was still not bridged.

Taylor's report on Thornton's brush reached Washington on May 9. Meanwhile American forces drove the Mexicans back across the river in the Battles of Palo Alto and Resaca de la Palma on May 8 and 9, although again it would be nearly three weeks before Washington learned of it. Polk drafted a message to be sent to Congress calling for a declaration that war existed by act of Mexico. It went to the Capitol on May 11. The next morning's *Public Ledger* carried a brief summary credited, "By Magnetic Telegraph" and datelined, "WASHINGTON, May 11, 2 P.M." The dispatch was sent from Baltimore by rail. This was the first time that a summary, rather than the entire text, of such a presidential document was used. The dispatch ended by saying that a copy would be sent by the evening mail.

New York received the news that the country was at war by telegraphic relay from Philadelphia. Washington correspondents

now became not only reporters of capital news, but agents to receive the mail from the South and forward its contents by telegraph. On May 12 the *Herald*'s editorial column said.

> We received yesterday morning by the Magnetic Tele-
> graph from Philadelphia, a despatch from our correspond-
> ent in that city, which contained some further intelligence
> confirmatory of the recent events on the Rio Grande frontier,
> and also giving us news from Washington of the extraordi-
> nary excitement that those events have created there, and
> of the probable steps that will be instantly adopted by the
> Executive and Congress. A terrible retribution awaits the
> Mexicans.

A series of items, each timed and giving information from Washington or from the Southwest, were credited as having been
mailed from Baltimore. The last, at "HALF PAST SEVEN
O'CLOCK, P.M.," said "The Telegraph has just confirmed the
report of the destruction of Thornton's command. We cannot say
more, as the cars are this moment leaving for Philadelphia, and
the North." A telegraphed summary of Polk's message was on
page 3.

Early in June construction crews set the last pole and connected the last stretch of wire on the link between Baltimore and
Philadelphia. The *Herald* of the 6th greeted the opening of the
wire with its natural ebullience. The first headline deck said:
"THE FIRST FLASH OF THE LIGHTNING LINE FROM
WASHINGTON TO NEW YORK." There were five more headline decks before the reader got down to the text. Such headlines
were now making their first appearance in the press.

> The lightning line from Washington to this city is com-
> plete, and we received the first flash—the first intelligence,
> at an early hour last evening—eighteen hours in advance of
> the mail.
> The completion of this line is of vast importance. It en-
> ables us to give in this morning's Herald, the interesting in-
> telligence from the Rio Grande, one whole day in advance
> of the old dog-trot way of receiving news from the South.

Not only war news flashed over the new electric wires. The
routine accounts of legislative steps and summaries of speeches
which had always been mailed were moved by telegraph as soon

as the lines were completed. Furthermore, on the day they opened and from then on the language of the congressional accounts was the same in all papers. It was obvious that the same reporters were preparing them for all, and that probably a single telegraphic transmission supplied all of the subscribing papers in a given city.

Files of such papers as the Philadelphia *Public Ledger* and *North American* and the New York *Herald, Sun, Tribune, Express, Courier and Enquirer,* and *Journal of Commerce* showed that exactness in congressional reports as soon as the telegraph opened. After 1847 the same language was to be found in those papers and in the Boston *Atlas* and *Courier.* After 1852, when the telegraph wires had stretched to more remote corners of the country, that was true also if the reports in the press of the eastern seaboard cities were compared with those in the New Orleans *Delta* and *Picayune,* the *Missouri Democrat* of St. Louis, the Charleston *Mercury* and *Courier,* and the Chicago *Times* and *Tribune.* It was no doubt true of practically all others.

It is not hard to come to a conclusion as to what must have happened. Use of the telegraph forced the press to reorganize some of its habits. Papers could no longer rely on the journals of other cities received by mail or horseback or locomotive express. Salaried or space-paid correspondents in the national and state capitals provided agents in those centers to file their copy on the wires. On the early systems the number of words that could be moved was limited. Use of the telegraph was expensive and caused publishing costs to climb. Reporters, therefore, had to cut down and paraphrase documents which formerly had been sent by mail or horse or railroad express and printed in full. Arrangements had to be made with the operating companies and increasing expenses met.

The early telegraph companies assumed from the start that newspapers would be among their leading customers.[1] In some cases, in the first year or two of operation, they had telegraphers forward the news found in their home journals to papers in other cities. There was some question as to whether or not the telegraph companies would remain merely the means of transmission, or would go actively into the business of reporting telegraph news with their own employees and selling it to newspapers. That happened in some other parts of the world. In this country, however, "telegraph reporters" appeared. They gathered the news and forwarded it by telegraph to any paper which would buy.[2]

In December 1846, for the first time, a president's regular message on the state of the Union, that annual index of the method of rapid news transmission, was telegraphed, in part at least. It was both summarized for wire delivery and expressed by railroad for the morning papers to print in full. The *Public Ledger* of December 9, 1846, said it had received the unusually long document by government express, but that "A brief synopsis of the message was transmitted to us . . . through the Magnetic Telegraph, and for the convenience of readers of the Ledger, we here append it."

Dr. Alexander Jones was a New York physician who added an interest in telegraph news to his medical practice. In the fall of 1846 he forwarded by wire to the Washington *Union* a story on the launching of a ship at the Brooklyn Navy Yard. In 1852 he published a book on the history of telegraphy in general and of news telegraphy in the United States. Between the story he tells and the evidence in the newspaper files it is possible to piece together the following as the probable story of early telegraphic congressional reporting.

At the time the first wires stretched northward out of Washington and west from Philadelphia there was already present in the capital a corps of stenographers who compiled floor proceedings for the Washington papers and for some of those outside. Some must have awakened to the possibilities and to have offered themselves for possibly lucrative new duties as soon as the telegraph opened. Furthermore the fact that only one wire was available probably caused the telegraphic companies to prefer a single transmission of that news which all newspapers would print. Therefore the "telegraph reporters" handled congressional proceedings for all journals reached by the lines. Individual correspondents filed short separate stories for their own papers although because of high tolls most of that special writing went by mail for several more years.

The telegraph reporters in different cities had organized by 1847 into a loose association to cooperate in filing dispatches and collecting fees. Jones, who continued to operate out of New York, seems to have taken a leading part in the organization. The sponsored history of the Associated Press, the present-day corporation which maintains a worldwide news-gathering network, says it grew out of a meeting in the office of the New York *Sun* in May 1848. The dramatized account draws on imagination, giving details of the meeting which cannot be verified. And it says that those at that meeting called their new creature by the name its descendant bears today.[3]

Actually the origin of the organization and the first use of the name are not clear. Some later accounts say that the Associated Press was founded in 1847, but those writers apparently had in mind the loose federation of telegraph reporters which Jones describes. Henry J. Raymond, an editor of the *Courier and Enquirer*, used the words *Associated Press* in a letter which he wrote on May 18, 1848, to refer to the loose affiliation of six New York papers which had been organized to deal with the telegraph companies.[4] After 1848 that loose affiliation was sometimes referred to in the newspapers of the day as the associated press (uncapitalized, apparently referring merely to the press, associated for this purpose), sometimes as the Associated Press (capitalized), and later as the New York Associated Press. After 1852 the news printed in newspapers which came from this association was usually described merely as "The General Despatch." When the organization was reconstructed in 1856 it was called "The General News Association of the City of New York." [5] The name Associated Press, however, was found with growing frequency in the newspapers and other records after 1852.

The circumstance and the exact date when L. A. Gobright became the Associated Press "agent" in the capital is also lost in records from which pinpointing is impossible. In his own book on his observations of the Washington scene, largely autobiographical, he neglects the point. His first reference to it appears when he discusses the Kansas trouble in 1857.[6] Other evidence makes it clear that he was the Associated Press agent by 1853 and probably earlier. The imperfect data and conclusions derived from a study of contemporary newspapers lead to the belief that the present large Washington bureau of the Associated Press originated under the circumstances described in the next three paragraphs.

The organization of telegraph reporters which Jones described was, as we have seen, in active operation in 1847. Its Washington associates were clearly among its most important members. Jones's book has a good deal to say about congressional reports. Gobright had reported congressional proceedings for the Washington papers and may have been one of those working with Jones. In his book the doctor-newsman wrote that the organization lasted only about a year, and then "we became the agent of the New-York Associated Press for all news of a commercial and miscellaneous character throughout the United States." That must have been in 1848, an outgrowth of the meeting in the *Sun* office.

The evidence of Jones's book and of the identical reports in the newspapers, therefore, seems to show that his organization of telegraph reporters, which had appeared a year or so earlier when the wires first started operating, moved into the Associated Press when Jones was retained by that group. Those on the Washington end went along too. The first reference to Gobright in connection with the Associated Press is to be found in an unofficial congressional directory published in 1853. In a list of reporters admitted to Congress, it named Gobright as the holder of a Senate seat for the New York Associated Press and James W. Sheahan as carrying out the same duty in the House for both the New York Associated Press and the Washington *Republic*.[7] The *Republic* had been President Taylor's official organ. This, however, was not the official directory printed by congressional order. That did not begin to list the press until 1860.

Gobright remained the Washington agent, sometimes alone and sometimes with one or two assistants, until his death in May of 1879. He saw the Associated Press replace the official journals as the medium for transmitting the complete text of official documents. It moved telegraphically extended start-to-finish accounts of congressional proceedings. Representing papers of varying political opinions, it avoided the highly opinionated flavor that then characterized newspaper writing, thus contributing to the objectivity that later marked the American press. Gobright reported Washington developments through disunion, Civil War, and Reconstruction.

Telegraph construction went forward rapidly. Not until 1860, however, were there enough wires or were their working techniques developed well enough for the press to rely on electricity instead of steam or horses to move the complete text of the annual message on the state of the Union.

Until Millard Fillmore became president, on Taylor's death

in August 1850, newspapers received the annual messages by locomotive expresses operated by the Post Office Department. The expresses did not leave Washington until the reading started at the Capitol. Fillmore sped up the system. In December 1850 he sent messengers in advance to deliver copies to the postmasters in New York, Philadelphia, Baltimore, Richmond, Boston, Providence, Albany, Rochester and Buffalo. The postmasters, in turn, gave them to the newspapers as soon as they were notified by telegraph that the document was being read.[8] Fillmore's last message, in December 1852, was taken in advance from Washington by eighteen special messengers to 119 cities and towns.[9]

Franklin Pierce used the same system although he did not send out so many copies. His final presentation of his views, in December 1856, went to 14 major cities.[10] James Buchanan, too, used this system but cut it back very sharply. His last, in December 1860, went in advance only to New York and Richmond.[11] When Buchanan penned that document, Lincoln was in Springfield. Before he left for Washington in February 1861 he wrote his intended inauguration address and had it printed in the office of the Springfield *Journal*. Then he took copies to Washington to discuss it with those whom he would appoint to his cabinet. Before March 4 the printed proof sheets had parts crossed out and new sections added. His secretary, John G. Nicolay, then made new copies by hand.

Lincoln refused to send out advance copies of his speeches or messages as his immediate predecessors had done. By now, however, the telegraph network was capable of moving the text. On March 4, 1861, a copy of the address was given to Gobright and sent in full to Associated Press client papers as far west as Chicago, St. Louis, and New Orleans.[12] This was the first to be so moved. Gobright apparently continued to receive a copy of the text coincident with its delivery. A note which he wrote on December 1, 1862, while the country awaited the message, seems to show what had become standard procedure. He wrote to Nicolay: "I will be on the lookout for you at the door of the Senate after you shall have delivered the Message to that body. Please have two copies for me in the envelope for better convenience of transmission." [13]

8. The Arrest of John Nugent

As the year 1847 drew to a close American troops were in Mexico City. Other columns had occupied New Mexico and California. Nicholas P. Trist, chief clerk of the State Department, was negotiating with diplomats of the defeated nation. On February 2, 1848, in the Mexican town of Guadelupe-Hidalgo, Trist and Mexican representatives signed a draft treaty.

In the summer of 1846 a correspondent who signed his writings "Galviensis" appeared in the New York *Herald*. The writer was John Nugent, a young Irishman. During the next two years his contributions appeared regularly. He and "The Doctor," the pseudonym of Dr. G. B. Wallis, wrote practically all of the *Herald's* mailed Washington correspondence during 1847 and 1848 and sometimes sent short telegraphic offerings. Probably, too, Nugent or Wallis wrote some of the material which appeared over such names as "Felix," "Ariel," "Allons," "Nous Verrons," and "Chee-Waw-Waw."

As was customary, then, the treaty text was, in theory at least, secret when it reached Washington. On February 22, 1848, Polk submitted it to the Senate, which debated it behind closed doors. It ratified the document on March 10, after amending it slightly, and the *Union* told the world that much. As a courtesy to Mexico, which had yet to ratify, the Senate insisted that secrecy, as far as the text was concerned, not be lifted. Actually the terms had become common knowledge.

The *Herald* of February 22, the morning Polk sent the treaty to the Senate, announced "what we believe to be authentic intelligence of a treaty of peace." The story gave a generally accurate summary of its provisions. The next day the telegraphic news column said that the treaty had gone to the Senate but that that body had adjourned before it arrived out of respect to John Quincy Adams. The venerable former president and diplomat, who closed a distinguished public career with long service in the House of Representatives, collapsed in that room on the 21st. He was carried to a couch in the Speaker's room and died on the 23d.

A telegraphic dispatch in the *Herald* of February 25 gave an article-by-article analysis of the presumably still-secret treaty. On March 11 the paper ran a series of one-paragraph items received by wire and timed at successive hours during the previous day. Each gave rumors which leaked past the closed Senate doors. The last, timed "March 10—9½ P.M.," said the Senate ratified by a four-fifths vote and gave the names of some of those who had voted for and against. "The injunction of secrecy is not yet removed," it said.

The *Union* was as cautious as was to be expected of the official organ. Saying that the treaty was ratified by a vote of thirty-eight to thirteen, it added that secrecy was still in order. It gave no provisions of the document. Two days later Bennett threw over the Senate restriction and involved his paper in a quarrel in which Nugent was arrested by the sergeant-at-arms. The Senate failed as it tried to force Nugent to reveal the source of secret information. On March 13 the *Herald* said it had had the treaty for nearly two weeks but had withheld publication from a regard for the public interest. It revealed it now because revelation could no longer be regarded as bringing influence to bear on the Senate's deliberations. The document text and an explanatory story followed. It said, truthfully, that the Senate had substituted different wordage for Article IX and had expunged Article X. The paper also gave what it said was the vote on ratification. The *Journal of Commerce* copied it the next day.

The *Herald* of the 16th printed a Washington letter dated the 14th which described humorously the reaction in the capital to the publication of the treaty and discussed guesses as to how the paper got it. The best guess, it said, "was that of a young lady, who could account for it in no other way than by a compact of 'peace, friendship and limits' between James Gordon Bennett,

Esq., and his Excellency, Don Lucifer Ampudia Beelzebub, of the Infernal Regions." Another letter said the Senate "are now in Executive Session supposed by some to be upon an investigation of the mystery of the publication of the treaty in the New York Herald." A few days later the paper published part of the president's confidential correspondence which had been submitted to the Senate with the treaty. On the 23d it explained in an editorial that all of the correspondence would have been published if the steam packet *Cambria* had not arrived from Europe with news of the revolution in France and the fall of King Louis-Philippe, which had crowded it out. The paper promised to publish the rest of the correspondence as soon as it could spare the space. It did not do so, however.

In a secret session that day the Senate adopted a resolution providing a select committee of three to inquire into the means by which the treaty and the message of the president and documents had been revealed.[1] The next day the committee reported that it had examined Nugent. He admitted that he was the *Herald* correspondent and that he knew from whom the treaty had been obtained. No senator, officer of the Senate, person connected with the Senate printing, or any third person connected with the families of any of these was responsible, he said. Asked who furnished it, he refused to answer. He regarded the publication as proper, he said, and he did not consider himself bound to tell where he got it. He gave a similar reply when asked the source of the documents which the *Herald* had promised to publish.

Nugent was confined from March 27 to April 28. Running through the Senate records, press accounts, and a court decision are opinions of the time on the right of a legislative body to confine a citizen and on aspects of freedom of the press. The question as to whether or not publication violated privilege, which had weighed heavily in eighteenth century legislature-press quarrels, occupied a minor place here. That battle had been largely won. The Senate claimed the right to force Nugent to testify, and to confine him until he did, on the ground that it had the right to find out if one of its own members, any of its officers, or any one in the office of the Senate printer had given away its secrets. It is clear, though, that some members were merely angry and were eager to find a scapegoat.

Too, the incident was fought out against the background of a presidential election year and shows individual relationships between a reporter and officeholder and the meddling of a reporter in politics of a type that has now disappeared. Nugent was close to Secretary of State James Buchanan. And he was believed to be Buchanan's tool as the secretary sought the Democratic nomination. When the convention took place a few weeks after Nugent was released, Buchanan lost to Lewis Cass of Michigan. Polk did not seek renomination, although the *Herald* and some other papers denied that he was sincere in his statements to that effect.

The Senate ordered the committee to continue its investigation and named two more members. Telegraphic dispatches to the *Herald* of the 25th and 26th and an editorial on the latter day discussed the committee's progress. The latter quoted a Washington letter to the Philadelphia *North American* which said that some senators suspected that Buchanan had given Nugent the documents. It added that copies had been given to two foreign ministers at the same time the original had reached the president and it implied that a diplomat may have been a source.

The committee reported on March 27 that Nugent's testimony "contains all the information we have obtained as to the manner and means by which the treaty and documents . . . have been made public." It quoted Nugent as having given a detailed and carefully worded answer again denying that he had secured the treaty and documents from the printers or any of the printers' employees. Asked if he could absolve all State Department officials, he refused to answer on the grounds that to do so would recognize the committee's right "to inculpate the head or any other officer of the State Department, a right which, with all due respect to the committee, I am disposed to question." Senator Simon Cameron read a letter from Buchanan, his fellow Pennsylvanian, saying that the latter understood suspicions were held that the department was responsible. Those suspicions were wholly unfounded, Buchanan wrote. He added that he and all department clerks were ready to submit to examination, and he hoped the committee would continue its investigation until no possible suspicion remained against him or others in the department.

The Senate spent the next two days debating procedure. It

acted with the doors closed although its journals were later published, so we know what took place. It finally ordered the sergeant-at-arms to arrest Nugent and to bring him into the Senate Chamber at 1:00 P.M. on March 30. Nugent was present, in custody, at the designated time. He admitted that he had copied the documents in his own handwriting in his room on G Street, between Thirteenth and Fourteenth Streets, Northwest, and had sent them to the *Herald*. Asked about their source, he replied, "I object to that question. Have I not a right to object to a question?" When the vice-president told him that he need not incriminate himself, he added, "I do not object to that question on the ground that it will criminate myself. I consider myself in honor bound not to answer it."

The *Journal* records a tedious proceeding that dragged for hours. Sometimes Nugent protested that he could not answer a question accurately because he did not remember. At others he simply refused to answer. But he did not reveal the source of the treaty and documents. Finally the Senate resolved that he was guilty of contempt and must be held "until he answers the said interrogatories or until the further order of the Senate." He was brought back the next day and asked if he had changed his mind about answering. There was another extended discussion about procedure. Finally, acting in accordance with a Senate resolution, the vice-president formally told Nugent that unless he could show cause why he should not be held in contempt he must be kept confined. Nugent answered that "From a confinement of two days in the close rooms of this building and from other causes," he felt unable to show cause, and therefore he submitted to the Senate's pleasure.

Robert Beale, the sergeant-at-arms, was brought in, sworn, and asked about his treatment of the prisoner. He confined Nugent, he answered, in the room of the Committee on Territories, although for the night he had taken him to his own home on Capitol Hill. The prisoner ate breakfast there and had other meals brought to him in the committee room. He had eaten well and had not complained of being ill. On Monday, April 3, after rejecting a motion to discharge Nugent, the Senate ordered the vice-president to issue a warrant to hold him. Nugent's next move was to ask the District of Columbia Circuit Court for a writ of habeas corpus. The writ was issued on April 3 and Nugent, Beale, and attorneys for both appeared before Judge William Cranch. Nugent's counsel argued that the Senate's power to punish by contempt was limited to its own members and that it should, in any case, not punish a citizen by proceedings in secret session. Counsel for the Senate argued its traditional authority. The court sustained the legislative body. It retained the common law powers enjoyed by both Houses of Parliament and the legislatures of the former colonies, the judge ruled. Nugent must remain under its orders.[2]

The *Herald*, of course, raged. Other newspapers were not far behind. Nugent's paper compared the Senate action to a tyrannous proceeding of the sort which, it said, Louis-Philippe had instituted in France and for which he had just been overthrown. It blamed the arrest on "the influence of certain candidates for the Presidency" and implied that Senator Cass and others had forced the investigation to embarrass Buchanan. On the 6th the *Herald* devoted more than four columns to excerpts from the Washington correspondence of other newspapers dealing with the case. Three of the excerpts are worth short discussions here.

The Baltimore *Clipper* Washington correspondent wrote that Polk had determined to secure renomination through the control of patronage, and that therefore Buchanan had hired "Galviensis" secretly to abuse the president. In return, the *Clipper* writer said, Polk had hired "Observer" to support his cause. "Observer" was Francis J. Grund, correspondent for the Philadelphia *Public Ledger*. He was a well educated, aggressive young immigrant from Germany, stout physically and noted for his peculiar manners. Certain private letters of his show him to have been bombastic, ambitious, perhaps not always entirely scrupulous, and peculiarly intolerant of Catholicism.[3] He praised Polk lavishly in the style that was characteristic of some of the journalism of the time.

When Nugent was arrested "Observer" was the only writer who supported the president and the Senate. The *Herald* protested, mentioning Grund by name. "Observer" replied in the columns of the *Public Ledger* of April 8 denying that he was Grund. It added that "Observer" knew Grund and "Mr. Grund knows Mr. Nugent as an educated gentleman, on whose account he has carefully refrained from making any reflection whatever."

The Washington correspondent of the Baltimore *Patriot* discussed the cordiality between Buchanan and "Galviensis." The senators, he wrote, knew that "Galviensis" had the treaty, that his correspondence had "teemed with laudation of Mr. Buchanan," and that he "has been the pet favorite of Mr. Secretary Buchanan, and, that he could at any time send in his card and obtain immediate admittance to the presence of the Secretary of State, when others, the senators included, could not get an audience because the secretary was engaged."

On April 13 the *Herald* printed the first of eight letters which were printed at irregular intervals under a heading, "Galviensis and the Senate." The dateline on each read: "Custody of the Sergeant-at-Arms of the Senate." The second, dated April 12 and printed on the 14th, was the only one which was more than a long, angry diatribe. It opened by insisting that Polk was insincere in saying that he would not accept renomination. It continued:

> Mr. Polk was excessively annoyed by these exposures, as well as at the general reflections on his conduct in the *Herald*. His friends waited on mine, and declared that if those censures were not stopped, Mr. Polk's interest throughout the country, would be thrown into the scale of the approaching presidential election against Mr. Buchanan, with whom I was known to be on terms of warm personal intimacy. I was remonstrated with by more than one member of the cabinet. . . . These gentlemen (doubtless they will all read this letter) will recollect my answer. I said—"I write for an independent journal, and I cannot suffer myself to be deterred by considerations of personal friendship or private interest from telling the truth."

Buchanan, he said, was among those who had asked him to cease attacking the president, but he had refused. The letter went on:

> The President and his friends were incapable of appreciating the noble and delicate sentiments of Mr. Buchanan, and when the treaty and accompanying documents appeared in the *Herald*, hoping to elicit something prejudicial to the Secretary of State, they resolved upon instituting an investigation; and accordingly on Wednesday, the 22d of March, the President sent a message to the Senate, apprising that body that the treaty with Mexico had appeared in the *New York Herald* with a part of the documents and the amendments of the Senate, and that the editor had promised to publish the remaining portion in a few days, and

recommending that means should be adopted to arrest the publication of this remaining portion, as it might tend to prevent the ratification of the treaty by the Mexican government.

Mr. Polk was never actuated by the motive he assigns for sending this message. . . . Under this absurd pretence he intended to conceal his design to injure the *Herald* and to destroy Mr. Buchanan.

The Senate finally gave up, although it made a face-saving gesture by attributing Nugent's release to his presumed illness. He was not ill although something to that effect had been said at one point. A motion to discharge him was made on April 19. It was tabled. On the 28th it was taken from the table, amended to include the words, "he being represented to be seriously indisposed," and approved. Nugent was released.[4] As was to be expected, the *Herald*, both editorially and in the last of the "Galviensis and the Senate" articles, boasted over the Senate's defeat. On May 3, in the last editorial on the matter, it gave what it called a "statistical table" of "leaky" senators. Its purpose, it said, was to show the folly of the whole proceeding and to show which senators normally gave the body's secrets to certain reporters. In tabular form it listed, in the first column, newspapers in New York, Philadelphia, Boston, Baltimore, and Albany. The second column listed the name of the correspondent of each, although those of the *Pennsylvanian* and the Albany *Argus* were given as unknown. In the third column were the names of the senators who were supposed to be the confidential sources of each correspondent. "The whig senators were . . . the most comprehensive leakers; but some of the democratic Senators were the most accurate leakers during these mysterious debates," it said.

The *Union* of June 2 announced that since the Senate had just lifted the injunction of secrecy it could publish the official vote on ratification, giving it as thirty-eight to fourteen. The *Herald*, three months earlier, had given it as thirty-seven to fifteen and had listed Senator Albert C. Greene, a Rhode Island Whig, in opposition. But he had voted aye. Otherwise the *Herald* was correct. On June 9 the *Union* announced that the Mexican Senate had ratified the treaty, and on July 6, after ratifications had been exchanged, it printed the text. The *Herald* had been accurate.

After an exhaustive examination of the records, the author of this book has been unable to ascertain how Nugent got the treaty. He believes, however, that Buchanan either gave it to him or connived at a scheme whereby he secured it from a foreign diplomat, and that the letter to Cameron was entirely a smoke screen. In the presidential race of that year Lewis Cass, the Democratic nominee, was beaten by General Zachary Taylor, the Whig standard-bearer. Eight years later Buchanan was nominated and elected.

9. The Press as Disunion Neared

Between the date on which the Senate ratified the Treaty of Guadelupe-Hidalgo and that on which the guns roared at Fort Sumter, the slavery controversy, corruption, and the normal growth of the nation were among the historic problems which shaped contacts between the country's press and its public servants. A woman sat in the Senate press gallery for one day, paving the way for others of her sex. The House moved to check an abuse in the use of its reporters' facilities. Another correspondent was seized, this time by the House, and refused to name the source of confidential information in spite of arrest and examination before the lawmakers. He was expelled from the gallery. And both chambers moved into the halls which they occupy today and the press was given part of its present facilities.

The woman who sat one day in the Senate press gallery, thereby establishing a claim to be the first Washington correspondent of her sex, was Jane Grey Swisshelm. Mrs. Swisshelm was a characteristic determined reformer. She was determined, self-righteous, intolerant, quick to attribute dishonesty to those of contrary beliefs, and lacking in humor. Her autobiography, which was published in 1880, shouts those characteristics on every page.[1] She was born in Pittsburgh and contributed to the *Commercial Journal* of that city during the Mexican War. Pressed by her family into a marriage which proved unhappy, she lived with her husband in Louisville for a few years. That city was the center of the trade in Negroes who were bought on the overstocked plantations of the border states and sold on the lower Mississippi, where there was a labor shortage. Mrs. Swisshelm was shocked by the cruelty of the trade.

She established the Pittsburgh *Saturday Visiter* (that is correct; she spelled the last syllable with an "e.") in January 1848 as an antislavery organ. In 1850 she and her fellow fighters for the cause watched anxiously while Congress threshed out the problem of civilian governments in the newly acquired Southwest. They regarded the failure, in the proposed compromise measures, specifically to forbid the extension of slavery into that area as a sellout. When Daniel Webster, in his seventh-of-March speech, supported the plan she took it on herself to fight against his winning the Whig presidential nomination in 1852. She persuaded Greeley to pay her five dollars a column for letters to his New York *Tribune,* and went to Washington. There she heard, as she described it in her autobiography, "of a family of eight mulattoes, bearing the image and superscription of the great New England statesman, who paid the rent and grocery bills of their mother as regularly as he did those of his wife." She also wrote that "one of President Tyler's daughters" had run away, had been recaptured, and on her "father's" orders had been sold to a slave trader. Meanwhile she decided to blaze the way for others of her sex and to invade the Senate press gallery. She approached Vice-President Millard Fillmore. "He was much surprised and tried to dissuade me," she wrote. "The place would be very unpleasant for a lady, and would attract attention. I would not like it; but he gave me the seat. I occupied it one day, greatly to the surprise of the Senators, the reporters, and others on the floor and in the galleries; but felt that the novelty would soon wear off, and that women would work there and win bread without annoyance." [2]

Her one day was that on which Senators Thomas Hart Benton of Missouri and Henry S. Foote of Mississippi engaged in a fight on the Senate floor during which the latter drew a pistol. The incident took place on April 17, 1850. Meanwhile Mrs. Swisshelm wrote a paragraph telling about Webster and the mulatto family. She showed it to friends who tried to persuade her not to send it. She wrote: "All the objections were for fear of the consequences to me. I had said God should take care of these, and mailed the letter, but I must leave Washington. Mr. Greeley should not discharge me. I left the capital the day after taking my seat in the reporters' gallery, feeling that the door was open to other women." The letter went into the *Tribune* without Greeley's having seen it. When he did the paper editorially apologized. Mrs. Swisshelm did not return to Washington as a reporter until the Civil War.

The New York *Herald* reacted with a characteristic Bennettism. On May 14, 1850, it commented on *Tribune* letters "said to be written from Washington by a certain Madame Swizzlehim, or some such name, who hails from Pittsburgh, and is considered a perfect cynosure of a literary lady." About Webster, it said, "she pours forth a flood of words and ideas that the lowest female being in the Five Points would be ashamed of applying to the meanest loafer in that awful region."

During these years a business built up of lobbying before Congress and the executive departments for private claims, the lobbyist earning a share of the final settlement. The agents advertised regularly in the capital newspapers. Some served both as newspaper correspondents and claim agents. Some who had developed congressional contacts through their work for the press capitalized on them by graduating to the more lucrative occupation. On December 13, 1852, Representative Edward Stanly, a North Carolina Whig, proposed a resolution adding a sentence to the rule for the admission of reporters. It would refuse admission to the press gallery of any one "who shall be employed as an agent to prosecute any claim pending before Congress." [3] "Right! Right!" members cried as his proposal was read. Stanly said men came into the House claiming to be reporters who had no connection with the press "but who constantly annoy us in talking about their claims." In some cases, he said, legitimate newspapermen were crowded out of press gallery seats by spurious reporters who were pressing claims. The resolution was adopted without a record vote.

By 1857 Congress had developed a policy of giving public lands to certain states and territories to subsidize railroad construction. The process was accompanied by intensive lobbying and whispers of corruption and payoffs to members. A story in the New York *Times* led to the detention of its correspondent by the House sergeant-at-arms under circumstances comparable to Nugent's arrest by the Senate. The correspondent was finally expelled from the press gallery. On the other hand three representatives resigned under fire as a result of the *Times* story and the consequent investigation.

James W. Simonton first went to Washington in 1844 as correspondent for the *Courier and Enquirer*. Six years later he took a press and type overland to California to establish a Whig paper. Finding the party already enjoying competent journalistic support he went to work for the *California Daily Courier*. Soon after Henry J. Raymond founded the New York *Times* in 1851 Simonton returned to the capital as its correspondent. The issue of January 6, 1857, published a long Washington letter dated the 3d which discussed critically some pending proposals for land grants. Quoting the text of a bill which was at that time in committee, it pointed out that the measure would grant to the Transit Railroad Company land for a line in Minnesota Territory. Other bills had made grants to a state or territory for the legislature to award to the companies which would build the lines. In inflammatory language, the letter challenged the House to investigate and said that "this bill is the special pet of that corrupt organization of insiders and outsiders whose evil influence upon the legislation of the present Congress has become almost as notorious as the Congress itself." It used such phrases as "Sodom and Gomorrah," "an individual hanging about the capital living upon ill-gotten gains," and "the slime of municipal corruption."

An editorial on the same day, referring to "our Washington letter this morning," said that a "new and magnificent land-stealing scheme is about to be brought upon the carpet in the House of Representatives." It denounced congressional corruption and intimated that former members of the body, using the floor privilege which the rules extended to them, were among the agents. "The testimony possibly may not be of the character which a court of law would admit," it said, "yet we have no fear but that we can present evidences sufficient to carry moral conviction to every honest heart, and thus bring the power of public sentiment to drive the criminals from the high places whose trusts they have dishonored." Congressmen sold out, it said, at $1,000 per vote.

On January 9 Representative William Henry Kelsey, a New York Whig, had the Clerk read the editorial. He offered a resolution calling for an investigation of corrupt combinations to be carried on by a select committee of five. Debate took most of the rest of the day. Representative Robert Treat Paine of North Carolina said that he knew that a corrupt proposal had been made to a member of Congress. Several protested that the House should not demean itself by acting on newspaper charges. Others felt that the fact that Raymond had been lieutenant governor of New York gave that paper special claim to consideration. One member echoed the common denunciation of newspaper correspondents when he described them as "those demented fragments of humanity that hang around this Hall merely for the purpose of gathering up every whisper and every word that may fall from the lips of a member, even in private conversation and trumpeting it through the land." The preamble of Kelsey's resolution was amended to credit the action to charges of a member, in recognition of Paine's remarks, and the resolution was adopted.[4]

In the course of the investigation the testimony of Simonton and Raymond discussed an issue which is still vital to newspapermen. At what point do reports of corruption or wrongdoing, perhaps not capable of being proven, establish themselves with enough justification in a reporter's or editor's mind to warrant being revealed to the world? Must the press wait until it can secure positive evidence of the type which is acceptable in court? Furthermore, it is clear that a reporter can get information more readily if his sources know that their identity will not be revealed. This is a long-standing press ethic. But are investigative bodies possessing the power of subpoena, such as legislative committees, courts and grand juries, required to respect that ethic? Should the reporter be punished if he adheres to it under questioning? Simonton and Raymond debated these points before the House committee in 1857. In the twentieth century several states have passed laws requiring their courts and legislatures to respect the reporter's right to refuse to reveal confidences.

The Simonton investigation had another result which has been invoked several times in the twentieth century. It was the immediate cause of legislation which makes refusal to testify before a committee of Congress the crime of contempt, to be prosecuted in the civil courts. The act has been invoked frequently in recent investigations.[5] The committee called several correspondents. Eliab Kingman testified that no corrupt proposition had ever been made to him. As to his knowledge of a corrupt organization, he said, "I know nothing of my own knowledge. I have heard rumors, for a great many years, of members being interested in this thing or that thing. I have seen it in every paper in the United States, but I do not know of any fact which tends to prove the existence of such a matter." James S. Pike was an independently wealthy man from Calais, Maine, who wrote for the New York *Tribune* as a hobby and to provide an outlet for his own strong antislavery sentiments. By now his writings, over the signature "J. S. P.," had made him one of the best-known correspondents in the city. He testified that he had no knowledge "strictly speaking" of corruption. He did say, however, that Representative Orsamus B. Matteson of New York had dropped a remark at one time which implied that Pike and other correspondents should be in a position to profit from inside information on land sales. Matteson resigned later after the committee recommended that he be expelled.

Raymond faced the investigators on January 14. He refused to admit that he had written the editorial in the paper of the 6th but said that as editor of the paper he accepted responsibility for it. Any knowledge on his part of corrupt proposals dealing with land legislation, he said, consisted of "only such information, at second hand, as leaves upon my mind no doubt of the fact asserted." That information was derived, he continued, "in part from our regular Washington correspondent, Mr. Simonton, and in part from other persons whose names I do not feel at liberty to give." He argued that although his information was not of the sort which might be admitted as evidence in court, it was still of a nature that justified a newspaper in presenting it in an effort to uncover wrongdoing. Simonton was summoned before the committee the next day. He admitted that he was the *Times*'s regular correspondent, writing over the signature "S." Asked if he knew of any organization among congressmen intended to arrange the sale of votes for legislation, he answered that he did not "of my own knowledge." "I have heard that there was such an organization, and from evidence conclusive to my own judgment, I have been satisfied that it did exist," he said.

The committee record tells of a long examination in which the members pounded at the witness with very little success. He told them that several congressmen had approached him asking if they could rely on his secrecy. "In my profession," he said, "such questions are put to me almost every day—I do not know whether the party approaching me desires to communicate public documents or news of interest to me—and I always, unless I have special reason for supposing that the particular individual has an improper proposal to make, accept their confidence." Having been assured of his secrecy, he continued, several members had asked him "to procure for them interests in particular measures, named by them, pending before the House, stating the amounts which they desired to receive." Simonton had always refused to help them.

There had been two direct proposals and several others had approached him under circumstances which led him to suspect that they wanted him to act as broker in improper negotiations. He had warded them off. He admitted that he had accepted a small payment several years earlier for helping a friend get a small private bill through the Senate. He also testified that he had once returned a loan when the lender asked help with a patent. Throughout that part of his examination which was printed he adamantly refused to reveal the names of those who had approached him, standing on the reporter's ethic. Debate in the House later showed, however, that he did give the committee some names although that part of the testimony was not printed. It was explained that Simonton had given those names only on promise that the committee would not regard his disclosures as evidence, but would accept them as merely individuals who might be helpful witnesses.

The day after his testimony the committee chairman reported to the House that Simonton refused to answer some questions. He offered a resolution directing the Speaker to issue his warrant for the correspondent's arrest. He also reported out of the committee a bill making refusal to testify before a committee of either house a misdemeanor liable to indictment and trial by any federal court of competent jurisdiction. It would be punishable by fines of up to $1,000 and jail sentence up to one year. The resolution for Simonton's arrest was adopted and the House went into debate on the bill. It was interrupted when the clerk of the sergeant-at-arms reported that he had arrested the writer and was ready to present him at the bar. While Simonton waited under guard the House debated procedure. Finally it directed the Speaker to ask "Are you ready to show cause why you should not be further proceeded against for the said alleged contempt;

and do you desire to be heard in person, or by counsel, now or at what time?"

Simonton asked and was granted permission to make a statement. His remarks take nearly four columns of the *Congressional Globe*. He maintained that he had a right to receive confidences which the House should respect and said that the committee had demanded that he give information that would not be legal evidence. The House finally voted 136 to 23 to order him held "during the balance of this session, or until discharged by the further order of the House, to be taken when he shall have purged the contempt on which he was arrested, by testifying before the committee." The next day the House passed the bill making refusal to testify a misdemeanor. The Senate passed it on January 23.

The committee brought Simonton before it again on February 4. This time he was asked in writing whether or not he had ever been solicited by any member of the Thirty-fourth Congress, directly or indirectly, "to make any arrangement by which the member was to receive any valuable consideration for his support of any measure." He was allowed to retire three times to consult his counsel, Senator Reverdy Johnson of Maryland. Finally he wrote in reply: "I cannot say, under oath, that I have, and never have intended to be understood so to mean." The committee reported the next day that the writer's answers were such as to make it unnecessary to hold him any longer. The House approved its recommendation for his release, so he was discharged. The committee further pointed out, however, that he had admitted that he had accepted something for helping a friend pass a private bill and said he had been promised compensation for backing a Wisconsin land bill, although he had not collected. It proposed, therefore, that he be expelled from the press gallery.

The House took up the expulsion resolution on February 28. Amended to include F. F. C. Triplett, it was adopted. Triplett had been admitted to the press gallery the year before as correspondent for the Louisville *Journal*. He had told the committee that although he had never been the agent for payment to procure the passage of land bills he had "been brought into contact" with members in that connection. He was not expelled for that reason, however. The committee found that he had agreed orally to pay to Representative William A. Gilbert of New York an amount on a sliding scale, possibly as much as $8,000, if Gilbert got the House to publish as a public document a book which Triplett had prepared on the bounty and land laws.[6] The committee also recommended that Matteson, Gilbert, and Representatives Francis S. Edwards of New York and William W. Welch of Connecticut be expelled. The three New York members resigned before the House acted. The move against Welch was dropped.

Simonton's examination took place in the old hall of the House, the room which is now Statuary Hall. The representatives had worked there since 1800 except for the five years after the British burned the building in 1814. Both Rounsavell and Davis had been examined in that room. But when Simonton appeared there the marble wings at the north and south ends of the Capitol, which house the present House of Representatives and Senate Chamber, were near completion. When Franklin Pierce took office as president four years earlier construction had started. Although work was going forward there was a dispute being carried on over the interior arrangement. Thomas U. Walter was the architect in charge and was proceeding according to his own plan, with work supervised by the Interior Department. Pierce transferred control to the War Department, and Secretary of War Jefferson Davis placed Captain Montgomery C. Meigs of the Army Engineers in charge. Meigs scrapped Walter's plan and went ahead with his own.

Under the War Department plan each wing is a three-story rectangle with the chamber occupying space in the center of the second and third floors. The Senate occupies the north wing and the House of Representatives that to the south. On the second floor of each wing a corridor adjoins the legislative hall on three sides and gives access to it. On the "attic floor," corridors on those same three sides have doors leading to galleries which look down on the lawmakers debating below. Outside of that corridor are offices or committee rooms. On the fourth side, on the second floor, the space between the legislative chamber and the outer wall is given over to lounges and retiring rooms for the members. On the floor above, Meigs planned that the central rooms in that area, which provide access to the galleries immediately above and behind the presiding officer, be reserved for reporters' work rooms.[7] Meigs's original plan for reporters remains in force. The open gallery behind the Speaker and the vice-president is, in each chamber, the press gallery. It is reached from the room behind it. That room remains, at each end of the Capitol, the working and rest area for the press. Since that time additional rooms, which were originally intended for committees, have been given to the press. Correspondents have formed the habit of referring to the whole area, both the rooms and the galleries proper, as the "press gallery."

On December 9, 1857, a committee was named to examine the new hall of the House of Representatives and to report when it might be occupied. The committee reported on the 14th that heating and atmospheric conditions made use of the newly-built chamber practical. The report said that a convenient desk in front of the Clerk's desk was available for the stenographers of the *Congressional Globe*. "And for the accommodation of the reporters of the public press, there is ample room in the gallery, immediately over the Speaker's chair and east of the railing." The committee recommended that that part of the gallery and the room behind it be set apart for their use and provided with desks. It also recommended that telegraph wires be run into that room.[8] On December 16, 1857, Speaker James L. Orr rapped his gavel to call the House to order for the first time in the room which it still occupies. Opening business was to make housekeeping arrangements.

Representative Charles J. Faulkner of Virginia said that the doorkeeper lacked enough men to guard all the entrances into the new room. Therefore, he moved that a select committee be appointed to report the number of additional messengers, pages and other officers and aides that would be necessary. A debate in which several members showed that they were anxious to provide comfortable and efficient press facilities was precipitated when Representative N. P. Banks of Massachusetts, who had been Speaker the previous session, moved that the committee also investigate accommodations for reporters who were not already provided for.

At this point Speaker Orr offered an explanation. He had found, he said, that no arrangements had been made for the press except for reporters for the *Globe*. (The *Congressional Globe* has had very little attention in this book. It was a privately

printed—by Blair and Rives—record of speeches as well as legislative steps which was subsidized by Congress. It gave way to
the *Congressional Record,* printed by the government, in 1873.)
Therefore the Speaker had instructed the superintendent to provide ten seats in the gallery behind the rostrum although he had
received between fifty and one hundred applications from newspapermen. The superintendent told him, he added, that seats in
that gallery could be elevated so that reporters could see and
hear everything better from there than from any other part of
the room. Faulkner's resolution, amended to direct the committee
to investigate press facilities, was adopted. He was made chairman.

Reporting from the committee a week later, he proposed a
series of resolutions. One would direct the Speaker to assign
galleries for the press, the foreign ministers, and the ladies. One
would direct the superintendent of the building to "cause the
reporters' gallery to be properly fitted up with desks and seats,
and convenience for taking notes." Another would provide that
the telegraph and reporters' rooms be reserved for the use of the
wire companies and the correspondents. Finally, the committee
proposed that the seventeenth, eighteenth and nineteenth rules
be rescinded and new ones substituted. One of these was the
rule governing admission of the press which had evolved between
1801 and 1852. The second of the new rules provided that "stenographers and reporters" be admitted by the Speaker to the
gallery over the rostrum. The precautions which had developed
over the years were written into this new rule. Among its provisions were: 1) that reporters not be admitted to the floor;   2)
that each must have written permission from the Speaker;   3)
that none be given that permission unless he state in writing for
what paper he was to report; and   4) that he be denied his seat
if he became a claim agent. The committee report was adopted
and the press gallery opened under these conditions.[9]

The Senate, too faced moving day. A week after the House
acted the upper body took its first step in that direction although
the actual change was not carried out for another year. A resolution on December 22, 1857, directed the Committee on Public
Buildings to submit a plan assigning the rooms in the Capitol
addition to the north. The report, offered on January 11, 1858,
and adopted on the 18th, assigned forty-five rooms to various

committees and provided that reporters and the telegraph should have number ninety-two.[10] This is the room in the "attic story" which had been intended for that purpose in Meigs's plan and which is still used by the press.

No more action was taken at that session. On December 23, 1858, the Senate ordered the superintendent to have the new chamber available by January 5, 1859. On the agreed date the Senate met for the last time in the historic chamber which had housed it since 1819. The Committee on the Library, reporting the assignment of galleries, said that "The center portion of the north gallery was reserved for such reporters of the press as may be admitted thereto by the authority of the Senate, except for the front desk, which was set apart for the reporters of the Senate." [11] After hearing the report the Senate marched in a procession to the new quarters.

The body was forced to adopt a new rule to govern the new facilities, as the House had done. Reported out from the Library Committee and adopted on January 11, the rule governing press provided: 1) that the seats in the reporters' gallery be numbered by the presiding officer; 2) that he may assign one seat to each Washington newspaper and one to such other daily newspapers as they may apply, "but if such papers have more than one reporter they may alternate, occupying only the one seat assigned to such newspaper"; 3) seats may not be assigned unless the presiding officer is satisfied that the applicant is a bona fide reporter; 4) and the presiding officer may make such further regulations as he deems necessary.[12]

The practice of listing reporters in the *Congressional Directory* originated two years later. The *Directory* was almost as old as Congress itself. Early issues were small pocket manuals giving little more than the names of the lawmakers, their Washington residences and their committees. As the years passed the editors put in more and more information which members of the two houses wanted in convenient form. The *Congressional Directory* for the first session of the Thirty-sixth Congress, in 1860, listed the reporters who had been accepted for admission to the two press galleries. Unlike the practice today each House listed its reporters separately. The Senate admitted twenty-three. Of those, six represented the District of Columbia papers, including the Alexandria *Gazette*. Kingman was there for the New York *Journal of Commerce.* J. T. Piggott reported the upper house for the Associated Press, and one man for the New York *Herald.* The *Tribune* was unlisted in either chamber's column although James S. Pike and James E. Harvey corresponded from Washington for that paper. Other papers represented in the Senate gallery included the Petersburg, Virginia, *Intelligencer,* the Raleigh, North Carolina, *Daily Press,* and the Cincinnati *Gazette.* On the House list were fifty-one names, including Poore and Gobright. The former reported for the Boston *Journal.* Three men were listed for the New York *Herald,* the only paper to require so many. In addition to the Associated Press, those who were listed wrote for forty-five papers in New York, Philadelphia, St. Louis, Cincinnati, Detroit, New Bedford, Chicago, Columbus, Atlanta, Ft. Smith, and San Francisco.

The year that this *Directory* appeared the new Republican party also put through legislation establishing the Government Printing Office, definitely taking that patronage plum out of the hands of an administration journal. In that year, too, Lincoln was elected and South Carolina started the secession movement. In April of the following year the shells rained on Fort Sumter.

10. The Civil War—1

The experience of the Civil War, of the two twentieth century wars and of such struggles as those in Korea and Vietnam shows that when a country with a free press tradition mobilizes, difficult contradictions appear. Warfare calls for unquestioning discipline among the armed forces and for a very broad reorganization of civilian life. Practically every citizen participates, with little questioning of governmental leadership in the case of a desperate struggle in which war has been declared. In the case of a debatable, undeclared conflict such as that in Vietnam, the proper place of public information and public opinion raises even more difficult questions. The American theory of a free press assumes that the public must know what its leaders are doing, and that the press must be free, within limits of responsibility, to discuss, comment on, and criticize goals and the steps being taken to realize those goals. Furthermore, with the national effort concentrated in government to the degree that it is in wartime, government must make positive arrangements to provide necessary information.

War raised four particular questions regarding the press: 1) To what extent should the press surrender the right to question leaders and criticize methods? If that right is adhered to and practiced vigorously is there danger that it will lead to fatal confusion and misdirection? Will it give encouragement to the enemy, giving him false hopes of the collapse of home front morale and cause him to fight on with greater determination?

If surrendered, does it allow leaders to relax their responsibility to the citizenry and to set up a compliant propaganda machine designed to keep themselves in power and to conceal their failures? 2) What provision should be made to release information as to the success or failure on the fighting fronts and the progress of civilian and industrial mobilization? 3) On the other hand, what and how much information can be made available to the citizens at home without giving helpful intelligence to the enemy? What powers can a free government keep to suppress or punish the publication of secrets without destroying democracy itself? 4) To how great an extent may government do its own reporting as against providing facilities for reporters to observe proceedings and present to the country facts which have not been channeled through and perhaps diluted by government sources? Assuming that it is desirable that the press send its own correspondents to the scenes of fighting and to observe steps in military and industrial mobilization, how much control should government exercise over them? What policy should guide censorship in the theatres of operations? And what arrangements should be made for reporters to meet their personal needs and to have channels of communication provided them?

The American Civil War was the first great conflict in which these questions presented themselves forcibly. Before the eighteenth century, warfare was a matter for professional soldiery and had less impact on the citizenry at large, except for those who lived in the occupied or combat areas, than have the twentieth-century struggles. The worldwide fighting between England and France and their respective allies as the nineteenth century opened made war involve practically total national participation. At that time the press was influential in circulating theories regarding public problems and in both reflecting and crystallizing informed public opinion. But it showed little enterprise in news-gathering. Between 1815 and 1861, however, newspapers both in Europe and in this country expanded their reporting and news transmission methods. The development of the railroad, steam navigation and the electric telegraph, together with commercial stimulation that added greatly to newspaper revenue, brought about a revolution in journalistic practices.

Newspapermen, soldiers, and civilian heads of government, therefore, had little experience to call on in solving the problems of public information and the press in April 1861. Moreover, in addition to the conditions which were discussed above and which always appear in warfare, their problem was complicated by others which were present in military organization, civilian government, and practices of the press which were peculiar to that time.

Those peculiar conditions were largely the outgrowth of the close political association of the average newspaper and the party structure which built the civilian government and the armed forces. Since Washington's administration the American press had stood on its constitutionally protected freedom to denounce, sometimes with imperfect regard for truth or responsibility, leaders of the opposition. Newspaper copy, whether on the editorial page or in the news columns, was highly opinionated. There was little tradition of responsible attribution of news material to its source. There was little tradition or thought of objective reporting. There were cases of exaggeration and deliberate efforts to destroy the public usefulness of statesmen who opposed the paper's position, sometimes without regard to the statesman's real merit.

Newspapermen, too, were driven by their home offices to search vigorously for exclusive stories because of the keen competition which then marked the press. Such great New York journals as the *Herald, Times, Tribune, World,* and *Journal of Commerce* were practically national institutions with nationwide circulation and reputation. They maintained that position by competing keenly for news, although each kept its own editorial character. Competition for local or regional circulation was particularly sharp in Philadelphia, Cincinnati, Chicago, and St. Louis. Papers in those cities sent correspondents to Washington and to the armies with orders to get exclusive breaks and to rush back from the fighting fronts and from the capital stories which were ahead of and more dramatic than those of the opposition. Reporters sought, and frequently secured, official connivance to gain their ends. To secure that connivance they used the weapon most conveniently available—that of published praise or criticism. The *Herald* in particular seems to have lauded those officials who were cooperative and damned those who refused to knuckle under to the paper's praise or threats. Others were not far behind. In this way reporters, both in Washington and with the armies, found it possible to play off the jealousies and ambitions of administrators, army officers, and clerks to secure information.

But secrecy is essential to military success. Responsible officers of the civilian government and responsible army officers realized it and took steps—untried ones in view of the lack of experience with this novel problem—to try to adjust to it. Responsible editors denied that they published information which would give "aid and comfort to the enemy," but they strove to keep ahead of their competition. As a result, northern newspapers, which circulated freely into the Confederacy, gave southern generals details regarding the position of individual corps and divisions of the Union army, battle plans and other essential military information which should have been kept secret. From Washington came stories of policy, personnel shifts, political maneuvering, the location and movements of army units, and other facts which Confederate officers must have read with interest.

Several studies have been critical of the press and have implied that the government should have been more repressive. One writer made the curious statement that the press stood on its rights "through a false notion" of the right of the people to know.[1] It is hardly a false notion that the people of a democracy have a right to know, but the amount of knowledge which may be allowed to reach them—and the enemy—may be debatable. An Army War College study in 1917 cited instances of damage to military operations through publication in the Crimean War, on both sides in the Civil War, and in the Spanish-American War. It said that there were two ways in which the press has a direct influence on the success of the army. First was the publication of military secrets. "Second," it said, "by criticism of the conduct of campaigns, the action of certain officers or exploiting others, the people will be led to lose confidence in the army with the result that the moral support of the people is lost." [2]

It is not easy to find the median point between these contradictory needs of military necessity and the position of the press. In the twentieth century, government has set up a combination of active propaganda, voluntary censorship, and accreditation and control of civilian newspaper, magazine, and radio and television correspondents at the fighting fronts and in Washington which grew in part out of the Civil War experience.

These problems being what they were—and are—and these press practices, both in Washington and in the field, being what they were, how did correspondents go about their work between 1861 and 1865? What steps did government take to make the necessary compromises? First, the means by which reporters sought and secured exclusive inside contacts. In selecting some noteworthy examples we may start with Samuel Wilkeson. In August 1861, when Wilkeson came to Washington to become chief of the *Tribune*'s bureau, the Union was reeling from the defeat at the first Battle of Bull Run and Simon Cameron was Secretary of War. Cameron was the machine politician from Pennsylvania who had found federal funds for Ritchie to buy Blair's *Globe* sixteen years earlier. He was applying his peculiar skill in political manipulation now to the Republican party. The ten months in which he headed the War Department were marked by inefficient management and the purchase of goods from manufacturers, notably in his own state of Pennsylvania, which fell short of specifications. Henry Villard, correspondent at different times for both the *Herald* and the *Tribune*, described him as the "typical American politician." Cameron "held himself a little too freely at the disposal of the newspaper men, to whom he was by far the most cordial and talkative of all the secretaries," Villard wrote.[3]

This was the man to whom Wilkeson presented a letter of introduction from C. A. Dana, managing editor of the *Tribune*. Soon he wrote to his paper: "Secretary Cameron gives day and night to the service of his country. The contracts made by him will defy the most unfriendly scrutiny." He clipped the article and sent it to the War Department chief with a note saying, "The satisfaction of doing justice to a wronged statesman, is not equalled by the pleasure with which I sincerely pay a tribute of respect to a maligned good man."[4]

Thereafter Cameron kept Wilkeson close to him. The secretary took the correspondent for a visit to his farm near Harrisburg. In October he actually sent a note to H. E. Thayer, the chief telegraph censor who was supposed to scrutinize reporters' copy to stop military information. The censor was directed to open the wire to Wilkeson without question. A few weeks later Wilkeson accompanied Cameron on a trip to Missouri and back through Kentucky. The correspondent sat in on some of the secretary's conferences with generals during that trip. The note-worthy instance was an interview with Brigadier General William T. Sherman in Louisville. The general was not told that the civilian accompanying the secretary and listening with deep interest to their conversation was a newspaperman.[5] Sherman was the most implacable enemy the reporters had among the high-ranking military leaders.

Back in Washington, Wilkeson scored repeatedly by sending to his paper copies of War Department reports ahead of competing correspondents. In some cases reports were printed in the *Tribune* before they reached the officer for whose eyes they were intended. Raymond protested to the secretary.[6] As a result arrangements were made by which the Associated Press became the channel for transmitting such official documents. The account of the incident in the New York *Times* of November 21, 1861, pointed out that the documents were to go to Gobright "—and to him alone." Disappearance of the official journal, the former medium for making public such official papers, had left the government without machinery to carry out that task. The Associated Press now did so.

At about the same time, Greeley made private arrangements through third parties for confidential information from the president. The go-betweens were James R. Gilmore and Robert J. Walker. The latter had been Polk's secretary of the treasury, the man who conspired with Cameron in the sale of the *Globe* to Ritchie in 1845. He was now close to the administration and a partner of Gilmore in planning a new magazine, to be named the *Continental*. They hoped Greeley would write for their publication and offered, as a special bribe, Walker's influence with the president. Lincoln was persuaded to take part in the plan in spite of the fact that it was the type of secret intrigue which he normally disliked. He wrote to Walker on November 21, 1861, a letter which Gilmore was authorized to take to New York and show to Greeley. "But all this must be on the express and explicit understanding that the fact of these communications coming from me shall be absolutely confidential—not to be disclosed by Greeley to his nearest friend, or any of his subordinates," the president wrote. "He will be, in effect, my mouth-piece, but I shall not be known to be the speaker."

Greeley had been a problem to the president. At first he

proposed to let the South secede, without coercion. Although the *Tribune* editorial page had swung around to support the war, it was by no means an uncritical supporter of administration policy in carrying it on. Recognizing the paper's influence, Lincoln hoped by this arrangement to buy Greeley's support. For several weeks thereafter *Tribune* editorials and correspondents gave the president unqualified backing. But such a plan was foredoomed to failure. Within a few weeks it broke down and Greeley's editorials returned to their former practice of occasional support alternating with harassment which did nothing to ease the heavy burden carried by the tall man in the White House.[7]

Two months later Cameron was pushed out of the War Department. In his place, the president named Edwin M. Stanton, a Washington attorney who had a reputation for cool efficiency. Cameron's departure opened the way for the *Herald* to seek the advantages which the *Tribune* had enjoyed while Wilkeson and Cameron worked together. Bennett's tool in this game was a man with a diverse past. Malcolm Ives had studied for the priesthood in Rome and Vienna, had been ordained, and had served a parish in Milwaukee. Later he married a Protestant girl and was unfrocked. He converted his wife to Catholicism only to have her leave him, refusing to live with a former priest. He joined the *Herald* staff in 1858.[8]

The James Gordon Bennett Papers in the Manuscript Division of the Library of Congress consist of confidential letters written to Bennett and to Frederic Hudson, the *Herald's* managing editor, from their correspondents in Washington and on the various fighting fronts. The collection includes one from Ives, written in Washington on January 15, 1862, which tells of conversations with Stanton and with General George B. McClellan which are almost incredible. The known related developments, however, seem to confirm much of what Ives wrote. At the time it was written, McClellan had spent six months organizing the Army of the Potomac, although he showed little vigor in seeking active contact with Confederate forces. The *Herald* supported him while the *Tribune*, which saw the war as an antislavery crusade, was cool because it doubted the general's sentiments on that point. Stanton's nomination had gone to the Senate but it was not yet confirmed. Ives wrote that he had been influential in bringing about Stanton's appointment and had been the one who first told the new secretary that his name was under consideration. The Senate approved the nomination on the day Ives wrote.

Marked "Confidential," the letter opened by saying that Stanton, "in accordance with the promise he had made me on the day of his nomination, last evening sent me word that he arranged an interview for me with Genl McClellan for last evening." It went into a long discussion of cabinet gossip which, it said, Stanton gave him. Finally Stanton left the reporter alone with the general. The letter continued:

After Stanton left McClellan's little study, the latter closed the door, and left me with him for three hours, closeted alone. With much feeling, and a manner so heartfelt, so evidently pure and sincere as to be absolutely touching, he began by saying that, on the previous day (Monday) he had been sent for to meet the President and a majority of the members of his Cabinet; that they had demanded, peremptorily, information concerning the manner in which he intended to carry on the campaign and that he had courteously but firmly refused to open his lips on the subject. "What I declined communicating to them," he said, "I am now going to convey through you to Mr. Bennett and Mr. Hudson; I am going to give you all the knowledge I possess myself with no reserve, and if you choose to take a pen you may take notes of what I am going to say, and I will willingly give you all the time you require to make the information complete."

The letter, which may, of course, have been largely untruthful or, at best, exaggeration, went on for page after page, quoting the officer as making almost saccharine remarks about Bennett and Hudson and how they had stood by him. Then it went into an extended discussion of tactical plans. In further letters during the next few days, Ives claimed the cordial support of Lincoln and of Secretary of the Treasury Salmon P. Chase as well as of Stanton and Cameron, and he said that Gustavus A. Fox, the assistant secretary of the navy, was "all right." He quarreled, however, with Simon P. Hanscom, chief of the *Herald* Washington staff. In one letter he said Hanscom had told War Department officials that Ives's connection with the *Herald* was only a local one in New York and that he had been given permission to come to Washington on private business. Hanscom described the business as "some damned speculation with combustibles." [9]

Three weeks after this conversation with McClellan, Ives was under arrest and his service to the *Herald* ended. He walked into the War Department on February 8 and demanded that he be allowed immediately to see the secretary. Assistant Secretary Peter H. Watson said that his superior was busy and that Ives must wait his turn with other callers in the anteroom. Then, according to the order for the reporter's arrest which Stanton issued two days later, "he conducted himself insolently, making threats . . . to Watson of the hostility of the New York Herald against the administration of the War Department unless he was afforded special privileges and furnished intelligence in the Department . . . the moment it was received by the Department in advance of all other papers." At another point Stanton's order said, "Newspapers are valuable organs of public intelligence and instruction, and every proper facility will be afforded all loyal persons to procure, on equal terms, information of such public facts as may properly be made known in time of rebellion." Ives was arrested that night in Willard's Hotel and taken to Baltimore, where he joined other political prisoners confined without trial in Fort McHenry.

His discomfiture occurred a few weeks after the *Herald* had a somewhat similar experience with another of its staff. The central character this time, too, had a curious background. Henry Wikoff was born in Philadelphia about 1813 and was said to be the son of a wealthy physician whose name he took. He was expelled from Yale for a prank, but graduated in 1832 from Union College and was admitted to the Pennsylvania bar two years later. He inherited a moderate fortune and went to Europe. For several years he moved on the fringes of that continent's aristocracy and stage circles. After receiving a decoration from the Queen of Spain he claimed the title of "Chevalier." In 1851 he pursued an American heiress to Genoa and tried to force her, at gun point, to marry him. She appealed to the British consul who had Wikoff jailed. Out of that experience he wrote a book, "My Courtship and Its Consequences." Henry Villard described him as "of middle age, an accomplished man of the world, a fine linguist, with graceful presence, elegant manners, and a conscious condescending way—altogether just such a man as would be looked upon as a superior being by a woman accustomed only to western society." [10] The *Herald* employed him in Washington, where he attached himself especially to Secretary of State William H. Seward and to Mrs. Lincoln. Again quoting Villard: "Wikoff showed the utmost assurance in his appeals to the vanity of the mistress of the White House. I myself heard him compliment her upon her looks and dress in so fulsome a way that she ought to have blushed and banished the impertinent fellow from her presence." Instead, she welcomed him to the White House.

Parts of Lincoln's first message to a regular session of Congress, in December 1861, were printed in the *Herald* the morning of the day the document went to the Capitol. The House Judiciary Committee, of which Representative John Hickman of Pennsylvania was chairman, tried to find the leak. Summoned before that group, Wikoff admitted that he had secured the document and sent it to New York. He refused to divulge its source, pleading "an obligation of strictest secrecy." The committee ordered the sergeant-at-arms to hold him. The president now intervened personally. He went to the Capitol and had a private meeting with the committee—an extraordinary act for the chief executive. Meanwhile Wikoff retained as counsel Major General Daniel Sickles, a former New York member of Congress who had created a sensation a few years earlier. Sickles shot and killed his wife's lover one afternoon near the Jackson statue in Lafayette Park. His victim was Philip Barton Key, the United States District Attorney for the District of Columbia and a brother of Francis Scott Key. On his trial Sickles successfully pleaded temporary insanity. He was to lose a leg at the Battle of Gettysburg.

While the reporter remained in custody, Sickles carried on talks with Wikoff, with a White House gardener named Watts, and with others at the executive mansion. Watts provided a way out. On February 5 he testified that he had seen the message in the White House library, read it, memorized parts of it, and recited them to Wikoff later. That story and Lincoln's visit led the committee to discharge Wikoff and hush up the matter. Washington understood, however, that Mrs. Lincoln had been Wikoff's leak.[11] The *Herald* published an editorial on February 16 denouncing Hickman. A confidential letter to Bennett from one of the paper's Washington staff two days later asked the editor to "have done with Hickman, or you will be the death of many of your best friends." It said Hickman and others threatened to retaliate by depriving Bennett's yachtsman son of his naval commission. No more such criticism appeared, although the incident was closed by then, anyway.

L. A. Whiteley, now chief of the *Herald*'s Washington staff, wrote on June 29, 1862, that Wikoff was involved in negotiations regarding a bid submitted to the War Department by the Savage Revolving Arms Company of Middletown, Connecticut. Wikoff had asked Whiteley to intercede at the War Department. The letter said that Wikoff claimed to be in the editor's confidence and that a brother-in-law of Bennett's was associated with the firm. Whiteley had no objection to calling at the department if he could be sure that what Wikoff said about his chief's connection were true. But he pointed out that "My effort to do so however diplomatically done may possibly compromise your independence towards a department you are assailing." [12] Ives and Wikoff were the only Washington correspondents whose efforts to arrange special favors brought about their arrest. We may look at one more of the several available cases of such activity. This one comes from another of the confidential letters to Hudson which are in the Manuscript Division of the Library of Congress.

T. M. Cook, who had covered the Battle of Mobile Bay for the *Herald,* wrote on November 3, 1864, from Washington. He apparently referred to an expedition which was then outfitting to attack Fort Fisher and Wilmington, North Carolina. At Whiteley's suggestion, Cook wrote, he talked to Assistant Secretary of the Navy Fox who thanked him for his account of the action in Mobile Bay. Cook asked for a note to Admiral Porter. "What I wanted," he wrote Hudson, "was to be placed on the Admiral's ship with facilities at my disposal to get away north in advance of the mass of correspondents or any of them." Fox hesitated, saying "something about Dahlgren getting into a scrape by sending a Tribune correspondent away specially with important news," but finally agreed to speak to Porter. Cook said he hoped arrangements could be made for him to get to New York twelve hours before Porter sent his dispatches to Fortress Monroe and "that the affair could be covered up." "I do not believe they will give me a special boat to get away in; they are afraid to do it; but I am satisfied that I shall be on the flagship exclusively, and then if an opportunity occurs Porter will assist me in giving other correspondents the slip." Later in the letter he added, "But I yet think the Navy Department could be induced to procure for us an outside vessel which we might call our own were Ashley or some other person who is on confidential terms there authorized to promise Fox that thereafter he and the Department would be exempt from attacks in the columns of the Herald—This thing is, of course, sub rosa."

Cook was not given the special privileges which he sought. At the first, and unsuccessful, attack on Fort Fisher the Navy provided all of the correspondents with a gunboat which Admiral Porter ordered to move about freely to points from which they could watch the operation, and none had any advantage over the others. No such press boat was provided for the second attack, on January 13, 1865. Correspondents were scattered among the several vessels taking part. But none was given special facilities to rush back the news ahead of his competitors.[13]

11. The Civil War—2

Having abandoned an official Washington paper as his outlet, Lincoln entered upon the presidency lacking such advantages as that form of journalistic support gave him, but free of its vexations. The Associated Press took over that part of the administration paper's function which had consisted of making public official orders and addresses. The news conference and the press secretary had to wait another half century.

Lincoln avoided favoritism to certain reporters or papers who might therefore have given him special backing. His dignity and sense of propriety, as well as his courage and his ability to keep his balance against the barking of the journalistic dogs which pursued him, kept reporters at a distance. He received them in the same way he received any other callers who visited the White House and sent in their cards. Only one writer enjoyed anything like the confidential relationship with Lincoln which Wilkeson enjoyed with Cameron. He was Noah Brooks, correspondent of the relatively uninfluential Sacramento *Union*. But the president's contact with Brooks was based on an old friendship and from a sincere personal liking. It had nothing to do with press connections. Brooks was a regular confidant of the president and frequently accompanied him on trips.

As to other correspondents, Gobright wrote that the president was generally courteous to them but gave none his complete confidence.[1] Newspaper files show little or nothing that could have come from the executive mansion in the way that news broke from Congress and the departments. There was nothing from the White House of the sort that twentieth-century newspaper readers expect. Gobright tells of two occasions when he called at the White House during the evening. It must have been a habit. At 10 o'clock one evening the reporter found the president just as the latter returned from the War Department. He said that he was relieved to learn that Grant, in command of the forces besieging Vicksburg, was in touch with N. P. Banks, who was leading an army upriver from New Orleans. Gobright said that he intended to telegraph the information and Lincoln replied, "That's right. The public ought to know good news." To the correspondent's dismay, however, the censor held up his dispatch in spite of the fact that the information came from the president.[2]

On another occasion Gobright was present when Lincoln received word of a military disaster. The president asked Gobright to withhold it. The report turned out to be false. The Associated Press agent called at the White House during the evening. Lincoln had heard nothing, but said he could not sleep and suggested that the two go together to the War Department. Reaching the telegraph office in the War Department building, the president was handed a telegram which had just arrived. It gave an unverified report that the troops at Vicksburg had been defeated and dispersed. Gobright wrote: "Mr. Lincoln read the telegram under the disadvantage of imperfect light. He was extremely nervous; his hands and legs shook violently; his face, upon which the gas shone, was ghastly. He again read the telegram, to fully satisfy himself of its purport." He asked Gobright not to send the story. The newsman pointed out that the telegram was not authoritative and was given only as a rumor which reached the telegraph office. The president expressed relief and again asked Gobright not to send the story. It turned out to be false.[3]

The Associated Press agent tells of one other direct contact with the president. This time Lincoln, happy over receiving good news, held an informal interview with a group of reporters which resembled a twentieth-century news conference. Gobright does not identify the story, but says that word had been received at the War Department of a Union victory. The secretary refused to release the information although rumors were widespread. A group of newsmen trotted to the White House where a cabinet meeting was just breaking up.[4]

The representatives of the press had no sooner sent in their cards to him than he welcomed them in a loud voice. "Walk in, walk in; be seated; take seats." Before they had time to announce the object of their visit, he remarked, "I know what you have come for; you want to hear more about the good news. I know you do. You gentlemen are keen of scent, and always wide awake." One of them replied: "You have hit the matter precisely, Mr. President: that's exactly what we want—the news."

He was more than ordinarily cheerful. As we had recently suffered a defeat in battle, this latest intelligence of which he was in possession evidently gave him much comfort. He was happy.

Leaning back in his chair and stretching his legs on the table, he took up a small piece of paper—memoranda— saying at the time: "I've already told this story half a dozen times, but I'll tell it again, as you haven't heard it." He then prefaced his narrative with a few explanatory remarks, in order that we all might more clearly understand it. He next alluded to what the telegram said, and made his comments, being very careful in separating this announcement in the dispatch from his own conclusions. . . . "Gentlemen," he said, "that's all there is about it. The public will be glad to hear it."

Instead of the president the principal wartime news sources in Washington were congressmen and cabinet members. Villard has left to us his experiences with them. In the summer of 1861, he wrote, he could always see the secretaries, usually immediately after office hours. At that time he found Cameron, Seward, and Chase the most accessible and communicative. Chase and Seward were peculiarly susceptible to newspaper flattery. "Seward was afflicted with an outright weakness in that respect," Villard wrote in his *Memoirs*. "The *Herald* made a regular practice of bestowing on him extravagant eulogies bordering sometimes on ridiculous exaggeration, in order to smooth the way to his confidence for its correspondents, and the recipient did not always succeed in concealing from them his grateful appreciation." [5] Gideon Welles, the former editor of the Hartford *Times* who headed the Navy Department, was perhaps the least communicative man in the cabinet. Therefore the reporters made their contacts with Assistant Secretary Fox, a former naval officer.[6]

Stanton, finally, was the keyman as the news source in wartime Washington. Through most of his term his attitude toward reporters was very different from that displayed toward Ives in January of 1862—if Ives were not telling untruths in what he wrote to Bennett. Villard wrote that after Cameron left the War Department "This change, while of immeasurable benefit to the country, proved a decided disadvantage to my profession; for whereas Cameron was always accessible and communicative—no doubt too much for the public good—his successor had the doors of the War Department closed to newspaper men." [7] Whiteley wrote to Bennett on March 30, 1863: "Stanton absolutely stinks in the nostrils of the people and the army. His manner has made him offensive to every one who approaches him. To me he is personally courteous, but to the 'Herald' inexorable in his hate." [8] Whiteley hoped that Major General Benjamin F. Butler might replace Stanton. Butler was the Massachusetts politician who owed his commission to his political strength, who cultivated the press, and who was a failure as a combat commander and showed no ability as a military administrator.

These were some of the conditions under which statesmen and reporters contacted each other in these four years. The government made fumbling efforts to limit the publication of news which might aid the Confederate forces. And late in the war Stanton developed a system for the release of news. His operation was the first such step taken by the government and may be viewed as the ancestor of today's large staff in the office of the Assistant Secretary of Defense for Public Affairs.

Soon after Fort Sumter surrendered, the government instituted censorship of the telegraph line between Washington and New York. The restriction was designed to prevent transmission and publication of military secrets although the rules allowed correspondents to file anything which was printed in the Washington papers. Mails were not censored, nor was the wire from Baltimore, so the reporters were subjected more to harassment and delay, in the first year of the war, than actual restriction in getting their copy moved.[9] Correspondents protested that the officers who were assigned to pass on their dispatches were capricious, lacked judgment of news, of literary quality, or of the nature of military secrecy.[10] Soon after he assumed command McClellan tried a system of voluntary censorship. He met with a group of newsmen on August 2, 1861. Resolutions which had been drawn up by the telegraph censor were adopted. On their part the reporters agreed not to send "any matter that may furnish aid and comfort to the enemy," and to ask their editors not to publish any such matter, either as editorials or correspondence. They also resolved: "That the government be respectfully requested to afford to the representatives of the press facilities for obtaining and immediately transmitting all information suitable for publication, particularly touching engagements with the enemy."

The resolutions were signed by McClellan and by Gobright and correspondents for papers in Boston, New York, Philadelphia, Washington, and Cincinnati. The telegraphic censorship applied only to Washington for most of the first year of the war. On October 22, 1861, Frederick W. Seward, assistant secretary of state and son of the secretary, wrote to the chief censor to "prohibit all telegraphic despatches from Washington, intended for publication, which relate to the civil or military operations of the government." His letter specifically exempted Gobright's file or any other stories containing the same facts as those offered by the Associated Press.[11]

The House of Representatives ordered the Judiciary Committee to investigate the telegraphic censorship of press dispatches on December 5, 1861. Its study dragged through the winter and was going on at the time Stanton was named secretary of war. Its report, issued on March 20, 1862, discussed McClellan's meeting of the previous August with correspondents and Seward's letter to the chief censor. It also quoted testimony by four correspondents, one of them Gobright. All gave examples of material which had been held up and which seemed to show that the censors had at times been motivated by political considerations as well as by military security in withholding dispatches.

The War Department had seized all of the telegraph lines in the country on February 25, 1862, while the committee's investigation was under way. After that date, the committee reported, it was "not aware of any interference on the part of the censor with any despatches except those of a military character." The investigators reached five conclusions. One said that "Despatches, almost numberless, of a political, personal, and general character have been suppressed by the censor, and correspondents have been deterred from preparing others because they knew they could not send them to their papers by telegraph." The report proposed to the House a resolution that the government should not interfere with transmission of telegraphic intelligence when it does not aid the enemy. The House did not act.[12]

The government's seizure of the telegraph lines in February of 1862 was one of the first results of Stanton's appointment as secretary of war.[13] Throughout the rest of the struggle the country's telegraph system was controlled by the War Department, and military censorship was invoked over the whole system. Actually, enforcement was never as drastic as the wordage of the orders seemed to authorize. No papers were seized, although several were suppressed for short periods and several editors were arrested.[14] They were normally released after a short detention. No Washington correspondents except Ives and Wikoff were arrested and no paper was suspended because of its capital correspondence. If Stanton became the principal enforcement officer in back of telegraphic news censorship, and if he was the object of reporters' hatred as Whiteley described, he was at the same time the man who made positive moves toward the systematic release of news.

From the beginning of the war Gobright and the special correspondents had received copies of certain of the telegrams received at the War and Navy Departments from the field commanders. It was not uncommon for a newspaper to receive, within a day or two after a major battle, brief dispatches from Washington giving the results. These dispatches consisted of complete copies of the terse telegraphic reports sent by the field commanders. Four or five days later the same paper would have an extended account giving battle details which were the work of its own correspondent at the front.

As an example, look at the Cincinnati *Gazette* of July 8, 1863. Four days earlier Union forces had successfully repulsed Lee's attack at Gettysburg and Pemberton's starving men had given up at Vicksburg. All of page one and part of page two of that issue were given to Whitelaw Reid's dramatic first-person account of the battle in Pennsylvania. On the third page was a column of telegraph news. At the top of the column was the single capitalized word, "VICTORY." After several headline decks, the text matter included a series of short telegraphic dispatches from

Harrisburg, Philadelphia, and Gettysburg giving rumors regarding Lee's retreat. There was one from Columbus that Secretary Stanton had sent to Governor Tod a telegram saying that Vicksburg had surrendered. On down the column the reader found:

Special Dispatch to the Cincinnati Gazette

WASHINGTON, JULY 7
NAVAL REPORT OF THE CAPTURE OF VICKSBURG
"U.S. MISSISSIPPI SQUADRON FLAG-SHIP
"BLACK HAWK, VICKSBURG, JULY 4, 1863
"To Hon Gideon Welles, Secretary of the Navy
"SIR: I have the honor to inform you that Vicksburg has surrendered to the United States Forces on this 4th of July.
"Very respectfully, your obedient servant,
"D. D. Porter, Acting Rear Admiral."

Additional telegraphic material in an adjoining column provided confirmation of the Vicksburg news:

"HEADQUARTERS, DEPARTMENT OF OHIO
"CINCINNATI, O., JULY 7
"Gen. Burnside: Official intelligence has just been received that Vicksburg surrendered to Gen. Grant on the 4th of July.
"Edwin M. Stanton
"Secretary of War."

In this case Welles became the Washington official who announced the happy news because it was a naval vessel, the steamer *M. L. Wilson,* which raced from Vicksburg to the end of the telegraph at Cairo, Illinois with Admiral Porter's official dispatch. The secretary of the navy confided to his diary that Stanton was angry. The secretary of war, he wrote, "craves to announce all important information." [15] As 1863 progressed newspaper files show that governors of loyal states and commanding officers of military districts received from Stanton frequent telegrams announcing military news. These telegrams often included the text of these preliminary reports from field commanders. Those governors or district commanders, in turn, made them available to the local press and to the Associated Press.

Meanwhile the strength and national leadership of the New York papers had caused the Associated Press to quote not only Gobright, but to send from New York summaries of the Washington dispatches and the work of army correspondents for the metropolitan journals. Early in 1864 Stanton started telegraphing news to Major General John A. Dix, commander of the New York military district, on the assumption that Dix would turn them over to the Associated Press. A biographer of the secretary described these telegrams as a "war diary," and said that they provided a truthful account of military events which thus reached the people in spite of Stanton's unpopularity with newspapermen.[16] At first they were telegraphed directly to Dix. From New York they were wired to the rest of the country, including Washington, a state of affairs which irked editors in the capital. On September 9, 1864, Lincoln wrote to the secretary that Washington publishers had appealed personally to him, and asked if the system might not be changed.[17] Thereafter they were made available at the source.

Some examples of news breaks late in the war will show how the system worked. In December 1864 the country anxiously wondered what had become of the army which Sherman had marched out of Atlanta and which had disappeared. Grant, directing the operations against Petersburg, sent to the War Department from his headquarters at City Point, Virginia, regular summaries of material taken from the Richmond papers. They circulated through the lines and complete files were kept in headquarters, while army correspondents sent southern journals to their own home offices. The New York *Times* of December 14 said, in its telegraphic column:

Secretary Stanton to General Dix

WAR DEPARTMENT
WASHINGTON, DEC. 13—8 P.M.

To Major General Dix, New York:—

The Richmond papers of yesterday report General Sherman at Bloomingdale, fifteen miles from Savannah, on Saturday, December 10. He is reported by this morning's Richmond papers, as will be seen by the following telegram from General Grant, *to be in line of battle not five miles from Savannah:*—

CITY POINT, VA., DEC. 13, 1864

Hon. E. M. STANTON, Secretary of War:—

Richmond papers of today contain the following:—

The Richmond *Dispatch* says:—"Sherman is near Savannah, probably not five miles distant. He has not yet made an attack. It is still doubtful whether he will do so or make for the coast southeast of the city. It is very certain he has not yet opened communication with the coast, though he may do so very soon."

LATER

Another paper states:—"There has been no direct communication with Savannah for several days, but we apprehend the wires have been cut between that place and Charleston."

U. S. GRANT
Lieutenant General

The severity of the weather has prevented any important movements by either side at Nashville.

Nothing of importance is reported to-day from the Armies of the Potomac or of the Shenandoah.

EDWIN M. STANTON
Secretary of War

A few days later correspondents at Fortress Monroe sent to their newspapers word that a patrol from Sherman had reached the coast and had communicated with naval vessels offshore.

For another example, see the *Herald* of April 4, 1865. The sensational headlines of that day were one column wide, but deck followed deck halfway down the page. To announce such glorious news, the paper devoted eleven headline decks of varied type sizes and styles before getting to the following:

Secretary Stanton to General Dix

WAR DEPARTMENT, WASHINGTON
APRIL 3—10 A.M.

To Major General Dix:—

The following telegram from the President, announcing the EVACUATION OF PETERSBURG, and probably of Richmond has just been received by this Department.

EDWIN M. STANTON
Secretary of War

The President's Despatch

CITY POINT, VA., APRIL 3—8:30 A.M.

To Hon EDWARD [sic] M. Stanton, Secretary of War:—

This morning Lieutenant General Grant reports Petersburg evacuated, and he is confident that Richmond also is.

He is pushing forward to cut off, if possible, the retreating rebel army.

A. LINCOLN

Secretary Stanton's Second Despatch

WAR DEPARTMENT

WASHINGTON, D.C. APRIL 3, 10 A.M.

Major General Dix:

It appears from a despatch of General Weitzel, just received by this department, that our forces under his command ARE IN RICHMOND, having taken it at fifteen minutes past eight this morning.

EDWIN M. STANTON
Secretary of War

Secretary Stanton's Third Despatch

WAR DEPARTMENT

WASHINGTON, D.C., APRIL 3—12 M

Major General Dix, New York:—

The following official confirmation of the capture of Richmond, and the announcement that the city is on fire, has been received.

EDWIN M. STANTON
Secretary of War

CITY POINT, April 3—11 A.M.

To EDWIN M. STANTON, Secretary of War:—

General Weitzel telegraphs as follows:

We took Richmond at a quarter past eight this morning. I took many guns.

The enemy left in great haste.

The city is on fire in one place. Am making every effort to put it out.

The people receive us with enthusiastic expressions of joy.

General Grant started early this morning with the army toward the Danville road, to cut off Lee's retreating army if possible.

President Lincoln has gone to the front.

T. S. BOWERS
Acting Adjutant General

Eleven days later Gobright worked at the office into the evening hours. He sent stories on the president's theatre party.

And he believed he was through for the day after he wrote that General Grant had decided to go to New Jersey with Mrs. Grant instead of joining the others at the scheduled performance of *Our American Cousin.*

The office door burst open. A friend raced in. Breathlessly he told Gobright that he was at Ford's Theatre when the president was shot. He rushed out and secured a hack to dash the six blocks down Pennsylvania Avenue to the Associated Press office.

Gobright quickly wrote out a short dispatch saying that the president had been shot and that the wound may be mortal. Then, going to the theatre he was allowed to pass through the cordon of troops which had already been established and he entered the presidential box. As he reached there, William Kent, a theatre employee, found the pistol which Booth had dropped. He handed it to Gobright. A naval officer demanded it but Gobright refused to give it to him and later turned it over to police. He walked across the street to the private home where the president lay dying and then returned to his office.

There he wrote a more extended account of the evening's developments. From time to time friends entered and gave him additional details. "Meanwhile I carefully wrote my despatch," he wrote in his book of memoirs, "though with trembling and nervous fingers, and, under all the exciting circumstances, I was afterward surprised that I had succeeded in approximating so closely to all the facts in those dark transactions." Lincoln was still living when the story was finished. Gobright returned to Tenth Street to watch outside the house for developments.[18]

The next morning readers throughout the country saw Gobright's dispatches describing the tragedy in the theatre. The actual announcement that the president had died, however, came through one of the Stanton-to-Dix telegrams:

WAR DEPARTMENT, WASHINGTON, APRIL 15

Major-Gen. Dix:
   Abraham Lincoln died this morning at twenty-two minutes after seven o'clock.

EDWIN M. STANTON
Secretary of War

12. Washington Correspondents and Correspondence: 1865–1900

If one compares a newspaper file of 1830 with that of 1865 he will notice very great changes in reporting, the style of newspaper writing, format and other characteristics. If he goes on to the newspaper of 1900 he will see that the change in the latter of these two thirty-five-year periods was far greater. The newspaper of 1865 was still largely that of 1830 with significant but not fundamental changes. By 1900, however, it had changed greatly. It had grown in number of pages, content, and variety of reader offerings, and had changed its style of news writing. Among other things, by now we see early forms of the "inverted pyramid" style, with emphasis on the "lead" or first paragraphs.

The changes reflected the rapid shift in the country's economic base from agricultural to industrial which took place in this period, and they consequently reflected the increase in revenue available to the newspaper as a result of the advertising growth which followed. Competition was still keen in 1900. (It was to diminish after 1920.) And while each newspaper had more money to spend in developing content to meet its competition, each was less dependent on political party than it had been before the Civil War. The public printing of the federal government was no longer available to a party tool after the Government Printing Office was established in 1860, and similar conditions were beginning to appear in state capitals and county seats. Party influence was still present but it was fast disappearing. At the same time, the crowded four- and eight-page papers of 1865 were being replaced by metropolitan journals publishing twenty or more pages with large headlines and heavy display advertising. Cheap newsprint made from wood was now available to replace the more expensive older rag stock paper. Thus there was space for more news.

Washington reporting moved with the changes. In 1865 the capital correspondent was expected to write highly opinionated essays supporting his party's position. If he did not back a political party, he wrote opinionated essays praising or criticizing public officials or policies. That praise or criticism was often intended to promote the paper's own ends. In 1900 he was becoming a reporter, with a tradition of careful objectivity as an essential characteristic of his trade beginning to take hold.

In 1865 the Associated Press moved as a routine matter the text of speeches, documents, presidential messages and proceedings on the floor of Congress. Little reference was made to committees. In 1900 correspodents were learning to discard the uninteresting and unessential in proceedings and documents and were developing a news writing style that was intended to offer for reader convenience shorter discussions of content. The routine accounts of congressional floor proceedings disappeared. And more attention was paid to committees. In 1865 many correspondents signed fictitious signatures at the bottom of their articles. They preserved the fiction of concealed identity although the knowledge of authorship was common. By 1900 that practice had ceased.

In 1865 politicians and statesmen spoke to the public through speeches or official documents, and reporters sent the full text or start-to-finish abstracts to their papers. The New York *Tribune* of August 20, 1859, was perhaps the first to introduce what became the interview when it printed a conversation which Greeley had in Salt Lake City with Brigham Young. During the next few years the *Herald* developed the technique a little more by printing, in question-and-answer sequence, conversations between its reporters and certain figures in the news. A noteworthy example was the interview between a *Herald* man and John Brown as the antislavery warrior lay in jail. After the Civil War several papers printed conversations between their capital correspondents and President Andrew Johnson.

By 1900 interviewing and publishing in direct or indirect

quotation the remarks which statesmen made to reporters had become a standard practice. Poore disliked it. Describing contemporary conditions as he wrote his book in the mid-1880s, he said, "While there is less vituperation and vulgar personal abuse by journalists of those 'in authority,' the pernicious habit of 'interviewing' is a dangerous method of communication between public men and the people." [1]

In 1866 the Associated Press rather than the Washington papers was the normal machinery by which the routine floor proceedings of the two houses were reported in the start-to-finish sequence which the press still used. On February 26 the House accepted a motion that the Speaker assign a desk on the floor to the Associated Press reporter. Representative Elihu B. Washburne of Illinois, the resolution's sponsor, said that it was desirable that the reporter be placed where he could hear accurately. [2] Seven years later the Senate followed suit. It adopted a resolution on March 12, 1873, on motion of Senator H. B. Anthony, of Rhode Island, chairman of the Rules Committee, giving that committee jurisdiction over the press gallery. Heretofore the press gallery had been governed by the presiding officer. The resolution also gave the committee power to provide a seat on the floor for Associated Press reporters. [3]

Thus the two houses took steps to continue a press practice which was rapidly losing favor. Public interest in debates and routine floor proceedings was falling off rapidly. By 1890 the large city journals no longer carried the old-fashioned accounts and the more conservative smaller papers were abandoning them. A Senate debate on February 28 of that year shows what was taking place. [4]

Senator Henry W. Blair of New Hampshire protested the lack of congressional accounts in the country's press and said that the Associated Press was failing in the duty for which its reporter was admitted to the floor. "The press has kindly intimated that the reason of the delinquency in serving the public with important matter such as sketches of dog fights, and prize fights, and that sort of thing, column after column, to the exclusion of what concerns the present and perpetual interest of the public at large, was that my speech was not entertaining," he said. Senator Joseph R. Hawley of Connecticut pointed out that the Associated Press still moved the stenographic reports in spite of the fact that more and more newspapers were abandoning them. Soon after this debate, however, that agency dropped them. Thus ended the practice which first brought reporters into the legislative halls.

In 1865 Francis A. Richardson moved from Baltimore to Washington and entered the press gallery. He joined the capital staff of the Baltimore *Sun* seven years later. In 1903, retired, he spoke before the Columbia Historical Society on the changes which had taken place during the years in which he served as a correspondent.[5] "The press galleries as a rule are comparatively free of occupants," he said. "Washington has become so fruitful in gossip and scandal, and intrigue, political and otherwise, that in contrast the ordinary debates can prove exceedingly dry reading. The gentlemen who declaim at the different ends of the Capitol are much aggrieved over this. I do not see how they can remedy it."

In 1865, he told the District of Columbia historians, he had been one of twenty-six newspapermen in the city. At the time he spoke there were more than two hundred. "In old Newspaper Row as it used to exist, there might be found any evening senators, representatives, cabinet ministers, now and then the vice-president, foreign ministers, prominent Federal officials from the large cities of the country, governors of states, etc." In 1903, he said, "no longer do senators, representatives, and cabinet members come to the newspaper offices. The correspondent must go after them."

Newspaper Row disappeared a half century ago. But it was the center of the city's press life for thirty years. Before the Civil War a row of brick and frame dwelling houses had been built along the east side of Fourteenth Street between E and F Streets. On the west side of that block stood Willard's Hotel. On the southeast corner of Fourteenth and F Streets, at the north end of the block, stood the Ebbitt Hotel. As the dwellers in those houses moved out, the rooms were rented for offices. Eliab Kingman took space in one of the before 1850. During the Civil War the New York *Tribune* correspondents worked from an office at Fourteenth and F Streets.

The telegraph office before and during the war was near the corner of Pennsylvania Avenue and Four-and-a-half Street. The Associated Press rooms were on an upper floor.[6] On May 7, 1869, the telegraph company moved closer to what was becoming the new center of the city's business, social, and political activity. It occupied a four-story brick building on the northeast corner of the intersection where Fourteenth Street, E Street, and Pennsylvania Avenue cross each other. Thus it was at the south end of the block which became "Newspaper Row," and the Ebbitt stood at the north end.

The hotels and bars attracted statesmen. Members of Congress were abandoning their former practice of taking rooms in rooming houses or "messes" and were occupying hotel rooms during the sessions. The hotels, bars, statesmen, and the telegraph office attracted newspapermen. A row of elm trees provided shade and made the sidewalk outside of the bars and newspaper offices a favorite place in warm weather to find friends and news sources and to exchange information. The Senate and the House Office Buildings were still in the future, so members lacked office space and tended to collect here. Newspaper rooms, the hotels and bars became gathering places for politicians, officeholders, and correspondents.

Soon rooms in all of the houses in that block were rented to reporters. Addresses listed in the press sections of the *Congressional Directory* between 1870 and 1900 are principally centered from 503 to 527 Fourteenth Street. Adjoining blocks also attracted newspaper offices. Locations along F Street, now one of the city's most valuable retail shopping districts, along G Street, and in the 1400 block of New York Avenue, which intersects Fourteenth Street two blocks north of F Street, are also listed. Newspaper Row remained here until about the turn of the century. Before the correspondents moved out, however, part of the character of the press operation there changed. As Richardson pointed out, news sources ceased to seek out correspondents as they formerly had. In 1907 there was gossip of a hotel project that would absorb the property, so the last of the correspondents moved to office buildings.[7] Eventually the houses which had sheltered the reporters were torn down to make way for the store blocks which now occupy the area. Today the National Press Building, which provides office space for a large part of the press corps, stands at the north end of the block. Recently, however, such news offices as those of the Associated Press and the Columbia Broadcasting System have gone farther to the northwest, along Connecticut Avenue or to the west of that thoroughfare.

13. The Press at the Capitol: 1870–1883

The country's rapid industrialization after 1865 coincided with a period of peculiarly corrupt public morals. Bribery, charges of bribery, and investigations of bribery were common and they marked some of the contacts between Congress and the press.

A reporter was forced to face the representatives in their own chamber again as they sought the source of a story in June of 1870. As in the cases in the House in 1812, 1838, and 1857 and in the Senate in 1848, the correspondent answered some questions and refused to answer others while the lawmakers went through the usual confused argument over privilege, the right of a reporter to respect confidences, and the power to expel from the press gallery. The House backed down. The spark this time was the effort of a revolutionary Cuban group to sell bonds in this country and to get the United States to recognize belligerency in order to help sales. A Washington dispatch to the New York *Evening Post* of June 6 said that a Mr. N. B. Taylor had been provided with between $30,000 and $40,000 by the Cuban backers and implied that the money was to be used corruptly. That and later stories in the *Evening Post* and the Washington *Evening Star* said that Taylor had contacted several members of the House but that it was not known whether or not they had accepted bribes. The stories gave the names of the suspected congressmen.

One was Representative Thomas Fitch of Nevada. On June 10 Fitch rose and had the Clerk read that paragraph of the *Eve-*

ning Post story. Saying that he understood that the correspondent responsible for the story was William Scott Smith, Fitch moved that the writer be "brought to the bar of the House to show cause, if he can, why he should not be expelled from the reporters' gallery for libellous statements reflecting upon the integrity of members of this House." In the debate that followed there was none of the general denunciation of the correspondents that had marked Davis's appearance in the House in 1838 or the Senate debate over the reporters' petition in 1839. Several of those who took the floor agreed that the story was libelous and that the House should not tolerate reporters in the press gallery who published unfounded defamatory statements about members. Fitch's motion was adopted.

The sergeant-at-arms thereupon seized the reporter. The debate that followed, while Smith sometimes answered questions and sometimes stood quietly looking on, required four pages of the fine type of the *Congressional Globe*. Asked why he should not be expelled from the press gallery, he submitted a three-paragraph answer in writing. His material, he said, was "based upon official documents which I saw, and the statements set forth in the dispatch were identical with those contained in said documents." Asked the nature of the official documents, he answered that they were affidavits which had been presented before a District of Columbia grand jury. But he refused to tell who had given them to him. A select committee was ordered to continue the investigation.

The committee reported on June 22 that Smith had been given documents which he understood were affidavits presented to the grand jury but which actually were false. If he were more experienced or were an attorney, the report said, he would have recognized their spurious character. It recommended that the move to expel him from the press gallery be tabled.[1]

In 1848 the New York *Herald* published the text of the Treaty of Guadelupe-Hidalgo in violation of the Senate's injunction of secrecy. Its Washington correspondent was held by the sergeant-at-arms and was examined in secret session by the Senate. In 1871 the New York *Tribune* and its Washington correspondents had an almost parallel experience. There were significant differences, however. In 1848 the *Herald* printed the treaty after the Senate had ratified it. In 1871 the *Tribune* published a treaty on the morning after the president submitted it and before the Senate considered it. In 1848 the legislators examined the correspondent in secret although the executive journal was published later. Most of the senators seemed to favor the proceedings and to be determined to uphold the dignity of the legislative body as against the press.

In 1871 the Senate's original resolutions which ordered that the reporters be detained and which set up a select committee to investigate were acted on in secret. On the other hand, the Senate's later debate, including that on the days when the *Tribune* correspondents appeared on the Senate floor, were carried on with the doors open and the galleries filled. This time several of the lawmakers said that after the writers had assured the committee that no Senator or officer of the Senate was responsible for the leak, the body had no power to pursue the matter further.

The debate and newspaper comments in 1848 gave some insight into the correspondent's relations with his news sources and the journalistic and political interplay of the day. There was less of that in 1871. The latter incident revolved around the Treaty of Washington, by which Great Britain and the United States agreed to submit several controversies to arbitration. The principal one was this country's claim to damages because the Confederate cruisers *Alabama, Florida,* and *Shenandoah* were built and outfitted in English ports. A Joint High Commission consisting of five delegates from each country was set up in February 1871. By April, details of the treaty were agreed upon. Drafts were printed for the confidential use of the commissioners on May 1 and 5, and an accepted text was signed on the 6th. President Grant called the Senate into special session, to convene on the 10th. He laid the treaty before it on that day.

The *Tribune* of May 9 devoted the first two columns on the first page to the "GENERAL PRESS DISPATCH" (the Associated Press account), which said that the treaty was signed and the Joint High Commission dissolved. "Although the Commisioners have been cautious in talking to persons outside of their own circle," it said, "the following points of the Treaty will be found to be correct." The summary that followed was generally accurate although the writer confessed to doubt on one point. That point proved to be in error. Another "GENERAL PRESS DISPATCH" quoted a story on the treaty's contents which was to appear in the

Washington *National Republican* of the same day and which, it said, "claims to be an authoritative official statement of the results of the labors of the Joint High Commission." Later stories said the State Department had given the story to the Washington paper.

The *Tribune* published the treaty text two days later. Most of the first page of the May 11 issue was taken up with the document and with an account of what the paper said had taken place in a secret session of the Senate on the previous day. That chamber continued to work with the doors closed. Throughout, however, the *Tribune* and other papers carried daily accounts which reputed to give the secret proceedings. The stories dealt both with the question of ratification and with the possible punishment of those responsible for giving the *Tribune* the treaty. The *Senate Journal* account of May 12 merely lists those present, records the routine motion for the next meeting, and says the body "proceeded to the consideration of executive business." [2] The *Tribune* of the 13th, however, had more detail. A special dispatch said that after the Foreign Relations Committee announced that it was not yet ready to report back the treaty "the Senate proceeded to the consideration of the far more important business of ascertaining how THE TRIBUNE obtained the treaty on Wednesday night." It said, correctly, that a select committee had been ordered to investigate the leak.

The committee held hearings on May 15, 22, 23, and 24. It examined twenty witnesses, including Zebulon L. White and Hiram J. Ramsdell, the *Tribune* correspondents. Among the other witnesses were George W. Adams, the New York *World* correspondent who occupied offices at 515 Fourteenth Street, across the first-floor corridor from those of the *Tribune*; Whitelaw Reid, the paper's managing editor; several senators; an assistant secretary of State, and two employees of the Western Union Telegraph Company. White and Ramsdell testified that they had come into possession of a printed copy of the treaty but that it was not one of those which had been printed by order of the Senate. They both swore that they had not secured it from any senator, officer of the Senate, or any one connected with the printing. They had copied it by hand between 10:00 P.M. and 1:00 A.M on the night of the 10th, they said, and had sent their copy to the telegraph office to be sent to New York. Then they surrendered possession of the printed copy. When they were asked where they secured it, each replied, "I respectfully refuse to answer." Adams testified that he had been offered a copy by each of two different individuals and thought that he could have secured it for three hundred dollars. One of those who offered it he did not know, and the other was a man who pledged him to secrecy. He refused to reveal the name even when threatened with arrest.

Reid told the committee that he did not know where his correspondents had secured the treaty. The two telegraph company agents said that they would refuse, even under questioning by a Senate committee, to reveal their relations with a customer. J. C. Bancroft Davis, assistant secretary of state, said that he believed the *Tribune* text was copied from the print that was run on May 5. He did not know how a copy could have reached the correspondents. The committee tried to track down the possibility that some of the copies which had been sent to members of the Senate Foreign Relations Committee might have fallen into other hands but it got nowhere. It gave up.[3] On May 16 the *Tribune* published a story on the committee's proceedings and an editorial which warned the group that it would achieve nothing. If its correspondents were confined, the paper said, "we shall simply double their salaries during their term of imprisonment, and fill their places with others at least as active."

On that day Senator Matthew H. Carpenter of Wisconsin, chairman of the select committee, reported in secret session. The injunction of secrecy was later removed from part of the proceedings, so they were published in the *Congressional Globe*. After pointing out that the *Tribune* correspondents refused to tell the committee where they secured the treaty text, Carpenter moved that the Senate order the sergeant-at-arms to arrest them and that each be examined before the Senate "until he answer for his contempt of the order of the Senate in the matter aforesaid and abide such further order as the Senate may make in the premises." The resolutions were adopted.

Although the *Congressional Globe* published that part of the proceedings which included the committee's report and the resolutions, it did not print the debate that preceded it. *Tribune* correspondents, however, moved copy on the presumably secret proceedings. Senators Charles Sumner of Massachusetts and Carl Schurz of Missouri, a special dispatch to the paper said, opposed continuing the investigation, "the latter, especially, it is said, defending the honor of the journalistic profession." Schurz was the liberal German-American leader who had been an editor of the German language *Westliche Post* of St. Louis and later edited the New York *Evening Post*. Senator Roscoe Conkling of New York was quoted as saying that the practices of newspapermen "were only to be classed with thieving, robbery, and Ku Klux outrages."

The next day the *Tribune* published more on the secret session, saying it had secured its facts "from a source which we positively refuse to divulge." Conkling, the story said, was twice led from the floor in angry tears but returned to carry on exchanges with Sumner. The account ended: "Here the honorable Senator again became incapable of articulation, and was carried home, upon which the Senate hastily adjourned." Conkling and the *Tribune* were at odds. The Senator was the leader of one faction of the party in New York state and the paper opposed him, supporting the branch led by Senator Reuben E. Fenton.[4]

White and Ramsdell were brought into the Senate in custody of the sergeant-at-arms on the 17th. Debate over what to do about them continued on every legislative day until the 25th. The doors were open and the galleries were filled when the Senate considered the cases of the reporters, although treaty debate was carried on in secret. It was ratified on May 24. Carpenter led in presenting the case against the correspondents. He argued that secrecy properly should cover such proceedings as treaty ratification. He and other speakers who favored pressing the matter insisted that in spite of the fact that the correspondents had absolved any senators or any one connected with the Senate from any guilt in releasing the document, the investigation should be pursued to support the Senate's right to privacy. The Act of 1857, Carpenter said, did not deprive the body of its powers of investigation and imprisonment in spite of its provision for court consideration of contempt cases. That was the law which Congress passed after the Simonton investigation. The two newspapermen were in the Senate Chamber, under guard, while Carpenter held forth. Finally they stood before the vice-president to hear the questions which the Senate had approved. Each correspondent asked and was granted a day to prepare his answers.

The next day, therefore, White, the chief of the *Tribune* staff, was asked his excuse for not answering when he was before

mr. Smith may notify in his paper that I have
recieved a letter from Capt. Lewis dated at St. Louis
Sep. 23. at which place himself, capt Clarke & their party arrived
that day. they had prast the preceeding Winter at a place
which he calls Fort Clatsop, near the mouth of the Columbia
river. they set out thence on the 27th. of March last & arrived at
the foot of the Rocky mountains May 10, where they were
detained until June 24, by the snows which rendered the
passage over those mountains impracticable until then.
~~he found~~ it 2575 miles from the mouth of the Missouri
to the great falls of that river, thence by land passing the
Rocky mountains to a navigable part of the Kooskooske
340. miles, of which 200 would admit good road, and 140 miles over
~~as South Latitude and banks of the Columbia in Colorado~~
tremendous mountains which for 60 miles are covered with eternal snows.
then 73. miles down the Kooskooske into a South Eastwardly branch
of the Columbia, 154 miles down that to the main
river of the Columbia, & then 413. miles to the Pacific
in all 3555. miles from the mouth of the Missouri
to the mouth of the Columbia. in this last river the
tide flows 183. miles, to within 7. miles of it's great
rapids, and so far would admit large sloops; and from
thence upwards may be navigated by batteaux & pirogues. he speaks of this whole line furnishing the most
valuable furs in the world, and a short & direct course for them
to the Eastern coast of China; but that the greatest part of
these would be from the head of the Missouri. he says
it is fortunate he did not send back from the head of
the Missouri any part of his force, consisting of 31.
men, as more than once they owed their lives & the
fate of the expedition to their numbers. one man of his
party had died before he reached Fort Mandan in 1805. every other
one is returned in good health. Capt Lewis expected to remain at St. Louis some
days, to settle with & discharge his men, & would then set
out for Washington, by the way of Vincennes, Louisville,
Abingdon, Fincastle, Staunton & Charlottesville. he is accompa-
-nied by the great Mandan chief, who is on a visit to Washington.
1543 Capt Lewis speaks of his colleague, Capt Clarke, in the most

See next page

affectionate terms, and declares his equal title to what
-ever merit may be ascribed to the success of that
enterprise.

By this note, Thomas Jefferson notified Samuel Harrison Smith of
the safe return of the Lewis and Clark expedition. Smith published
in the National Intelligencer *an account in almost identical language, and that, in turn, was picked up in other newspapers around
the country.* —Reproduced from the collections of the Library of
Congress

*Thomas Jefferson sent Samuel Harrison Smith notes on material
which was to be used without being attributed to its source. One
such is presented here.* —Reproduced from the collections of the
Library of Congress

Th. Jefferson to mr Smith

The inclosed paper seems intended for the legislative as well
as Executive eye; but certainly not to be laid before the former in a
regular way. the only irregular one would be in the newspapers. but
this must depend on it's merit and your opinion of it. there are
a few just ideas in it, but they are as a few grains of wheat in a bushel
of chaff. I know not from what quarter it came, there being no postmark
on the cover. do with it as you may think it worth or want of it.

1513   Oct. 23. 1802.

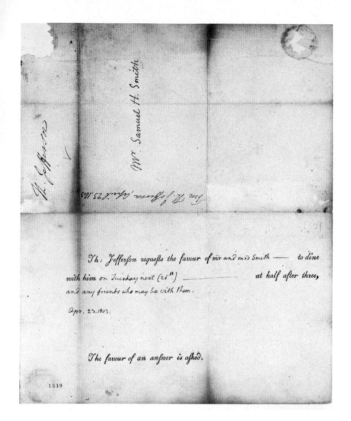

Note from Thomas Jefferson inviting Samuel Harrison Smith to dine at the White House. — Reproduced from the collections of the Library of Congress

In 1858 those reporters who were admitted to the House of Representatives press gallery received elaborate and ornamental credentials. Today they are issued a small card which can be carried in a billfold. — Reproduced from the collections of the Library of Congress

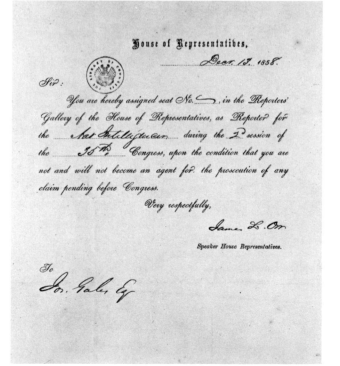

L. A. Gobright, the first Washington "agent" of the Associated Press. His book on his Washington experiences gives a graphic account of the night of President Lincoln's assassination. —Ben: Perley Poore, "Washington News," Harper's New Monthly Magazine, January 1874

This picture of Ben: Perley Poore appeared as the frontispiece in his Perley's Reminiscences of Sixty Years in the National Metropolis, *which was published in 1886*

James W. Simonton, Washington correspondent of the New York Times *in 1857. He was arrested and examined by a Select Committee of the House of Representatives after he sent to his paper some articles charging some members with corruption and was expelled from the press gallery.* — Ben: Perley Poore, "Washington News," Harper's New Monthly Magazine, January 1874

"Mack" interviewing President Andrew Johnson. The correspondent was J. B. McCullagh, and his articles, published in the Cincinnati Commercial *of April 1 and 6, 1868, are among the first examples of a presidential interview.* — Ben: Perley Poore, "Washington News," Harper's New Monthly Magazine, January 1874

Newspaper Row. The east side of Fourteenth Street between E and F Streets, in 1874. — Ben: Perley Poore, "Washington News," Harper's New Monthly Magazine, January 1874

Detail from the painting The Florida Case before the Electoral Commission, *by Cornelia Adele Fassett, which shows the hearings in 1877. The proceedings were held in the room in which the Senate sat before 1857 and which is now unused. The painting hangs in the gallery-floor corridor of the Senate wing of the Capitol, near the east door of the Senate press gallery and near the Senate radio and television gallery. Shown here is the gallery which was reserved for the press.*

Portrayed are many of the correspondents mentioned in this book. The man with the heavy beard, third from the left in front row, is Ben: Perley Poore. The bald man with the beard to the left of the clock is H. V. Boynton. On the other side of the clock, in the first row, sits Mrs. Jane Grey Swisshelm. Beside her is L. A. Gobright. The two ladies to Gobright's left, in order, are Mrs. S. J. Lippincott and Miss Austine Snead. F. A. Richardson is in the second row behind Mrs. Swisshelm. — Reprinted from the collections of the Library of Congress

One of Gobright's twentieth-century successors as chief of the Washington Bureau of the Associated Press. Byron Price served as news editor of the Washington Bureau from 1922 to 1927, and as chief from the latter date to 1937. He was executive news editor of the Associated Press from 1937 to 1941, and directed the Office of Censorship during World War II, and afterwards served as assistant secretary-general of the United Nations. —Wide World Photos

James Reston of the New York Times is one of the capital's most perceptive students of the relationship between press and government. Of his numerous writings, some of which touched particularly on that problem were The Artillery of the Press, published in 1967, and "The Press, the President, and Foreign Policy." in Foreign Affairs, July 1966. The latter was based on the 1966 Elihu Root Lectures which he gave before the Council on Foreign Relations. He was chief of the Times Washington Bureau from 1953 to 1964, associate editor from 1964 to 1969, and then vice-president. He continues to make the capital his headquarters. — Photograph by the New York Times Studio

Shown prior to a CBS "Special Report" on Vietnam, January 21, 1968, are: (l. to r.) CBS's Dan Rather, Senator Gale McGee (D., Wyoming), the late Senator Robert Kennedy (D., New York), Edwin O. Reischauer, former ambassador to Tokyo, and CBS's Marvin Kalb. — Reni Photos

President Nixon held his televised news conferences in the East Room of the White House. He stood on a slightly raised platform facing the reporters with nothing in front of him but the microphones. This is the conference of March 5, 1969. — Wide World Photos

the select committee. He replied with an extensive elaboration of the argument which all newspapermen upheld then and continue to uphold. Confidential relations with news sources were necessary and ethically correct, he said. He argued that the relations of a reporter with sources were similar to those of a client with an attorney, a patient with a physician, and a dying man with a minister of the Gospel. He said he had been informed that the copy of the treaty which he saw was not Senate property but was one of forty or more copies which had been printed for use of the State Department and the administration. He was willing to swear that it was received neither directly nor indirectly from any one connected with the Senate, but he refused to commit himself beyond that. Ramsdell was led through a similar examination with the same result.

There the matter deadlocked. Carpenter argued that the Senate could order the two held even after adjournment, which would take place within a few days. He suggested that the reporters be held "for forty years" if necessary and that they be placed in the District of Columbia jail. Several defenders argued that the Senate should proceed no further, once the correspondents had denied that any of its officers or members were responsible. They held that the reporters' right to secret information should be respected. Finally a resolution was adopted which ordered them held until they were willing to testify, even after adjournment, if necessary. The resolution also ordered the select committee to remain in being subject to call when the two indicated that they had changed their minds.

Greeley was in New Orleans, and apparently wrote none of the editorials with which the *Tribune* damned the Senate day after day. Correspondents who replaced White and Ramsdell, meanwhile, sent long stories on the floor action as well as on the proceedings of the select committee when it resumed hearings on May 22. The two prisoners, however, wrote nothing to compare with Nugent's "Galviensis and the Senate" articles in 1848. A telegraphed dispatch on the 23d said the correspondents' imprisonment was not unpleasant. They were confined in the Pacific Railroad Committee room, were visited daily by their wives, friends, and senators, were given books and flowers, had excellent meals sent in from the Senate restaurant, and carried the key themselves.

On Monday the 22d Senator Henry Wilson of Massachusetts, who had been one of the correspondents' defenders in the debates, moved that they be discharged when the session adjourned. A few minutes later Sumner moved that they be released immediately. The two resolutions lay on the table until Thursday when Wilson's was called up and precipitated another debate. Unsuccessful efforts were made to amend the resolution to provide that the release of the pair should not be construed as limiting any prosecution that the district attorney might bring. Finally, on Saturday, Wilson's motion was adopted. White and Ramsdell were released. The Senate adjourned, ending the session, a few minutes later.[5]

Three years later the House ordered an investigation of rumors that congressmen and reporters had been bribed or improperly approached by lobbyists who had secured a large subsidy for the Pacific Mail Steamship Line. During the proceedings, which dragged through the House and through the Ways and Means Committee during the winter of 1874 and 1875, several correspondents were questioned about their relations with the lobby group. Testimony was introduced showing that the promoters had paid four newspapermen sums ranging from $5,000 to $30,-000. The committee was unable to get satisfactory explanations from them as to why they were paid that money.

Some company officials were quizzed in the committee and before the whole House and one was confined in the District of Columbia jail. No newspaper correspondent was punished, but when the investigation was over the House adopted a resolution that any reporter who had taken a bribe in connection with legislation should be expelled from the press gallery. The resolution was not, however, invoked against any of those who had been named in testimony before the committee.[6]

Charges of corruption and a move to expel a reporter were heard again in 1884. No such incident has taken place since then. The correspondent involved this time, and his brother and nephew, were for many years among the most respected leaders of the capital press corps. Henry Van Ness Boynton, normally described as "General" Boynton, was born in West Stockbridge, Massachusetts, and studied in Cincinnati and at Kentucky Military Institute. When the Civil War broke out he trained recruits in Cincinnati and was later commissioned as major in an Ohio regiment. He fought through the Tennessee campaigns, commanded four regiments at the Battle of Chickamauga, and was wounded at Missionary Ridge. Leaving the army, he joined the staff of the Cincinnati *Gazette* in December 1864 and became a member of that paper's Washington staff immediately after the war. He corresponded for the *Gazette* and its successor, the *Commercial Gazette*, until 1896. In 1901 he became chairman of the District of Columbia Board of Education and devoted his remaining years to school matters.[7] His younger brother, Charles A. Boynton, was chief of the Washington bureau of the Associated Press in the last years of the nineteenth century and into the twentieth and Charles Boynton's son, Charles H. Boynton, also served the Associated Press for many years.

Charges of corruption against Henry Van Ness Boynton arose out of a California land claim and out of a quarrel over an incident in which the press gallery was opened one night to the general public. Every year since 1866 there had been introduced into Congress a private bill designed to redress a man named William McGarrahan, who claimed a very large tract of land in California under a Mexican grant. Part of the property had been conveyed by the United States to various purchasers, including a mining company, apparently as a result of confusion over McGarrahan's title. The bill had been reported favorably by a House committee and in March 1883 lay on the House calendar. Boynton was not personally acquainted with McGarrahan. He had been favorably impressed after reading the committee report on the bill and had written some articles supporting it. The claimant thereupon appealed to the reporter.

On February 27 Boynton sent to Speaker J. Warren Keifer a note asking him to recognize Representative Dunnell of Minnesota to call up the McGarrahan bill for a vote. The writer carefully pointed out that he had no personal interest in the measure but thought McGarrahan the victim of a rich corporation. Keifer and Boynton conversed in the Speaker's office on either February 28 or March 1, 1883. A year later, in testimony before a House select committee, each told a different story of that conversation.

Keifer testified that Boynton came into the office, delayed until some other visitors left, and then had the Speaker direct his clerk to leave the room. When they were alone, he testified, Boynton vigorously urged that Dunnell be recognized to call up the

McGarrahan bill. His testimony said that Boynton spoke loudly, sometimes angrily, and said that there were millions in the Mc-Garrahan claim. Boynton expected personally to make a great deal out of it, the Speaker said, and hinted that the latter might be cut in. Boynton denied that he had made any such corrupt advance. He called in the Speaker's office that day, he told the investigating committee, because a brother of one of his paper's editors was threatened with the loss of a patronage post as register of the land office at Walla Walla, Washington Territory. Boynton did not know President Chester A. Arthur, he said, and hoped the Speaker might intercede at the White House. He testified that as he entered the room he said: "General, I took the liberty of sending you that note in reference to McGarrahan the other day, to fulfill a promise made him. I have no interest in it." After Keifer said that some one would be recognized, Boynton continued, nothing more was said about the McGarrahan case and the conversation turned to the patronage problem.

Three nights later a curious incident took place. Before the Twentieth Amendment to the United States Constitution was ratified the short session of Congress ended at noon on March 4 of every odd-numbered year. The last week was marked by day and night sessions, confusion, excited crowds in the galleries, hurry in enacting necessary legislation and stepped-up activities by lobbyists who hoped to get their bills through with the least possible debate in the last-minute rush. Correspondents raced back and forth between the press gallery and the tables in the adjoining rooms where they wrote their copy. The Speaker's power to recognize members to call up action gave him extensive control of proceedings. It was customary to arrange in advance for recognition.

That was the state of affairs on the night of Saturday, March 3, 1883. Representative James A. McKenzie of Kentucky sought and was granted recognition. He asked unanimous consent "that the reporters' gallery may be thrown open to the occupation of the wives and friends of Congressmen, who are now unable to obtain seats in the other galleries." He could only have gotten the floor by prior arrangement with the Speaker. Angry correspondents later said that in the confusion which prevailed most members probably did not hear McKenzie or understand what was involved. Keifer heard no objection and ruled the proposal adopted.[8] Crowds moved into the press gallery, hindering the reporters in their work.

Late that night Representative J. C. Burrows of Michigan stepped to the rostrum to ask that he be recognized to move that the press gallery be cleared of visitors other than reporters. Keifer refused. As the session dragged into the early morning hours the sightseers disappeared. Reporters, however, knew that before noon, when the session would end, the visitors would return, making it nearly impossible for them to work. About 2:00 A.M. William E. Barrett, correspondent for the Boston *Advertiser* and Boynton's fellow occupant of the same office on Newspaper Row, approached the Speaker and asked again that Burrows be recognized. Barrett later told his fellow reporters that during the conversation Keifer said, "I don't care a God Damn for the press."

The Speaker delivered his customary valedictory and banged his gavel for the last time at noon on Sunday. Five minutes later about fifty angry newspapermen gathered in the press gallery, with W. B. Shaw of the Boston *Transcript* presiding and John B. McCarthy of the Baltimore *Sun* and San Francisco *Chronicle* acting as secretary. After a short debate and over some opposition, they approved a resolution condemning Keifer. The six "whereas" clauses recited the events of the evening, including Barrett's plea to the Speaker and the latter's profane answer. The four main clauses condemned McKenzie and Keifer as acting "in violation of the Rules of the House and of common courtesy to the press," and condemned the Speaker for his language to Barrett. The resolution was published in the Washington papers the next day. Keifer followed it up with a long denial that he had been rude. His statement appeared in the *National Republican,* a loyal party organ, on March 7.[9]

As one of his last official acts, Keifer discharged a House stenographer named Tyson and appointed in his place Benjamin P. Gaines, a relative. Gaines was in a position to draw $3,750 in salary for little or no work during the congressional recess.[10] Correspondents, already angry, seized on this situation to add to the denunciations which were pouring from their pens. Keifer was from Springfield, Ohio, not far from the home office of Boynton's paper, and until this time the Speaker and the reporter had been friends. On March 3 Boynton telegraphed an angry story to his paper describing the opening of the press gallery and denouncing Keifer. The former friendly relations between the two ceased.

The Forty-eighth Congress met the next December with the Democrats in control of the House. A subcommittee of the Committee on Accounts investigated why Tyson lost his job. The former Speaker appeared before a secret session on January 19, 1884. According to a story on the "secret" meeting which appeared in the next day's Cincinnati *Commercial-Gazette*, Keifer denied that he had fired Tyson and said that the story was instigated by correspondents who were angry because he had defeated a bill which they were trying to lobby through the House. His testimony became generally known. On the 21st the *National Republican* published an interview in which Keifer implied that the correspondents, one of whom was Boynton, were angry about the failure of their bill and therefore built up the story about the discharged stenographer out of revenge. Most of the interview, however, attributed the reporters' resentment to the opening of the press gallery.

After an angry exchange of letters between Keifer and Boynton, which was printed in the Washington papers, the reporter asked Speaker Carlisle for an investigation.[11] On January 29, Representative J. H. Hopkins, a Pennsylvania Democrat (Boynton's paper was a Republican organ, but independently so and a supporter of reform forces in the party), offered a resolution that Boynton, who held a press gallery seat in accordance with the rules of the House, had been charged by a member with having made a corrupt advance intended to influence the member's official action. The resolution pointed out that such charges would justify the reporter's expulsion from the press gallery and called for a five-man select committee to investigate.[12]

During debate, Keifer told his story that Boynton had approached him in his office, called him a fool for not making money, and implied that he would be paid off liberally if he recognized a member to call up the McGarrahan bill. He indicated that the measure involved lands worth as much as $80,000,000. The measure was amended to authorize the select committee to investigate whether or not any reporter holding a seat in the press gallery should be expelled, and was passed. Hopkins was named chairman of the committee.

In the eleven days in which they sat, the investigators heard sixty-five witnesses. The testimony, plus documentary exhibits and the final briefs filed by two attorneys, was printed in 395 pages. It ranged over the whole quarrel between Keifer and Boynton and went into detail regarding the opening of the press gallery. The committee reported on April 1 that the correspondent enjoyed an "unsullied reputation," and referred to criminal records of two witnesses whom Keifer had called. One had been charged at one time with running a house of prostitution in Washington. It offered a resolution that "the charges against H. V. Boynton are not sustained by the evidence and that there is no ground for any action by the House." [13] It was adopted without debate on April 11. [14]

14. The Press at the Capitol: 1884–1969

Every year the thousand Washington newspapermen who have been admitted to the press galleries of Congress elect some of their number to the Standing Committee of Correspondents. In even-numbered years they elect two, and in odd-numbered years, three. Those named serve for two years. Thus the committee consists of five, elected for overlapping terms. In accordance with the rules of the two houses the Standing Committee governs the press galleries, under the supervision of the Speaker of the House and the Senate Committee on Rules and Administration. It passes on applications for membership. It selects the press gallery employees. It arranges with the responsible authorities in each chamber for improvement in the gallery facilities and supervises press arrangements in committee rooms. And it engages in certain other governing duties.

Since 1943 it has kept careful records, which are preserved by Joseph E. Wills, superintendent of the Senate press gallery. His files also contain an irregular collection of minutes and correspondence some of which dates from as early as 1911. They contain nothing, however, from the nineteenth century. But there are records which make it possible to piece together the probable story of how and when it began.

As we have seen, the rules governing admission to the press gallery which were drawn when the House of Representatives moved into its present quarters in 1857 gave the Speaker control. The vice-president, as president of the Senate, enjoyed similar power in the upper chamber. The latter, however, transferred that responsibility to the Rules Committee in March 1873. There was a never-ending pressure by lobbyists and claim agents to secure admission to the press gallery and to other correspondents' prerogatives. Some department clerks engaged in part-time newspaper correspondence. Some reporters used their press gallery contacts to branch out into such sidelines as lobbying, pressing claims, and selling tips to lobbyists and speculators. Members of the two houses were annoyed to have the privilege which they extended thus prostituted. Those correspondents who did not engage in such practices sought to exclude those who did. The burden on the Speaker and the Rules Committee must have been great and the cause of a good deal of complaint. The answer seemed to be to give authority to a policing group of the reputable correspondents, subject to check by the responsible authority in each house. That happened about 1877.

Records can be found of the following events:

1. Washington correspondents met on November 5, 1877, to select a committee to confer with Speaker Samuel J. Randall about the assignment of seats in the House press gallery.[1] Who the committee members were and what happened at their conference, we do not know today.

2. There was another meeting in April 1879, this time in the New York *Times* Washington office. Those present adopted rules prepared by the executive committee regulating admission to the reporters' gallery in each house. The *Evening Star* of April 4 said, "The old executive committee of last year was reelected, consisting of Mr. George W. Adams, Gen. H. V. Boynton, E. B. Wight, L. Q. Washington, and William C. MacBridge."

3. Five days later Adams sent a note to Speaker Randall. "Please sign the accompanying tickets for admission to the Reporters Gallery as approved by the Standing Committee of Correspondents on the gallery," he asked.[2] This seems to be the earliest record now to be found which uses the words *Standing Committee of Correspondents*. It shows that the committee was in effective operation by then.

4. In the report of the committee which investigated the quarrel between Boynton and Keifer are listed five regulations which Keifer had signed on being elected Speaker in 1881. The first repeats much of what had been in the 1857 House rule that reporters desiring admission petition in writing to the Speaker, name the paper which employs them, and agree not to act as claim agents. Others name the Standing Committee of Correspondents as the body which is ordered to govern the gallery and see that members conform to the House rules. One forbids admission to the gallery to clerks in the executive departments or to any one whose principal employment is not to report for daily newspapers. This is the earliest record to be found which specifically names the Standing Committee as the governing group, operating under authority granted by the Speaker. The rules were signed by the five-member Standing Committee, headed now by Boynton.

5. The story which Boynton filed on the night of March 3, 1883, blasting Keifer said that James G. Blaine and Randall, during their respective terms as Speaker, had extended special help to the correspondents. "Under Speaker Randall," he wrote, "new rules were adopted and better facilities extended than were ever enjoyed before." Blaine, a Maine Republican, was Speaker from 1869 to 1875 and Randall, a Democrat from Philadelphia, from 1876 to 1881.

6. During the session which convened in December 1879 the House rewrote its rules. The provision governing the press gallery was essentially the rule of 1857 although it was considerably abbreviated. The changes must have been worked out in cooperation with the correspondents, and the meeting of the previous April would seem to have been part of a general program of revision. The requirements that applicants specify in writing the name of their paper and the part of the gallery which they would occupy was removed. So was the clause forbidding gallery privileges to claim agents. Although those sections were taken out of the House rule, however, they were present in the regulations drawn by the Standing Committee, obviously in cooperation with the Speaker and the Rules Committee. The rule of 1879 did, how-

ever, specifically authorize the Speaker to admit two Associated Press reporters to the floor.

From these records the student of press corps history may conclude that Randall, possibly as early as 1877, or perhaps in conjunction with the rule revision of 1879, drew the five-point set of regulations given in the Boynton committee report. Probably he worked with the reporters in preparing them. In so doing he acted under the authority of the House rule giving him control over the press gallery. He, in turn, delegated that authority to what must then have been a new group, the Standing Committee of Correspondents.[3] On succeeding to the Speakership in December 1881, Keifer accepted the same regulations as had his Democratic predecessor.

The session which saw Keifer and Boynton quarrel also saw the Senate extend official authority to the Standing Committee to govern the press gallery, subject, still, to supervision by the Rules Committee. That committee started in November 1883 to prepare an extensive revision of regulations governing precedure in the upper house. It adopted new ones on December 1 and the Senate approved them on January 16, 1884. Rule 34 in the new compilation reaffirmed the Rules Committee's power to govern the Senate wing of the Capitol. And it directed the committee to "make such regulations respecting the reporters' gallery of the Senate as will confine its occupation to *bona fide* reporters for daily newspapers, assigning not to exceed one seat to each paper." [4]

The committee next drafted new regulations under its authority to govern the north wing of the building. They were approved on March 15. Included as Rule 4 were provisions assigning parts of the gallery to the public, to the ladies, the president, senators' families and diplomats. They set aside the gallery in rear of the vice-president's chair for reporters. Rule 5 was in language almost identical to that of the regulations which Randall and Keifer had approved in the House, except for different paragraphing and the fact that it recognized the Rules Committee, rather than the Speaker, as the governing authority to which the Standing Committee was responsible.[5] It is obvious that the committee had accepted the action which had been taken earlier in the House. From 1884 to the present the rule laid down by the

Senate committee in the annually published compilation of rules for the regulation of the Senate wing of the Capitol has been that agreed to by the Standing Committee of Correspondents and the Speaker. Since 1888 they have been published under the press list in each issue of the *Congressional Directory.*

In the twentieth century the Standing Committee shouldered an additional duty. The Republican National Committee asked it to handle arrangements for the press section of its national convention in 1904, and it has done so at every such quadrennial conclave since. The Democratic National Committee has done so since 1912. The Standing Committee's records show that as the date of each convention has approached, some of its members have gone with the party's committee on arrangements to inspect the site and make advance preparations. Then the press group has combed the thousands of applications for credentials in order to single out those who have a valid right to attend. When the delegates convene, the superintendents of the two press galleries supervise the convention press facilities.

Speaker Thomas B. Reed approved slight amendments to the regulations governing the press gallery in 1891. One added section directed the Standing Committee to report to the Speaker violations of the provisions, and another provided that the press list in the *Congressional Directory* be limited to correspondents filing copy by telegraph. The 1896 *Senate Manual* showed that the upper house, too, had rewritten its Rule 4 in the *Rules for the Regulation of the Senate Wing of the U.S. Capitol* to conform. This added a sentence saying that "Correspondents entitled to the privileges of the Press Gallery may be admitted to the Marble Room under such regulations as may be prescribed by the Committee on Rules."

As the nineteenth century closed, the Associated Press was the only telegraphic news service operating effectively, although several smaller agencies tried to compete. Early in the twentieth century, however, strong rivals appeared and demanded the rights on the floor that were granted to the older agency. Several times the rule was amended to meet the newcomers' demands. Such action was taken formally only in the House. The Senate made no specific provision to this effect in the rules but extended the courtesy by action of the Rules Committee.[6]

The Standing Committee was recognized as the governing

body of the press gallery only by the Speaker and the Rules Committee, without specific provision in the Standing Rules of either body, until 1916. Its minutes show that in 1914 there was correspondence between its members and the House Rules Committee about the promotion of one of the press gallery laborers to the rank of messenger. On December 21, 1915, Representative Benjamin G. Humphreys, chairman of the Democratic Patronage Committee, wrote to the Standing Committee that his group was prepared to give the correspondents control over the press gallery employees. On January 8, 1916, the Rules Committee reported out a substitute for Clause Two of the press gallery rule. It was the same as the older except that it added: "and the supervision of such gallery, including the designation of its employees, shall be vested in the Standing Committee of correspondents, subject to the direction and control of the Speaker." [7]

Although the Senate made no specific provision in its rules to admit press association reporters to the floor, as did the House, ever since Senator Anthony's resolution of March 1873 it had granted that privilege to two from each by action of the Rules Committee. By 1929 the custom which brought about that courtesy, that is, daily transmission of start-to-finish summaries of floor proceedings in the nineteenth-century style, had long since been discarded. Indeed, the current generation of correspondents did not remember that such a practice in legislative news writing had ever been followed and did not know why press association reporters had been admitted to the floor. In that year the question became entangled in the latest of the wrangles between the Senate and the press.

As in 1848 and 1871 the discussion grew out of publication of the Senate's "secret" proceedings. The offending reporter this time, Paul Mallon of the United Press, was questioned by the Rules Committee. True to the tradition of Nugent, Simonton, Ramsdell, and White, he refused to reveal the identity of his leak. He was not, however, arrested as his predecessors had been. Instead the incident was capitalized on by a group of solons led by Robert M. La Follette, Jr., of Wisconsin and Wesley L. Jones of Washington who made it the occasion to change the rules.

On November 30, 1928, a few months before he was to leave office, President Coolidge sent to the Senate the nomination of Roy O. West as secretary of the interior. Charges by western

Republicans that West was a tool of the electric power interests heightened interest in the nomination. Under the rules the Senate debated and voted to confirm the nomination in secret session on January 23. A few days later Mallon secured what he wrote was an accurate roll call of the vote and the story went to all United Press client newspapers. The Senate took no action. Off the floor, however, there was extensive discussion. Senator Charles Curtis of Kansas, chairman of the Rules Committee and vice-president-elect, told a New York *Times* correspondent that he might move to deprive press association reporters of their right to the floor. He later changed that to threaten only the United Press, but he did not actually press the case.[8] The Standing Committee of Correspondents met and found that Mallon had done nothing unethical.[9]

Inaugurated as president on March 4, 1929, Herbert Hoover called Congress into special session. Senate business included confirmation of the executive's nominees for office. Attacks on the "power trust" led by Senator George Norris of Nebraska, and the senatorial split between the conservative "Old Guard" and the progressive group of western Republicans meant that the nominees had a stiff gauntlet to run before they could be confirmed.

Irvine L. Lenroot had been a senator from Wisconsin from 1918 to 1926, when he was defeated for renomination. Coolidge nominated him for judge of the United States Court of Customs and Patent Appeals on February 14, 1929. The selection was greeted both on and off the Senate floor by charges that Lenroot had been associated with former Secretary of the Interior Albert B. Fall, who was convicted of criminal charges growing out of the Harding administration scandals. Lenroot's confirmation was still bogged down when the session ended on March 4. Hoover resubmitted his name on April 22. On May 17, after a secret session which lasted six and one-half hours, the Senate confirmed him. The debate and the vote were withheld. Mallon broke it again. The United Press moved, under his by-line, what it said was the forty-two to twenty-seven vote on Lenroot's confirmation and gave the names of the senators voting pro and con. It was published in client papers, including the Washington *News*, on May 21.

Before this story appeared the gage had been thrown down

to the Senate by one of its own members on the question of continued secret sessions to consider executive nominations. On April 22, Senator Jones introduced a resolution providing that executive nominations be considered in open session unless the Senate should vote to close the doors.[10] That was where things stood on May 21 when Mallon's story on Lenroot's confirmation was published. In the Senate that day there was a long debate in which the question of whether or not the body should take some kind of punitive action was tangled up with the opposition to continued secret sessions.[11] The Rules Committee met the next day. It voted to withdraw from the United Press the privilege of the floor. It decided to call Mallon before it at a later session although members took it for granted that he would refuse to divulge his source.[12] And it drew a resolution that Mallon's story "is a breach of the privileges of the Senate, made possible only by a violation of the rules of the Senate by some Member or officer of the Senate. . . . and deserves and should receive severe censure and punishment."

Senator David Reed of Pennsylvania introduced the resolution when the Senate convened later that day. LaFollette took advantage of its introduction to raise the question as to whether or not the rules actually admitted press association reporters to the floor. His purpose was both to defeat the Rules Committee decision to withdraw the privilege from the United Press and, by derision, to support moves for open executive sessions to consider nominations. He read the rule listing those having the privilege of the floor and pointed out that it said nothing about press association reporters. Vice-President Curtis, as a former Rules Committee chairman, as well as Senator George H. Moses of New Hampshire, who then presided over the committee, and Senator Lee S. Overman of North Carolina, its ranking minority member and chairman in years of Democratic control, both said they had inherited the practice of issuing cards to two reporters for each press association. None knew how the custom had originated. None was aware of Senator Anthony's resolution of 1873.

While this discussion went on before a jammed gallery, Fraser Edwards, a Universal Service reporter who possessed a card admitting him to the floor, strolled in. LaFollette, who had probably arranged the matter with Edwards, called the chair's attention to his presence and demanded that the rules be enforced.

Vice-President Curtis held that Rule 33 must be interpreted strictly and that press association reporters must be barred in spite of the Rules Committee's custom.[13]

On the 23d LaFollette introduced a resolution adding to Rule 33. It would include among those having the privilege of the floor two reporters each for the Associated Press, the United Press, and the International News Service, and one for the Universal Service, not more than one reporter for each to be on the floor at the same time. In debate LaFollette tried to embarrass Senator Reed by pointing out that the Pennsylvanian's secretary, Theodore Huntley, was a former Washington correspondent of the Pittsburgh *Post-Gazette* and had once sent to that paper an account of a secret Senate debate. LaFollette implied that Reed had been the leaky senator that time.

On Monday, the 27th, the Rules Committee called in Mallon. The reporter, attended by counsel, read a statement denying that the committee could subpoena him. Senator Reed Smoot of Utah said they could not conduct an active investigation without a directing resolution by the Senate and that for all of the floor discussion no such action had been taken. During the hearing, which was public, Mallon refused to reveal his source and said that he would not approach an officer or employee of the Senate for information. Thus he implied that a senator had given him his material. In reply to questions by Senator Hiram Bingham of Connecticut, Mallon said that a reporter's principles would cause him to protect a news source and to respect a request not to publish material given in confidence. Thus, it was made clear, if a senator had given him the roll call vote it was with full knowledge on the lawmaker's part that it was to be published. Ethics did not, Mallon said, bind the reporter to respect the Senate's secrecy rule.[14] In the regular session of the Senate later that day Senator Moses, as chairman of the Rules Committee, pointed out that the meeting was public "and I think all present will agree that it was fruitless." Senate debate over Mallon recurred irregularly for several days more and finally dropped off inconclusively.[15]

On the other hand the Senate considered a rash of proposed resolutions bearing on the several issues raised. It finally adopted a rule which provided that executive nominations be considered with the doors open "unless the Senate in closed session, by a majority vote, shall determine that a particular nomination, treaty, or other matter shall be considered in closed executive session." It provided, however, that any senator might make public his own vote if he so desired. LaFollette's proposal to admit press association reporters died in committee.

In 1947 and 1949 the rules governing the press galleries underwent the most extensive overhauling that they have had since they were first drafted between 1877 and 1884. The cause, in 1947, was the application for admission to the press gallery by reporters for a group of Negro papers which brought out several weeklies and one daily. Although their application was the immediate spark, pressure on the Standing Committee to admit writers for labor groups and for the State Department, as well as the question of correspondents who represented foreign government propaganda agencies, called for a reexamination.

The question about admitting representatives of the Negro press revolved around the rule that the press gallery be limited to those filing telegraphic stories for daily newspapers. The Negro journals, in most cases, were published once a week. Standing Committee minutes show that as early as November 18, 1943, it discussed a letter which the Associated Negro Press had sent to Speaker Sam Rayburn applying for membership in the press galleries. Merriman Smith, United Press White House correspondent, told the committee at that meeting that the White House Correspondents' Association had received a similar letter. The Association had referred the matter to Stephen S. Early, the president's press secretary. The Standing Committee felt that the applicants failed to qualify under the rules governing the correspondents at both the Capitol and the White House. It postponed action, however, pending further information.

The minutes of September 27, 1945, show that Harry S. McAlpin had applied to represent the Atlanta *World*, the only daily paper among the associated group of Negro journals. A subcommittee was appointed to investigate the daily file of that paper and its weekly associates, but six weeks later that subcommittee reported that pressure of other work had prevented an adequate study. A subcommittee member reported that McAlpin had left the *World* but that Louis R. Lautier had applied to represent the Negro Newspaper Publishers Association News Service. The Standing Committee again postponed action.

Finally the Rules Committee intervened. (It had become the Committee on Rules and Administration under the 1946 Congressional Reorganization Act.) It called a special meeting for March 18, 1947, to consider Lautier's application. The Standing Committee met the previous day and prepared a statement that it had rejected the reporter for the Negro weeklies under the current rules limiting membership to those covering dailies. It recommended that possible amendments to open the door within the rules be studied. The Senate Committee failed to act on the proposal for a study but issued Lautier a card for admission to the Senate press gallery.

The Standing Committee met again the next day. The minutes record that "Members freely expressed their indignation at the arbitrary action of the Senators in ignoring the Standing Committee's recommendation for a one-month study" and referred to "the obvious political motivation behind the Senatorial order." It wrote to Senator Wayland Brooks of Illinois, the committee chairman, that "the unprecedented action of the Senate Rules Committee in overruling the Standing Committee places Mr. Lautier in the incongruous position of being credited to one press gallery and not to the other." Therefore, the letter said, Lautier was being issued a card for both galleries. But it protested that the senators had still failed to provide a satisfactory solution for the problem.

Since the Rules and Administration Committee had acted on Lautier's application as an individual instance, although it was contrary to the rules as interpreted by the Standing Committee, the latter group decided to revise the press gallery regulations to conform. It called a special meeting of the press gallery membership for May 8 to consider a statement which it had prepared. And it proposed an additional paragraph in the regulations to admit a carefully limited number of reporters for weeklies. The new provisions would admit not more than two correspondents for each bona fide news association which regularly serviced news of national affairs to a substantial number of weekly newspapers. Those papers must be entitled to second-class mailing privileges, be sold regularly for profit, and pay for the service. And the proposed addition would forbid that they be interpreted to admit writers for publications for special economic, labor, or business interests. The proposed addition was accepted by the press gallery membership and then by the Speaker and the Rules Committee.

Meanwhile other groups were knocking at the press gallery doors. As a result, further changes were written in 1949.

In 1943 the Office of War Information, the agency set up to coordinate government information activities during World War II, applied to have its own reporters admitted to the press gallery. The minutes for November 18 say that "Mr. Paul Frederickson and Mr. M. F. Stonehouse, O.W.I., appeared before the committee and gave detailed statements concerning the type of news O.W.I. was handling from the hill." (The word "hill" is common Washingtonese for the Capitol.) After discussion, "it was unanimously agreed that this committee was without jurisdiction in this matter as the rules governing the Congressional Press Galleries clearly prohibit the use of the galleries by Government agencies."

Six years later the State Department tried. In 1949 the Office of International Information, a predecessor of the United States Information Agency, applied to have its reporters admitted. At about the same time writers for the Labor Press Association, a service providing news for union newspapers, sought accreditation. The Standing Committee debated the two applications on June 27, August 15, August 25, September 8, and October 17, a series of called meetings entirely out of the ordinary in their frequency. The committee members' uncertainty spread to the whole accredited membership of the press galleries. William S. White of the New York *Times*, chairman of the committee, felt that both the labor group and the State Department representatives should be admitted but that the number from each should be carefully limited. Admission of the State Department's reporters in particular, he felt, was necessary as the Standing Committee's part in patriotic support of this country's international program. He and some others, both in and outside the Standing Committee, felt that the current regulations forbade the applicants' admission but that they should be revised.

Meanwhile some correspondents outside the Standing Committee determined to oppose any easing of the barriers. They privately approached members of the Senate Rules and Administration Committee with plans to override the Standing Committee.[16] This tense situation was reflected in the Standing Committee's meetings. The minutes show motions made, seconded, amended, withdrawn, points of order, appeals, motions to table and discussion among the five members which read almost like the journal of one or the other of the two houses of Congress itself as a confused and intricate legislative problem is fought out. The Rules and Administration Committee met with some of the correspondents, but only directed the Standing Committee to work out the necessary changes with individual objectors among the gallery membership. The Standing Committee finally prepared a new draft of the regulations and submitted it to Senator Carl Hayden of Arizona, chairman of the Rules and Administration Committee, and to Speaker Samuel Rayburn. On October 19 both approved them.

At the meeting on the 17th White resigned as chairman of the Standing Committee. In a statement, he said that he did so because he felt that a minority of the accredited correspondents, in going over the heads of the Standing Committee to the overseeing Senate committee had made it impossible for the Standing Committee to work properly.

The result of Lautier's admission in 1947 and of the debate in 1949 was that the old regulations accepted by the Speaker and the Senate Rules and Administration Committee were dropped. They were essentially those which Speaker Randall had approved after 1877 and had been amended only in minor detail in seventy years. The new regulations set out in more detail than had been done heretofore the structure of the Standing Committee. Becoming a sort of constitution and bylaws, they provided that it consist of five members. At the election in January 1951 the three candidates receiving the highest number of votes were to serve for two years and the next two, for one year. After that an election would be held each January, to name three men in odd-numbered years and two in even-numbered years. Furthermore the Standing Committee was not to propose a change in the regulations except on petition in writing signed by not less than a hundred accredited members of the press galleries.

The old limitation of membership to those filing copy by telegraph for daily newspapers was taken out. Now membership was limited to those whose "principal income is obtained from news correspondence intended for publication in newspapers entitled to second-class mailing privileges." Other clauses forbade members of the press galleries from engaging in paid publicity or promotion or from prosecuting claims.

The Standing Committee voted on October 28 to admit Nathan Robertson and Alvaine Hamilton, the applicants from the Labor Press Association, which its motion carefully pointed out was "an association of newspapers entitled to second class mailing privileges." But when the applications of William C. Bourne and Joseph M. Sittick of the State Department were considered, the committee voted "That the applications did not come within the rules governing the press galleries and could not be approved." On February 9, 1950, Jack C. McDermott, chief of the International Press and Publications Division of the State Department, asked a further hearing. But on June 1 the Standing Committee voted unanimously to reject the department's request. The minutes of this meeting ended: "Being informed that the St. Louis Browns had defeated the Nats 5 to 4, the meeting adjourned, subject to call of the Chair, at 11:52 P.M. EDT."

15. The Press at the White House: Lincoln to Nixon

When Lincoln abandoned the administration press organ he left the presidency at loose ends as far as its public contacts were concerned. But it did not make much difference. The thirty years after 1865 saw the White House occupied by relatively colorless men. They possessed neither the personal spark nor the governmental leadership to inspire deep interest by the press and the public. They led the nation, nominally, but correspondents devoted their attention to the Capitol.

Lincoln's successor occupies a peculiar spot in press history. Andrew Johnson was the first chief executive to grant interviews. In their time, correspondents regarded the articles signed "MACK," which were published in the Cincinnati *Commercial* of April 1 and 6, 1868, as an interesting innovation.[1] A recent study, however, shows that "MACK" (he was J. B. McCullagh, later the famous managing editor of the St. Louis *Globe-Democrat*) was not the first. The real innovator was Colonel Alexander K. McClure, a Pennsylvania journalist and politician, who published the first presidential interview in the *Franklin Repository* of Chambersburg, Pa., on October 31, 1865.[2]

Press and presidential relationships from Johnson's retirement in 1869 until William H. McKinley entered the White House on March 4, 1897, were so limited that we may dismiss them without further attention.[3] The latter's administration, however, saw the beginning of a shift toward more regularized press relations and a greater volume of news from the president. It was at this time that the correspondents and the executive started working out the practices which today keep his family, personal and social life as well as his political and administrative acts under greater public scrutiny than that faced by any other head of a state.

Developments in both the press and the presidency brought about the changes. By 1900 the former was separating from close political party association and was becoming more and more a business enterprise dependent on news for its circulation and on the booming advertising which resulted from the country's rapid industrial growth for its financial support. Correspondents were more nearly objective writers of news than political essayists. Vigor in ascertaining facts was replacing cooperation with politicians who enjoyed a paper's support. Newspapermen, therefore, demanded closer access at the White House for all instead of a favored few party supporters.

Meanwhile the presidency was changing. The assassin who shot McKinley at the beginning of this century sent into the White House the first of three aggressive personalities who have done much to shift the center of governmental power away from the Capitol. But even if the two Roosevelts and Woodrow Wilson had not entered the stage, other pressures would have thrown more power and responsibility to the presidency. Worldwide tensions since 1890 have thrown foreign relations into the American ken to a greater degree than has been true since 1815. Foreign policy is the responsibility of the president and his selected servant, the secretary of state, with Congress having relatively little influence in spite of senatorial power to advise and consent. Demands for increased governmental service, for regulation of business and for welfare programs has brought a corresponding increase of executive agencies directed by the president and a greater White House leadership in proposing legislation to Congress.

By the middle of the twentieth century a fourfold set of practices had developed for White House coverage. It involved 1) the news conference, in which reporters meet as a group with the president, ask questions, and either note the answers for publication or are given information which they are pledged to keep in confidence; 2) the maintenance full time at the executive mansion of newsmen who interview presidential callers as they leave and thus try to secure through this secondary channel an insight into the executive mind; 3) a press secretary, usually a former newsman, employed by the White House to prepare and release formal statements, to receive and try to answer correspondents' queries in the periods between the regular news conferences, and to advise the president on his press relationships, and 4) certain informal arrangements such as contacts between individual reporters with members of the White House staff and the executive's family and sometimes interviews between selected correspondents or groups of correspondents with the president to the exclusion of others.

One of the traditions of the press corps is that William W. Price, a Washington *Evening Star* reporter, took the first step toward establishing the present-day system of White House coverage. In 1895 he stationed himself at the mansion and began interviewing presidential callers as they left. The present wings to the east and west had not been built yet and the president's office was on the second floor of the old part of the building. Those who had appointments entered through the Pennsylvania Avenue portico. Price and other reporters who soon followed his example stationed themselves at the entrance. A press corps legend says that they sometimes stood on the sidewalk, in good and in bad weather. Later Price was admitted to the second floor corridor outside the presidential office.[4] During the Spanish-American War Fred A. Emery of the Associated Press waited in the first floor corridor. His service had a direct telegraph wire to its office in the Star Building and maintained a telegrapher as well as Emery at the White House.[5]

Coming after the colorless McKinley, Theodore Roosevelt was a welcome change for the correspondents. Aggressive in personality and in politics, he made far more news than did his predecessors. Also, correspondents saw more of him personally than they had seen of the others although he did not hold formal press conferences of the type which developed later. There is a story that he sometimes admitted groups of correspondents to talk while he was being shaved. As the valet labored over his chin with a straight razor the excitable president would talk and would gesture with his hands. The reporters watched, fearing that a finger or the presidential throat would come into destructive contact with the razor's working edge. That did not happen.[6]

Before Roosevelt succeeded to the presidency the reporters

who followed Price's example made a sizeable little group waiting to waylay callers as they left the office. Roosevelt ordered that space be made available to them. In 1904 the building underwent drastic reconstruction. The present west wing was added to become the executive offices. A room adjoining the secretary's office was made available to the press.

On the day Roosevelt returned from McKinley's funeral in Canton he called the chief Washington representatives of the then three major telegraphic news services in. He promised cooperation with those reporters who respected his confidences. On the other hand, he promised that if any correspondent violated that confidence or wrote anything which he felt should not have been used, he would punish him by withholding legitimate news from him.[7] This rule characterized much of Roosevelt's contact with the press although its enforcement varied. Individually or in groups, correspondents could see him at almost any time, and he would talk freely, leaving much to their judgment as to what was confidential and what could be used. Anxious to continue the blessings of the arrangement, they remained cautious and were particularly careful not to attribute their news to him. They did not write: "President Roosevelt said today that. . . . " On several occasions he is said to have used the correspondents to spread stories which he wanted published to secure an effect or to test public reaction. When it suited him he followed up his first statement with a flat denial and sometimes denounced the unlucky reporter who had believed him the first time.[8] A story which is dubious but which demonstrates what some reporters thought of his attitude says that he once gave some correspondents an announcement with one hand while he held in the other a denial which had been prepared for release the next day.[9] He would consign to his "Ananias Club" those whom he condemned for writing stories which he denied.

Thus he left to William Howard Taft, his handpicked heir, a collection of reporters housed in their own White House working quarters and accustomed to frequent access to the executive presence. Furthermore, the practice of interviewing callers as they left the president was well established. Taft has been credited with having originated the press conference. But the meetings which he had with the correspondents in the early years of his administration were not like the more formalized sessions which have since developed. When Taft was secretary of war under Roosevelt a group of reporters formed the habit of calling on him at 4:00 P.M. He talked freely, sometimes to the point of indiscretion in giving away cabinet secrets.[10] His geniality cooled, however, under the responsibilities of the presidency. When a group of those correspondents who regarded themselves as personal friends from his secretary-of-war days called on Inauguration Day, a secretary told them that the former relationship would no longer continue. Nevertheless he tried, for a time, to hold weekly meetings with the press. They were scheduled for 4 o'clock, but the president would sometimes make the writers wait until 6 or later before he appeared.[11] Eventually they were abandoned. Taft continued throughout his administration, however, to give his confidence to Gus J. Karger, correspondent of the Cincinnati *Times-Star,* which was owned by the president's brother, Charles P. Taft.[12]

Then Woodrow Wilson appeared, bringing a political party shift and a broad legislative program of reform. Holding a formalized press conference eleven days after his inauguration, he explained to the assembled reporters that he hoped they would try to help the public understand the issues and also would become a channel to "tell Washington what the country is thinking."[13] He planned to meet the correspondents twice a week. Wilson's innovation, however, proved satisfactory neither to himself nor to the reporters. For the president's part his academic dignity and sense of his own intellectual leadership was upset by contact with a press group which was not always respectful. He was angered by newspaper speculation over his family affairs, particularly regarding his daughters' real or rumored romances. His conception of what should be reported differed from that of the newsmen. He was unable to adjust to the fact that journalists are interested in what he described as the personal and trivial as well as in the serious problems of government. He felt, too, that most of the press opposed his program and that therefore the representatives who faced him were hostile.

The reporters, for their part, found the intellectual, reserved former professor very different from that vigorous extrovert, Theodore Roosevelt, and the likeable Taft. For one thing, they did not like the fact that the frequent informal calls by individual reporters which Roosevelt had permitted were now at an end, making the press conferences their only direct contact. And they did not like the academic attitude with which he seemed to lecture them. In 1915, after the *Lusitania* was sunk, Wilson abandoned the conferences. Thereafter Joseph P. Tumulty, his secretary, remained the sole channel for White House news.

Out of the need for regulating admission to such a novelty as the formal press conference grew the White House Correspondents' Association. David Lawrence, columnist and publisher of *United States News and World Report*, who covered the early years of the Wilson administration for the Associated Press, wrote to this writer in July 1953:

> *I remember very well the occasion of its origin. The question arose as to accrediting correspondents at the White House press conferences. At that time the only organization which did any accrediting was at the Capitol, namely, the Standing Committee of Correspondents. This was a large and unwieldy group and obviously not everybody in it was eligible to go to a presidential press conference. It became necessary to make sure that men who regularly covered the White House were admitted because the space was limited. That is how the White House Correspondents' Association started.*

The association drew a charter and had it suitably engrossed, signed and framed in a large frame bordered on all four sides with oval photographs of the original members. That charter still hangs on the White House press room wall. It states that the primary purpose of the association "shall be the promotion of the interests of those reporters and correspondents assigned to cover the White House." Membership is limited to those whose duty it is "to primarily cover, and who are directly responsible for handling, the news and events of the White House." And the charter limits the privilege of the press room to members and to those regularly accredited to the press galleries of Congress. Price was the first chairman, Lawrence was the first vice-chairman, and William B. Metcalf of the Baltimore *Sun*, secretary-treasurer. Eleven names are signed as charter members.[14]

Since each president makes slightly different arrangements for press relations the White House Correspondents' Association has never been granted the authority over the executive mansion press room that the Standing Committee of Correspondents exercise over the press galleries of Congress. Indeed, the records of the Standing Committee contain several references which show that sometimes it eyed with interest the news center at the other end of the downtown stretch of Pennsylvania Avenue. Some of its members felt that they should assume the responsibility for the White House as well as the press galleries. In 1918 there was correspondence between Gus J. Karger of the Cincinnati *Times-Star*, then chairman of the Standing Committee, and George Creel, the wartime chairman of the Committee on Public Information, about resuming the presidential press conferences and about having the Standing Committee govern them. Nothing came of the correspondence, however, in spite of the fact that Creel was interested.

When Franklin D. Roosevelt became president the association started the custom of annual dinners for him, and he accepted every year. All presidents since then have also done so, with a year skipped occasionally when there were problems which made it hard to arrange. In 1952 the late Joseph H. Short, Truman's press secretary, wrote to this author that "in my twenty-one years in Washington the main function of the Association has been to hold an annual dinner for the President of the United States."

On March 4, 1921 there was inaugurated a president who differed in nearly every way from his predecessor. Where Wilson was intellectual and reserved, Warren G. Harding was of ordinary mentality and cordial with those whom he regarded as friends. Where Wilson had positive goals which he wished the government to achieve under his leadership, Harding sought less clearly defined ends and was content to follow the lead of others. Where Wilson demanded the cooperation of the correspondents to bring the country to his way of thinking, Harding, himself a publisher, was more familiar with the working of the reporters' minds and wanted to make them his friends. He reinstituted the twice-a-week press conferences which Wilson had tried and abandoned. He asked that questions be submitted in writing in advance, and the rule that he was not to be directly quoted was understood. On the other hand, although questions were written, the president permitted further discussion. His manner was affable and friendly and an atmosphere of mutual liking prevailed. In December 1921, however, a press conference incident caused a flurry among members of Congress and the delegates and newspapermen attending the Conference for the Limitation of Armaments.

The gathering convened on November 12. By mid-December it was known that the United States, Great Britain, France, and Japan had agreed on a separate pact guaranteeing the status quo for ten years in the Pacific for "insular possessions and insular dominions." Certain senators criticized the pact as a guarantee that this country would go to war to protect the home Japanese islands. They asked whether or not the American delegates, in their secret negotiations, had agreed to such a construction. They had so agreed, and the press had said so, but the attitude of members of Congress made the matter delicate. This was the situation when the reporters trooped into the executive office at 1:30 P.M. on December 20.

In answer to a written question the president replied that he understood that the pact applied to the Japanese homeland no more than it applied to the mainland of the United States. Within an hour his remark was known at the Capitol and various embassies and conference rooms and had been cabled around the world. Intense excitement resulted. Charles Evans Hughes, secretary of state and chairman of the American delegation, hurried to the White House. At 7:30 P.M. the White House issued a correcting statement. It opened with the explanation that "When the President was responding to press inquiries at the afternoon interview today he expressed the opinion that the homeland of Japan did not come within the words 'insular possessions and insular dominions' under the four-party agreement." It said that he had learned from the United States delegation that they had agreed to a contrary understanding and added that "the difference in view in no wise will be permitted to ambarrass the conference or the ratification of the agreement." Some writers have said that Harding permitted oral questioning in his early press conferences and started requiring that queries be written in advance only after he was embarrassed by this slip.[15] He became more cautious, but written questions had been asked before that time.

Moving to the White House after Harding's sudden death in 1923, Calvin Coolidge continued to receive the press twice a week, as had his predecessor, but was adamant about requiring that questions be submitted in advance, in writing. Furthermore, he allowed no discussion of the question as to whether or not material could be directly quoted, such as had marked some of Harding's sessions. As the reporters, between fifty and one hundred in number, stood silently in the executive office taking notes, the president leafed through the pile of written queries and answered those which he wished to answer, ignoring the others. He would not permit attribution to him, either directly or indirectly. The correspondents, therefore, launched the fiction of the "White House spokesman" as the source of material which came from the lips of the president himself.

The reporters disliked it. Probably many supported the sentiments voiced by Frank R. Kent of the Baltimore *Sun* in a harsh magazine article and one by Oswald Garrison Villard of the New York *Evening Post* in another which was more restrained but critical.[16] They agreed that "silent Cal" was not silent, but was sometimes garrulous. In the monologue which he delivered to the unspeaking reporters, they said, he gave little news but at times discoursed at length on trivial matters. And except for these sessions, he kept the press at arm's length.

Like Taft, Hoover came to the White House after he had built up a reputation for cooperation with the correspondents while he was a cabinet member. As secretary of commerce he had developed a departmental publicity structure which became the model for those set up later by other executive agencies. In addition, he was at that time personally approachable and cooperative. He became, however, the most distant and most repressive president, as far as the press was concerned, who has held office in this century.

This was due, in part, to his misfortune in occupying the White House during the early depression years. Confused by events and angered by criticism, Hoover took steps which caused his press relations to deteriorate while secretaries whom the press regarded as inept did little to ease the situation. By 1933 he had formed the habit of canceling press conferences on short notice and had all but abandoned the system.

At his first one, which he held the day after he was inaugurated, Hoover indicated that these meetings would be more productive of news and that a greater measure of attribution to their source of his statements would be permitted than had been the case under Coolidge.[17] He suggested that the White House Correspondents' Association appoint a committee to meet with him and improve relations.

Hoover was not the man to take the blows which descended upon him and still keep the good nature and poise in meeting reporters which he had shown in happier days as secretary of commerce. The result was a series of irritating incidents and attempts at news suppression which resulted in fewer and fewer press conferences and greater and greater strain between the president and the press. At times he received certain reporters privately, excluding others. Among those receiving this special privilege were Mark Sullivan, politically conservative syndicated columnist, Frank Kent of the Baltimore *Sun*, Richard V. Oulahan of the New York *Times*, Roy Roberts of the Kansas City *Star*, and Roy Vernon of the Chicago *Daily News*. Other correspondents felt that anything initiated by such an important news source as the president should be given to all, without playing favorites, and were angered by this selectivity. Another irritation was laid at the secretaries' door. Reporters filed written questions to be answered at press conferences but believed that they had not reached the president. Hoover was annoyed by the persistence with which the correspondents clung to him during his weekend trips to the headwaters of the Rapidan River and at stories that the cars in the presidential party sometimes drove at excessive speeds. And in 1931 he tried almost literally to order the press to print nothing about an evening White House meeting with Congressional leaders. It was a request, or an order, which was not respected.[18]

In July 1931 a committee of correspondents called on the president to try to improve relations. They submitted five requests, as follows: 1) that the written questions reach the president; 2) that on long motor trips arrangements be made for the correspondents to file stories; 3) that advance release be provided of radio speeches; 4) that better press arrangements be made at the Rapidan camp; and 5) that the press be informed of Hoover family activities. The call resulted in temporary improvement. But when conflicting statements from the White House and from Albany regarding certain correspondence between the president and Governor Franklin D. Roosevelt of New York seemed to imply that the White House had been guilty of an untruth, the old conflicts reappeared.

Consequently Hoover held fewer and fewer press conferences in his later years and relied more and more on "press statements" issued from a secretary's office. A tabulation which was published in 1934 showed that during twelve months covering parts of 1929 and 1930 he held twenty-three press conferences and issued eight press statements. For corresponding parts of 1932 and 1933 he held only twelve press conferences and issued twenty-six press statements.

Probably few men ever have or ever will reach the presidency who have displayed or will display the adeptness in dealing with the press that was shown by Franklin D. Roosevelt. Kennedy may have equaled him. Quick-thinking, well-informed as to his aides' activities, good at verbal fencing with the reporters, possessed of a genial friendliness and knowledge of the newspapermen's thinking greater than that of most men in public life, Roosevelt was able to face open questioning at press conferences until he died.

His administration was not, however, entirely a correspondents' honeymoon. Roosevelt protested at times, as had his predecessors, at what he regarded as reportorial inaccuracy or misplaced emphasis. In his later years he showed an increasing desire to avoid the constant scrutiny of the press. Furthermore, his continuing battle with publishers and editorial writers, most of whom opposed him and his policies, was reflected at times in his relations with the White House newsmen. These flaws, however, do not alter the fact that he was able more effectively to keep the news channels open than had any president preceding him. He held open press conferences with questions submitted orally instead of in writing. At the first, on March 8, 1933, he announced that his answers would come in three categories: 1) material which could be attributed to him, but not in direct quotations; 2) material which could be used but was not to be attributed; and 3) material given for the correspondents' information but which was not to be published. Reporters laughed with him when he remarked, "I do not want to have to revive the Ananias Club." [19]

Thus the written questions submitted before the conference were at an end. Furthermore, under the new rules reporters could write: "President Roosevelt said today in a press conference that . . ." followed by a summary in indirect quotation, instead of

"It was learned today at the White House . . ." or "The White House spokesman revealed today . . . ." One former rule to which the president clung, however, was stated in that first conference as follows: "Then in regard to news announcements, Steve and I thought that it would be best that straight news for use from this office should always be without direct quotations. In other words, I do not want to be directly quoted, unless direct quotations are given out by Steve in writing." [20]

"Steve" was Stephen S. Early, the "press secretary." Presidents' secretaries had always been important in press contacts. But before FDR there had been no one on the White House staff whose duties were entirely devoted to news. When Roosevelt brought Early, who had served with both the Associated Press and the United Press, into the executive office he assigned him responsibilities dealing with the press and radio. The president carefully kept his press secretary informed and, in turn, he listened to Early's advice as to the release of news and contacts with reporters. The country came to accept stories attributed to "Stephen S. Early, press secretary to the President," and summarizing material which he gave out in a daily session with reporters as carrying practically as much authority as those credited to Roosevelt himself.

Correspondents looked forward to happy years with White House news channels carefully kept open. Soon, however, differences crept in. The critics who wrote at that time argued that the president was less interested in keeping the public informed as part of his conception of public duty than he was in using a deft public relations touch to gain his own ends. Furthermore the president, as well as many other New Deal leaders, reacting to the fact that a majority of the country's editorial pages opposed his policies and reelection, sometimes made countercharges against the press.[21] He was genial most of the time, but truculent and evasive at times. He laughed off without answering some embarrassing questions. In his later years he resorted on occasion to a smiling, but nonetheless barbed, order to a correspondent to "go into the corner and put on the dunce cap" when he was pinned down. During the war he pleaded security in making some trips without his normal accompanying group of newsmen.

In November 1940, a few days after he had been elected for the third term, he ordered Secret Service men to bar Paul Mallon, whose syndicated column had been critical, from a press conference. Correspondents blamed the act on Early's being out of the city at the time and therefore not in a position to forestall a display of petulant temper. The order was rescinded after Early's return.[22] In the last few years there were a few cases of press conference cancellation, but they were maintained with considerable regularity until the last fatal trip to Warm Springs.

Roosevelt also provided the reporters with better quarters. The original White House press room was barely nine feet by twelve, and was located to the left of the main entrance to the executive offices. That wing was badly damaged by fire in 1929. When it was repaired the press room was enlarged. The office wing was extensively rebuilt in 1934. Thereupon the press received a larger room at the northwest corner of that extension, equipped with desks, typewriters, direct telephone connections to the offices of the telegraphic press associations, and such recreational facilities as card and chess tables.[23]

The room remained essentially unchanged for nearly thirty years in spite of the very great growth of the press corps in that time. In 1961, however, it was extensively remodeled although it was not enlarged. From 1934 to 1961 it was essentially one large, open room. In the reconstruction partitions were added, breaking part of the area up into smaller cubicles to give some privacy to separate booths for the telegraphic press associations and some newspaper staffs.

By 1970 the press room had become very crowded and reporters protested the lack of space as well as imperfect heating and air conditioning. Some broadcast facilities had already been provided near the swimming pool in the west wing, between the main building and the executive offices. The pool had been installed for President Franklin D. Roosevelt. Nixon, who was uninterested in swimming there, determined to provide new press facilities at that site. By April the pool had been covered, although the work was done in such a way that future presidents, if they so desire, may have the press facilities removed and again exercise in the water. The new press facilities provide multiple-room space on two levels for reporters' desks, direct-line telephones, broadcast booths, two comfortably furnished lounges, coin venders for snacks and drinks, and other comforts and conveniences. Glass-partitioned rooms or booths are built in for the

Associated Press, United Press International and the major foreign news agencies, and newspapers that maintain full-time staff members at the White House. Desks and telephones are available for reporters who appear there on a part-time basis. The work cost $574,000. The room was given an informal dedication on April 13 when former President Johnson breakfasted with Nixon. After their breakfast, the two visited the new press facilities and chatted with reporters.

Harry S Truman brought to the presidency poise and self-assurance in meeting the press but less of the smiling geniality which had marked his predecessor. He did not try to laugh off embarrassing questions or to order his questioner to don the dunce cap. Instead, his crisp "no comment" ended the matter when he was asked questions which he was unwilling to answer.

His first press conference, on April 17, 1945, was attended by 340 correspondents. He announced that he would continue to allow the open oral questions and the attribution, not in direct quotation, to which the reporters had by then become accustomed. Where Roosevelt had normally held two conferences per week, Truman reduced them to one. Although the day and time were sometimes shifted to conform to important news developments, normally they were held on Thursday—at 10:30 A.M. one week to give the afternoon papers the break, and at 4:00 P.M. the next out of deference to the morning papers.

He rehearsed carefully for each press conference. As the meeting hour approached every week he called on his secretaries and cabinet chiefs for information on the answers to the probable questions. His press secretary then held a practice session with him, firing the questions which were expected and coaching him on the answers. The press secretary had gained some hints as to what to expect through his own daily contact with reporters. Only after such preparations did Truman face the one hundred to two hundred newspaper and radio writers who normally attended.[24] Presidents who have followed him have also carefully prepared for their sessions with the newsmen.

Truman also continued the practice of maintaining on the White House staff an experienced newsman, a former Washington correspondent, to direct his press contacts. Early left to enter private business soon after Roosevelt died. On April 20, 1945, the president named to the post Charles G. Ross, who had been a childhood friend in Missouri. Ross had served as head of the Washington bureau of the St. Louis *Post-Dispatch* and later as an editorial writer on that paper. He died on December 5, 1950, and was succeeded by Joseph H. Short, who had worked on newspapers in Vicksburg, Mississippi, on the Associated Press staffs in Richmond and Washington, and later in the Washington bureau of the Baltimore *Sun*. He died suddenly on September 18, 1952. His assistants carried on the work of the office through the four remaining months of the administration.

Until 1950 press conferences were held in the president's office, with the reporters standing in a close-packed crowd of up to three hundred men and women grouped around the executive desk. Roosevelt sat down, flanked by Secret Service men and by secretaries and cabinet and bureau heads to whom he sometimes referred questioners. Truman stood up. In April of 1950 Truman suggested that the White House Correspondents' Association set up a committee to consider another location. On the 20th he announced that in the future press conferences would be held in an ornate conference room of the old State, War, and Navy Building across the street to the west of the White House. In the new meeting place there was room for two hundred folding chairs. The attending reporters were expected to sit instead of standing in an informal group as in the past. Microphones scattered about the room and on the table in front of the president carried the voices of all participants to a loudspeaker system and to tape recorders. In the past those present had asked questions without identifying themselves. Here each was required to precede his question by stating his identity and his press connection. The first meeting in the new location was held on April 27, with 278 news and radio reporters present.

Dwight D. Eisenhower came into the White House as the leader of the party of Coolidge and Hoover. In his relations with the press, however, he followed the trail blazed by his immediate Democratic predecessors. He named a press secretary, but his choice was not, as had been those of Roosevelt and Truman, a former Washington correspondent. To the post he named James C. Hagerty, a former New York *Times* reporter who had worked on the publicity staff of the Republican National Committee during the 1952 campaign.

Where Truman had seemed actually to enjoy the give and

take of the news conferences, Eisenhower appeared to shoulder them as one of the necessary, difficult burdens of a difficult post. He continued his predecessor's open questioning, and continued to meet the reporters under the Truman rules in the ornate room in the building to the west of the White House. In his manner there was none of Franklin D. Roosevelt's laughing evasion, and there was none of Truman's "No Comment." Eisenhower tried to answer every question, and maintained a serious manner. Reporters protested, however, that his replies were sometimes extended evasive discussions which lost their grammatical structure and wandered all around the subject without giving positive information.[25] And he continued the rule that he must be quoted only indirectly. At least he did so at the beginning of his administration. His contribution to press-presidential relationships, however, was to grant permission to radio and television stations to broadcast approved parts of the news conferences. But they did not go on the air live. Tapes and film were released only after Hagerty reviewed them. And once they were approved, newspapers as well as the radio and television stations were allowed to quote directly those approved parts, using the president's actual words in quotation marks.

Truman had ordered the Army Signal Corps to record his later press conferences on tape to preserve them for the White House archives. Early in Eisenhower's administration Hagerty told radio news writers that he hoped he would be able to arrange for more direct news for broadcast than had been made possible until then. On December 16, 1953, the pres conference proceeded as usual. As it ended, press association reporters and those who covered for the afternoon papers rushed to their direct-line telephones in the corridor outside the conference room. In the downtown offices of the telegraph services, dictation boys, headsets in place, were already waiting, and the first bulletins were on the wires within seconds. The stories which they moved carefully avoided the use of direct quotations.

During the afternoon, however, Hagerty announced that approved parts of the tape would be made available for radio broadcast and that newspapers could use direct quotations from those parts. Some reporters protested that such a late release of direct quotation worked a hardship on afternoon papers which had gone to press before Hagerty had examined the taped remarks and had given his approval. The press secretary, however, was adamant on that point.

Heretofore reporters had been allowed only to go from the news conferences and write: "President Eisenhower told a news conference today that he would . . . ." That was still true of those who rushed from the room to give their news to the world within minutes after the session closed. But writers for newspapers with later deadlines and for late-in-the-day newscasts could now say: "President Eisenhower said today, 'I will . . . .'" And evening radio newscasts could project the president's voice into the country's receiving sets.

Another year passed before the system was extended to the television screen. In January 1955 it was announced that cameras would record the conferences for possible video broadcast and for newsreels. But the cameras would not be allowed to transmit the scene straight to the nation's homes. Again the film must be reviewed before release and only that part authorized by the press secretary allowed to be used. And direct quotations were allowed only after the transcript had been examined. Scaffolds were built into the high-ceilinged room so that the cameras could be placed above the reporters' heads, looking down on the president and his questioners. The first to be so recorded was on January 19. The news shows on the broadcasting chains that evening presented in the nation's homes the image and words of the president as the correspondents saw and heard him. Of the thirty-three minutes recorded, film requiring twenty-eight minutes and twenty-five seconds was released. During the rest of Eisenhower's administration the part of the film made available for broadcast was normally either complete or so nearly complete that the expurgated sections were negligible.

John F. Kennedy's affability and his contacts with reporters led many to regard him favorably personally, and probably that attitude crept into their copy. That affability, self-confidence, and ability to think on his feet, which were put to use both in his televised news conferences and in other contacts with journalists, no doubt did much to build his popular image in the country and the world. On the other hand, several writers scored what they regarded as presidential press management. Kennedy, these critics charged, was less interested in keeping the press and public informed than in using a deft public relations touch to push his program.

The innovation which stands out as the great contribution of his administration to press-presidential relationships was the televised news conference. He inherited a practice which had evolved through successive administrations from the conferences with questions submitted in advance in writing under Harding and Coolidge, to the free-wheeling informal give-and-take but indirectly-quoted sessions with Roosevelt and Truman, and the filmed, but carefully checked, meetings of Eisenhower. To go on to the televised conferences, broadcast live with direct quotation permitted, was a natural next step for a self-confident young president who felt that he could handle the situation.

He changed the rules in a few particulars. Instead of meeting in the ornate room of the former State, War, and Navy Building, Kennedy met the reporters and faced the television cameras in the larger auditorium of the new State Department building. And he no longer required that each questioner identify himself and his paper. The conferences were by no means favorably received by all of the press. Some newspaper and magazine reporters protested that they were actors in a show staged for the benefit of television. They as well as the radio and television correspondents felt that the use of the large State Department auditorium separated the reporters from the closer contact with the presidential personality that they had enjoyed when the meetings were held in the White House office. Each was limited to one question. With more than three hundred press, magazine, radio and television correspondents for American and foreign media present there was competition for the president's attention which gave him power to recognize certain of the competitors and thus exercise a measure of control. And once a question was asked, it was impossible to follow it up with further queries to develop the theme or to clarify an ambiguous and unclear reply.

By 1970 the televised news conference had become institutionalized although, as will be discussed later in these pages, neither Johnson nor Nixon held them as frequently as did Kennedy. In 1970 George E. Reedy, who had served for nearly a year and a half as Johnson's press secretary, published a book in which he wrote critically of the practice. He said:

The most graphic illustration of the effects of TV upon our government can be found in the White House press conference. When televised, this has become as spontaneous as a Javanese temple dance, but without the grace which makes the latter a deeply moving experience. . . .

There are rarely more than twenty questions, and only one to a correspondent. They are not controlled, although this has been tried with disastrous results on one or two occasions, simply because controls are not necessary. The president dominates the scene completely. The lead questions are easily predictable. The "follow-up" questions—the kind that narrow down generalizations or pinpoint evasions —are nearly impossible in a situation where 200 to 400 correspondents are clamoring for recognition and where time is limited. Any president who has done his homework will emerge unscathed, with a generality for the "tough" questions and a rebuff for the "impertinent" questions. It is a breeze.[26]

Kennedy enjoyed the process, Reedy wrote, but Johnson dreaded it, although each emerged from each such session with an improved public image. Nevertheless, "for all the public learns about a chief executive's thinking, the newsmen might as well sit in the front lobby and dutifully file the press releases handed out by the press office."

Arthur Krock of the New York *Times,* in a rasping magazine article, charged that "A news management policy . . . has been enforced more cynically and boldly than by any previous administration." [27] Those facts which Krock saw as boldness and cynicism were also commented on by other writers who did not find fault with them in the same manner or to the same degree as did he.[28] All agreed that Kennedy's contacts with reporters were far greater than those of Eisenhower, and were perhaps greater than those of any president in the last half century or so. Richard Rovere, correspondent of the *New Yorker,* wrote in the issue of March 30, 1963, that "By almost any quantitative measure . . . the opportunities for getting news from responsible officials are greater than they have been at any time in the last twenty years, and are perhaps greater than they have ever been."

The televised news conferences were not Kennedy's only reporter contacts. He had made many personal friends among the press corps during his days on "the hill." He kept these contacts, seeing some of them socially or more often talking to them in a friendly manner by telephone. More than any president up to that time he received newsmen in groups in his office in an informal way unlike regular news conferences. Rovere wrote that "Mr. Kennedy enjoys the company of newspapermen as Mr. Eisenhower enjoyed the company of businessmen." And in addition to his contacts with journalists assigned to the capital he held frequent luncheons with delegations of visiting editors. Krock condemned this practice. On December 16, 1962, the president held a special interview in his office with a correspondent of each of the three major television chains. The taped interview, "A Conversation with the President," was broadcast on all three networks on the following evening. Fred Friendly, CBS news chief, hoped that more such conferences would be held, but it was not done again.[29] Johnson held two similar interviews with reporters from the television chains.

Rovere wrote that under Kennedy opportunities for getting news were greater than they had been for the preceding twenty years. James Reston of the New York *Times* wrote about President Johnson: "No President in the history of the Republic has ever devoted so much time to reporters, editors, and commentators." [30] These statements characterize much of the writing about the press relations of these two men.

It can be said in a study such as this that whereas Kennedy came into office enjoying the personal liking of much of the press corps, Johnson entered on the responsibilities of the presidency after he had earned, during his years at the Capitol, the dislike of some reporters.[31] Furthermore, he is a man of great sensitivity. To follow to the high office a wealthy, poised, and handsome young man who was surrounded by aides who idolized him and who were sometimes supercilious about the successor created strains which affected Johnson's attitude toward the executive office in general and his relations with the press in particular.[32]

Johnson held fewer televised press conferences than did his predecessor although he did continue the practice irregularly. Some of them were held in the White House East Room instead of the State Department auditorium. And he introduced a new use for video. A television theatre was placed in the Fish Room of the White House. There he met visiting groups and had his speeches recorded for news broadcast. Swearing-in ceremonies for newly-named government officials, and occasions such as the presentation of medals to Vietnam veterans were filmed for broadcast on television news shows, and the president made them the occasion for appropriate remarks. The rose garden, too, was at times used in this manner.

Johnson did, nevertheless, cultivate personal contacts with reporters. As Reston wrote, to a greater extent even than Kennedy had done, he talked to selected journalists individually or in small groups. From time to time he called White House reporters into his office for what amounted to informal small-group news conferences. And at times he was joined by correspondents—and the television cameras—for walks and talks in the White House grounds.

Like Johnson, Nixon had in the past come to be disliked by some of the press corps. Coolness between them reached a peak during his campaign for governor of California in 1962, bursting out in a bad-tempered display on his part on the day after his defeat. But during the campaign of 1968 and during his early months in the White House he improved the relationship. An editorial in *Editor and Publisher* of February 15, 1969, said: "President Nixon's performance in the area of information during his first month in office is receiving high grades from experienced newsmen on the Washington beat."

He continued the Kennedy-Johnson practice of news conferences televised live, holding the first on January 27, 1969, one week after his inauguration. During his first year in office he held eight full-scale televised news conferences and three informal press briefings. During the first four months they came fairly regularly, a few weeks apart. Later they were separated by as much as three months. For instance, after holding a televised news conference in June, he waited until September 26 for the next and then skipped until December 8.

At that December 8 meeting he was asked about his future plans by a reporter who, in his question, emphasized the fact that nearly three months had passed since the previous such session. The president replied that he expected to call in the reporters and appear before the television cameras only when it seemed to him that there was significant news to be laid before the public. He limited his reporter contacts to the formal news conferences or the occasional press briefings. He did not meet individual newsmen in the way both Kennedy and Johnson had done. He held the meetings before the correspondents and the video cameras in the White House East Room, bearing himself with cultivated ease on a slightly raised platform with only the microphone on its stand before him. He did not take a position behind a lectern on a table as his predecessors had done.

One early innovation, which had not been attempted by earlier presidents, was a news conference devoted entirely to a single topic. On March 4, 1969, after he returned from Europe, he appeared before the correspondents and television cameras to discuss, live, foreign relations and the results of his meetings with European heads of state. Ronald L. Ziegler, his press secretary, announced beforehand that he would entertain questions on no other subject.

His interest in the use of television was made evident before his inauguration. He made a show out of the announcement of his cabinet, with a special program on December 11, 1968. And he uses the auditorium in the White House for televised ceremonies in the same way that Johnson did. Formerly called the Fish Room, that chamber is now designated the Roosevelt Room. He reinstituted a practice which Kennedy had followed but which Johnson had abandoned. When the president travels, normally the regular White House correspondents follow in another plane. Kennedy worked out a pool arrangement whereby a small number of reporters and photographers went in the presidential plane itself, and they were required to report to the rest of the correspondents anything that happened en route. The other writers still followed in a separate aircraft.

Nixon and the press have arranged a pool of seven reporters and two photographers to cover for the press associations and the broadcasting chains and who accompany him personally in *Air Force One*. And during his European trip and on a later trip to California he talked with them informally and socially during the flight. Before leaving for Europe, however, he gave the correspondents a luncheon which, one of them told this writer, turned into "backgrounder." That is, he discussed some of the problems incident to the flight, giving the reporters information for their own guidance but which was not intended to be written.

Eisenhower's successors have followed his lead in going outside the ranks of Washington correspondents in naming the press secretary. Reporters felt that Hagerty was part of the White House force of advisers, taking an active part at times in the formulation of policy. In particular he was credited with favoring full publicity for such things, for example, as the president's heart attack in Denver and his other illnesses. Correspondents gave him high marks for competence and for knowledge of administration programs. They attributed to him the decision to televise edited transcripts of the news conferences.

Kennedy named to the post Pierre Salinger, a former San Francisco journalist who had been on his staff in Senate days. In seeing more of the press through direct contact than did Eisenhower, however, he served to some extent as his own press secretary and relied to a lesser extent on Salinger than Eisenhower had on Hagerty. Salinger, however, was credited with actively urging the president to hold the televised news conferences. Salinger was called on, too, for a delicate task beyond the duties of the press secretary. It was he who went to Moscow in 1962 and held private conversations with Nikita Khrushchev.

Johnson had a series of press secretaries, selecting them from aides who had worked for him in the past, but who had little or no press experience. Salinger held on until March of 1964 and resigned to run for the Senate from California. George Reedy, a Texan and long-time aide to the former senator and vice-president then took over. In July 1965 he was assigned to other duties and was succeeded by Bill Moyers, an ordained Baptist minister and School of Journalism graduate, also a Texan. He, too, had worked for Johnson in prepresident days. In January 1967 Moyers resigned to become publisher of *Newsday* and was succeeded by his assistant, George C. Christian.

For many years Herbert Klein, a former San Diego newspaperman, handled Nixon's press contacts. Newsmen, therefore, assumed that he would become the White House press secretary when his boss entered the White House. Instead, Nixon created a new post, that of communications director for the administration and installed Klein therein, giving him an office and staff in the White House Executive Offices Building. As press secretary he named Ronald L. Ziegler. A native of Covington, Kentucky, Ziegler had lived in California and had worked for an advertising agency, but had had no news experience. He was assisted, however, by Gerald L. Warren, a former staff member of the San Diego *Union,* who thus brought something of the experienced newsman's point of view.

16. The Press in the Departments

The perspective of more than one hundred and fifty years points up several shifts in the emphasis and volume of Washington news found in the newspaper files. Through much of the nineteenth century Congress occupied most of the space given to the capital. The attention devoted to the president varied according to the personality and press contacts of the individual who happened to occupy the White House at any given time. The Supreme Court has never been a major news source. A very marked change in the twentieth century has been the increased attention given to the executive departments. There are two reasons for that increase. One is the mere fact that the importance of the departments, the number of workers employed in them, the volume of work they do, and its effect on the lives of Americans has very greatly expanded. The second reason is that those departments employ information specialists.

In 1947 Representative Forrest A. Harness of Indiana, one of many critics, said that the government kept 45,000 "propagandists" at a cost to the taxpayers of $75,000,000 per year.[1] Other efforts to estimate the cost of the government information services, press bureaus, publications divisions, public relations offices, propaganda mills, or whatever names are applied to them have been made but are unreliable. In 1967 the Associated Press estimated the annual cost of government public information at $425,000,000.

By the mid-century a very large part of the Washington news which reached Americans originated in mimeographed "handouts" from departmental information offices. A few highlights of their growth in the Departments of Agriculture, Commerce, War, and Navy (and Defense) will show the major lines along which they moved in all divisions of government. It started in the Department of Agriculture. That department was established, to be headed by a commissioner, by an act of Congress in 1862. The act instructed the new agency to "acquire and to diffuse among the people of the United States information on subjects connected with agriculture in the most general and comprehensive sense of that word." The commissioner issued an annual report containing a wide variety of agricultural information. The reports were the ancestors of today's *Yearbook of Agriculture*. Later, in addition to the annual report the commissioner issued monthly statements in pamphlet form.[2]

In February 1889, as Cleveland's first administration drew into its final weeks, Congress extended the department's powers and placed it under a secretary with cabinet rank. On March 7 the incoming president, Benjamin Harrison, named Jeremiah M. Rusk to that post. After ten months in office, observing that he had received forty thousand letters of inquiry, he determined to provide the public with an improved information service.

His first report discussed at length the problem of getting to farmers the knowledge of improved practices which was being developed by the department's research. To achieve that end he established a Division of Records and Editing. Furthermore, in that first year he started sending to press associations, agricultural papers and other journals advance sheets summarizing the contents of the department's publications.[3] Thus originated what the Washington correspondent calls "handouts."

The next decades saw a swift upswing in the field of "press agentry" or "public relations." The same years saw a quickening buildup in government bureaus. The Interstate Commerce Act of 1887 was the first of a series of laws which placed the government in new fields of business regulation and of public welfare and research. A stream of congressional acts set up new agencies with duties that could be made effective only if there was broad public knowledge of their activities and purposes. The newcomers who were brought in to man them had before them not only the example of the Department of Agriculture but they observed with interest the new and rapidly developing public relations techniques used by business and by professional and pressure organizations.

Although Secretary of Agriculture Rusk had shown an interest in newspaper contacts from the beginning, for nearly twenty years the reports of himself and his successors, in setting out the work of the Division of Records and Editing, told only of the distribution of the department's own publications. In 1910, however, the report of the Division of Publications (an expanded successor to the Division of Records and Editing) said: "This Division maintains a list of agricultural and other newspapers and periodicals to which are sent copies of all publications issued by the Department in editions permitting such distribution, and a smaller list of Washington correspondents, to which copies of practically every important document are mailed promptly upon issue." During the previous fiscal year the Division had issued 124,850 mimeographed copies of 126 press releases.[4]

Congressmen disliked it. Members of the two houses have reacted on the floor or in committee with repeated criticism since 1908. The first debate on the press bureaus showed the lines on which both the attacks on and the justification of this activity were to take then—and still take. On March 30, 1908, the House was debating the Agriculture Appropriation Bill. While the clauses dealing with the Forest Service were up, Representative Franklin W. Mondell of Wyoming offered an amendment providing that "no part of this appropriation shall be paid . . . for . . . the preparation of any newspaper or magazine articles." A point of order was made that the amendment would limit the legal mandate to accumulate and diffuse information. Mondell replied that he had no objection to a proper bureau of publicity but he argued that the Forest Service had been paying for magazine and newspaper articles which exaggerated the value of its work and belittled its critics, especially those in Congress. The point of order was overruled. Representative Charles F. Scott of Kansas, chairman of the Agriculture Committee, said that he had written to Forester Gifford Pinchot after he heard of complaints. He offered Pinchot's answer for the *Record*.

The Forest Service, Pinchot wrote, had assigned two men, who were sometimes assisted by a third, to the preparation of press material. The long letter, written by a man who was obviously angry at criticism, maintained that this publicity was entirely proper and denied that it exaggerated the service's importance or belittled its critics. By newspaper release, it went on, the service spread valuable knowledge of improved forest practices which would have cost far more if it had been published and distributed at government expense. Scott, opposing the amendment and defending Pinchot, said that at the Department of Agriculture there were "a dozen or more men regularly employed in similar work for the other bureaus." Mondell's amendment was adopted.[5]

There was a flurry in the House over the maintenance of a "press bureau" in the Census Bureau in 1910. Representative Joseph T. Robinson of Arkansas introduced a resolution on January 18 calling on the bureau for information about the employment of a publicity man and raising a question about the legality of such work. The director of the bureau testified before the Committee on the Census, at a hearing on the resolution, that he had indeed hired a man who had worked on Washington newspapers and later in theatrical publicity. He felt that by spreading widespread information about the decennial count which was about to take place it would be easier to find competent census takers and that their work would be made easier. No further action was taken in spite of Robinson's further protests.[6]

Two years later the question was brought up again in the House. Having heard that the Bureau of Animal Industry was lax in enforcing the meat inspection laws, Representative John M. Nelson of Wisconsin introduced a resolution for an investigation. The day before the Expenditures Committee held a hearing on his move a circular was issued, he said, from the office of the Secretary of Agriculture "charging mercenary motives to this distinguished woman who furnished me with information." He referred to Mrs. Caroline Bartlett Crane, a minister from Kalamazoo, Michigan, who had become nationally known for her fight for better conditions in the slaughterhouses.

Therefore on May 20 Nelson introduced a second resolution. It charged that a "press bureau is maintained at public expense in the Department of Agriculture" by which public funds and stationery "are being daily used in circulating private, garbled, and misleading reports among the newspaper correspondents; . . . and to members of Congress" and "similar press bureaus are maintained in other departments of the Government at great public expense." It called for a special committee of five to investigate and "to make recommendations to the House as to what steps are necessary to protect public funds from newspaper exploitation without warrant of law." [7]

The resolution was referred to the Rules Committee which held a hearing the next day. Appearing as the first witness, Nelson told of his experience with the releases concerning the meat investigation. He charged that the Department of Agriculture had developed an extensive press service which, as far as the meat investigation was concerned, had tried to "befuddle, mislead and deceive the public." He recruited three correspondents to testify. The first was Charles P. Hunt who represented several Arizona newspapers. Hunt told the committee that the only legislative authorization for departmental press agents was the provision for a Bureau of Publication in the Department of Agriculture. Other departments, he said, were employing them under other names. The Bureau of Education had asked the Civil Service Commission to hold an examination for press agents under the title of "editorial assistants," he said, while the Census Bureau had a man employed as a "special agent" and other departments called their publicity experts "editorial clerks." The Bureau of Soils, the Bureau of Biological Survey, the State Department, the Bureau of Public Roads, the Smithsonian Institution, the National Museum, and the Post Office Department, he said, employed press agents under various guises.

Both of the other correspondents who testified implied that Department of Agriculture press agents had issued releases reflecting on the character and purposes of witnesses appearing in the meat investigation and on Representative Nelson himself. Isaac Gregg of the New York *World* blamed a man named John R. Bowie, whom he described as "the press agent of the Department of Agriculture." (Gregg later became a departmental information officer.) Charles W. Thompson of the New Orleans *Times* gave the committee more detail on what he called attempts at disparagement although he said that criticism of that type was the exception rather than the rule among the department press agents. Referring to the pending meat investigation, Thompson said that some one named Burroughs was to testify. The press agent, he added, brought to Thompson's office photographic copies of letters which reflected on Burroughs's character. He wished Thompson to send the material to his paper. The correspondent refused either to look at the material or to write a story on it. The press agent, he added, refused to leave the office until Thompson threatened to kick him out. The committee took no action and Nelson's resolution died.[8]

Congress then wrote what was intended to be limiting legislation which applied to the entire governmental service. That measure is still on the books but is ineffective. Today, indeed, many of the information offices have specific legislative authority and operate on appropriations granted specifically for that purpose. Others get around the law of 1913 by various pretexts. It came up on September 6 while the House was considering a deficiency appropriation bill. Representative Frederick Huntington Gillett of Massachusetts offered an amendment providing that no money appropriated "by this or any other act" be used for "the compensation of any publicity expert unless specifically appropriated for that purpose." He read to the House a Civil Service Commission circular for a "publicity expert" in the Office of Public Roads to be paid eight dollars per day. The amendment was adopted and went through the Senate without change. Whereas the 1908 action was limited to the Forest Service, this applied to all departments.[9]

Propaganda was an active weapon used by all belligerents in World War I. When the fighting was over, government officers had before them the experience of the Committee on Public Information, this country's contribution to wartime government news services. Some were eager to apply that experience in peacetime. The years after 1920 were the years in which that experience bore fruit.

When the Department of Commerce transferred some of its files to the National Archives it gave the student of government public relations history major assistance. Much of the correspondence between 1918 and 1930 which deals with publicity was gathered in one file. That file provides a ringside seat from which the student sees how Secretary Herbert Hoover and Dr. Julius Klein, director of the Bureau of Foreign and Domestic Commerce, built up a public information structure which was designed to provide for American businessmen, through the press of general circulation as well as through trade papers and direct contact, the fullest possible data on foreign trade.

In that file is an order issued by the secretary on February 18, 1914, requiring that all press notices be issued through the office of the chief clerk. Before 1919 there was established an Editorial Division with duties similar to those of the similar branch in the Department of Agriculture. It issued reports which were gathered from departmental representatives abroad and condensed them into the small publication, *Commerce Reports*. After the war, in the late years of Wilson's administration, a movement developed to expand the information service.

There was correspondence in August 1918 between O. P. Hopkins, chief of the Editorial Division, B. F. Cutler, chief of the Division of Foreign and Domestic Commerce, and E. St. Elmo Lewis, an executive of a Detroit advertising agency. The latter prepared a memorandum on how to organize a publicity setup but expressed doubt that a capable man to head it could be secured for the $3,600 per year which seemed to be available. Hopkins wrote a memorandum to Cutler on August 29 saying:

> Mr. Lewis's plan is a very ambitious one, but I believe it is sound. Only a very ambitious plan will put the Department before the country as it should be put. Perhaps Mr. Lewis is the Moses who can lead us out of the Wilderness of Obscurity.
>
> We have missed getting any big war work that we could carry on as our own. We have merely been assistants to war organizations that have taken all the credit to themselves. We have a chance to get back in the running by bringing the reconstruction work to focus in this Bureau. If we miss that chance, we are through.

In this confidential memorandum is expressed a department worker's dream of glory—through a public information program. Critics of the department services attack the idea that public funds should be used to build up a service's importance and carry on the battling which is present in interdepartmental jealousy. Those in the public relations departments deny that such is their purposes, saying they are only providing information to which the country is entitled.

Lewis's and Hopkins's ideas were not carried out immediately. Not until the administration changed were steps taken to move actively in this direction. The secretary whom President Harding named to head the department built a strong publicity structure. Herbert C. Hoover, backed by the political strength of the expanding American manufacturing industry of the 1920s, made the Bureau of Foreign and Domestic Commerce the largest branch of the department. Dr. Klein, who was placed in charge late in 1920, regarded it as a reporting agency whose principal duty was to see that information gathered by its foreign representatives reached the affected businessmen.

Commerce Reports was given an expanded new format in September 1921 with a mailing list of Washington correspondents, trade paper editors, and businessmen. A former department clerk, Paul Croghan, took charge of publicity and developed a "press room" which became a popular and convenient gathering place for Washington correspondents. This press room became a model for similar spots in other departments. Here they were given typed "press memoranda." Soon these were dropped in favor of increasing numbers of mimeographed releases. Capital reporters believed that the publicity given the Department of Commerce in these years did much to secure the Republican nomination for president for Hoover in 1928.[10]

An officer of the Pittsburgh Chamber of Commerce wrote in February 1922 for material which could be broadcast over a novel instrument—Radio Station KDKA. Croghan adjusted rapidly as he saw the possibilities in radio. By January 1923 stations were using department material in Springfield, Massachusetts, New York, St. Louis, San Francisco, Chicago, Cincinnati, New Orleans, and Atlanta. By July 1932 Dr. Klein, then assistant secretary of commerce, was himself making weekly broadcasts. Croghan's activity paid dividends. On February 27, 1930, he sent to Secretary Robert P. Lamont, whom Hoover had named to his own former post when he moved on to the White House, a memorandum based on a daily check of eight hundred daily newspapers and three hundred weeklies. From September 1929 through February 1930, he said, he collected 50,534 clippings, which represented 22.1 percent of the space given to all government departments. "Having in mind the traditionally independent attitude of the hard-boiled, sophisticated group which comprises American journalism," he wrote, "I think we are all safe in assuming that press reception is the best available criterion as to the real value of the innumerable activities in which the Department is engaged."

The Department of Agriculture also used the radio. The 1923 report of the secretary said that broadcasting as a means to disseminate market information "has been given a thorough trial during the past year and has fully demonstrated its value." [11] David F. Houston, secretary of agriculture under Wilson, set up an Office of Information attached to his office. Department publications were insufficient, he said in a statement at that time, and therefore a more popular form of dissemination was necessary. Material from those books and pamphlets he ordered to be prepared in simple news form, mimeographed, and given to the newspapers, particularly in the special districts to which it applied.[12]

The present Office of Information was established on May 1, 1925, by Secretary William M. Jardine. It gathered into one division all of the department's publication, press and radio activity. The first director was Nelson A. Crawford, who had been a Kansas newspaperman and a member of the faculty of the Kansas State College of Agricultural and Mechanical Arts. He was soon succeeded by Milton S. Eisenhower, whom one writer credits with having established the department's information policy on a firm foundation.[13] During the next fifteen years Eisenhower became well known in Washington's press and official life—more so at that time than an older brother, a West Point graduate.

A brief sketch put out by the United States Army describing the evolution of its public relations activities says that at the outbreak of the Spanish-American War an unnamed newspaper correspondent persuaded the War Department to put information for the press on a bulletin board outside the office of the secretary of war. In 1904 the adjutant general issued the first press release to newspaper correspondents, and that practice continued until June 1916.[14] On that date an aide to the secretary of war, a major named Douglas MacArthur, was designated as press release officer for the War Department.[15]

Both of the departments which then administered the armed forces and which today, combined into the Department of Defense, have a very large public information structure, lagged behind those agencies that had scientific and practical information to disseminate. The War Department set up a small news bureau, operated by civilians and attached to the office of the secretary, during the first World War. On October 14, 1921, a Press Relations Section was added to the intelligence branch of the General

Staff.[16] The United States Navy provided slightly greater service to the press. Secretary Josephus Daniels, a newspaper publisher in private life, established a Navy News Bureau during the War. During Harding's administration Assistant Secretary Theodore Roosevelt, Jr., created an Information Section in the Office of Naval Intelligence. This office maintained a small press room in the Navy Building and handled press contacts until 1939. Then it was enlarged slightly and renamed the Public Relations Branch of the Office of Naval Intelligence. Subsidiary offices were established in all naval districts.[17]

The State Department, too, organized a new press information structure in 1921. Henry Suydam, who had been a war correspondent and later a representative of the Committee on Public Information in the Netherlands, wrote to Secretary of State Hughes suggesting that dispatches from diplomatic representatives abroad should be given greater press attention. Hughes set up both a Division of Publications and a Division of Current Information. He placed Suydam in charge of the latter. The division remained small, with barely a large enough staff to answer telephone calls.[18] Meanwhile Michael J. McDermott was becoming familiar with State Department machinery. He was to become the personification of the successful government information officer, whom correspondents trusted and whose name, as the source of news, carried authority almost equal to that of the secretary himself. He became assistant chief of the Division of Current Information in 1924 and was placed in charge three years later.

Thus before Hoover entered the White House, these departments and others whose public relations history is not chronicled here made the information representative a standard fixture in a government office. Those like Agriculture and Commerce, which were ordered to carry on research and disseminate the results, built the largest staffs and used not only newspaper releases and radio but engaged in extensive original publication. Their offices, too, answered queries from individual citizens and sometimes from members of Congress. They made contacts with the motion-picture industry and with writers of books and of magazine articles. Other departments, such as State, War, and Navy, limited their service, with staffs designed to do little more than to relieve the secretary of the duty of answering individual correspondents' queries and to issue limited numbers of releases.

Meanwhile the relationship between cabinet officers and the press was moving in a direction similar to that of the presidency. In the nineteenth century contacts had been personal, with the heads of executive departments making independent arrangements with individual newspapermen. As Woodrow Wilson formalized the press conference, with all reporters admitted at set times, some department chiefs followed suit. During World War I, Secretary of War Newton D. Baker saw the press once a day. General Peyton C. March, the chief of staff, did so once a week. Secretary of the Navy Josephus Daniels received reporters twice daily during part of the war. In the morning he went to the old office of the secretary in the State, War, and Navy Building and held a press conference there. After the Navy Building was opened on Constitution Avenue (it was B Street then), he worked there in the afternoon and again talked to reporters.[19]

While departments were expanding their information branches after 1920, cabinet members further developed the press conference idea. Secretary of State Hughes normally scheduled two a day although sometimes he had an assistant secretary take one of them. After he resigned, succeeding secretaries cut them back to one a day.[20] At the same time the conference became a fixture in other departments although they were normally less frequent. When the writer of this book joined the Washington staff of the Associated Press in May 1933 a session with the newsmen at least once a week was regarded as normal for each department and independent office head.

Then the German panzer divisions swept across France and British fighter pilots fought the Luftwaffe to a standstill. President Roosevelt asked Congress to speed up American defense and the State, War, and Navy Departments, which had been comparatively out of the public eye during the years in which the country was preoccupied with domestic problems, prepared to expand. By now the administration had extensive experience with public information systems. Although more than a year was to pass before we entered the war, steps were early taken to inform Americans of the need and of the moves being taken to meet it. The information staffs of both the War and Navy Departments went through repeated reorganizations during 1939 and 1940 and expanded rapidly. Secretary of War Henry L. Stimson established the War Department Bureau of Public Relations on February 11,

1941. This bureau handled the burden during the war. A reorganization in the autumn of 1942 expanded the News Division, consolidating therein what had been the press, pictorial, publications, radio, intelligence and analysis, and continental liaison branches.

Ten officers and civilian associates maintained daily contact with about two hundred correspondents of the press, radio, and magazines. About a hundred telephoned questions were answered daily. Total personnel, including clerks and administrators, numbered thirty-three at the beginning, climbed to fifty, and dropped off to twenty-seven in 1947. With Secretary Stimson holding weekly press conferences, it fell to the Bureau of Public Relations to arrange the details, including the agenda, and the notification of the newsmen. The bureau also arranged press conferences with other department executives. Between five hundred and nine hundred mimeographed releases were issued every month during the war although these dropped to about two hundred after V-J Day. Navy public relations moved through nearly parallel channels. Expansion in 1939 found this duty still handled by the Public Relations Branch of the Office of Naval Intelligence. On May 1, 1941, Secretary Frank Knox, who was in private life the publisher of the Chicago *Daily News*, established the Office of Public Relations.[21]

The State Department, too, had to expand. McDermott remained in charge of a growing Division of Current Information. When the Office of War Information was established to coordinate information during the struggle, the State Department, like the War and Navy Departments, retained control of the release of its own press material although it cooperated with the OWI in certain other aspects of its overall task. The staff of McDermott's division climbed to fifteen officers and included about fifty other workers.[22]

In 1944, with Secretary of State Cordell Hull ill and Edward R. Stettinius actively directing the department, McDermott was given the title of special assistant to the secretary for press relations. Although the principal function of the Division of Current Information had always been press relations, it also carried on certain other public contacts. Stettinius set up the Office of Public Affairs to take over those other duties. Thus McDermott, as assistant to the secretary for press relations, was allowed to devote his time entirely to contacts with the press and radio and to providing a summary of press reaction for the department. When James F. Byrnes became secretary of state in July 1945 he found facing reporters' questions a strain. In place of his predecessors' daily press conferences, therefore, he refused to schedule more than one a week and ordered McDermott himself to take charge of the daily delineation of department news for newspaper and radio correspondents. But they insisted on being allowed to quote an official source for their information. Therefore, McDermott told them to use his own name, and thus became the identifiable official department spokesman.

The State Department press structure was reorganized when the Republican administration took over in 1953. McDermott was named ambassador to El Salvador, and he died in August 1955. The title of special assistant to the secretary for press relations was abolished although McDermott's staff structure remained largely intact and was folded into the Office of Public Affairs. This structure, with only minor changes, remains in effect. The News Division operates under the direction of the assistant secretary of state for public affairs. The chief of the News Division holds a daily press briefing with correspondents, and his name appears in their stories as the authoritative source of their information. The group that met him every day in 1971 included a large force of correspondents for the foreign press. This daily conference has replaced the daily session with the secretary of state which had been held by those who preceded Byrnes.

The relationship between the secretary of state and the press which is outlined here reflects what has been a general movement in the cabinet departments and independent offices. Half a century ago and more, as we have seen, department heads saw correspondents on an informal and personal basis. A greater distance between the administrative heads of government and the press developed when the regular press conference became the point of contact. That coincided with the development of the information services and the practice of the information officer replacing his chief as the spokesman. Press conferences became less frequent. Those newsmen who protest that the public relations men serve as a barrier between the reporter and the responsible department head see in this development support for their argument.

Secretary of State Dulles normally held news conferences every two weeks when he was in Washington and talked to reporters frequently during his many trips abroad. Secretary Rusk did so about once a month. Until September 1967 they were televised under rules similar to those which applied to President Eisenhower's filmed conferences. That is, cameras recorded the meetings. But the films could not be used until the transcript had been checked and the films released. The department did not attempt to forbid reporters to use direct quotations on what the secretary had said, but warned them that they did so at their own risk.

On September 8, 1967, this rule was changed to authorize immediate use of the secretary's voice and image on news broadcasts. Robert J. McCloskey, deputy assistant secretary of state for public affairs and director of the Division of News, wrote to this author on September 20, 1967, however, that "We will continue to reserve on the possible necessity of adding to or amending the official transcript, but where it is not necessary we will authorize his remarks for immediate broadcast." [23] Selections from the film of the secretary of state's news conferences are normally used on the regular chain news shows. They are seldom broadcast live. McCloskey has told television news chiefs that if they wish to do so they should indicate that wish in advance. On two occasions under Rusk such agreements were made.

Taking office with the administration of January 20, 1969, Secretary William E. Rogers waited until April 7 to hold his first news conference. McCloskey wrote to the writer of this book on April 4 that Rogers would follow the same rules as those which applied under Rusk as regards filming the conference and direct quotation. Selections from his first conference were presented on the chain news shows that evening.

The information offices of the War and Navy Departments remained in existence as those bodies became the Department of the Army and the Department of the Navy within the new Department of Defense in 1947. And the new Department of the Air Force, which had built an extensive information branch when it was still the Army Air Corps during the war and after, kept that service in being. When James Forrestal was named the first secretary of defense in September 1947, a reorganization of the information service was one of the matters to which he gave early attention. On October 10 he set up a Public Relations Advisory Council consisting of newspapermen and information officers of the services. An Office of Public Information was established on July 19, 1948, and a press room was set aside in the Pentagon on August 11. These were temporary steps. An organization designed to be permanent was created by an order which was signed on March 17, 1949. It established the Office of Public Information for the National Military Establishment as part of the Office of the Secretary. An assistant to the secretary of defense was detailed to serve as Director of Public Information and as principal advisor to the secretary and to the War Council on public information matters.[24]

The Office of Public Information has been brought under the assistant secretary of defense for public affairs and has tried to bring under its control, instead of leaving it up to the information branches of the three services, most information for the press, radio and television, magazines, books, and motion pictures insofar as those matters are handled at the Pentagon. Each of the three services, however, maintains a structure which controls information officers at each base and installation throughout the world. On November 28, 1969, Harold Willens, organizer of a businessmen's group opposed to the Vietnam war, said on a national television program that the Department of Defense maintained 6,130 public relations men.

The secretaries of defense have habitually held a news conference about once a month, leaving their spokesmen in the Office of the Assistant Secretary to speak for them at other times.[25] That was the policy of both Robert S. McNamara and Clark Clifford, and was followed by Melvin Laird in the early months of the Nixon administration. Laird issued an order on March 7, 1969, saying "I intend that the Department of Defense shall conduct its activities in an open manner, consistent with the need for security." At another point the order said: "I want to emphasize that the sole purpose of . . . planning and coordination will be to expedite the flow of information to the public. Propaganda has no place in Department of Defense public information programs."

Throughout the development of the government information services there have been varying degrees of control exercised from the White House. Neither the president nor his press secretary, however, has ever attempted to dictate the appointment of departmental information officers. In the larger departments an incoming secretary, as the administration has changed, has often named as his information chief a man who had been associated with him in a public information capacity in his prior experience. Sometimes he was a Washington correspondent who covered that official's actions in earlier years. But if the top man changes with the administration in the major departments, the bulk of the office force continues in existence, giving continuity of service and advice by men who make a career of it. Many come up in the Civil Service without news experience.

Nevertheless it has become customary for the president's press secretary to keep in touch with departmental information officers and to try to bring about unity of information policy. Salinger, for instance, held regular weekly meetings with them. On being named press secretary to the president, Ziegler was not extended the authority that Salinger and Hagerty had exercised over the departmental information officers. That duty devolved on a new office which Nixon created—that of director of communications for the federal branch.

Herbert Klein, who has been named to the post, had been editor of the San Diego *Union* and had been associated with Nixon since 1946. He was given a staff of eleven aides and carpeted offices in the Executive Office Building (formerly the State, War, and Navy Building across West Executive Avenue to the west of the White House). Each of his senior assistants is assigned certain of the departments and independent offices. Each morning the aide talks by telephone with the information officer of those branches and thus keeps informed as to the news situation. Occasionally, but only on rare occasions, a release is prepared in Klein's office to be put out by a departmental office. As a result, Klein is able to coordinate information policy and avoid the conflicts and inconsistencies which sometimes appear. He has, moreover, been given credit for urging reluctant officials in the new administration to pursue a liberal news policy. Within the first weeks in which he held office he persuaded some cabinet officers and others who had avoided reporters to make themselves available and to talk more freely than they otherwise would have.[26]

Newsmen have regarded this attempt to coordinate information from the White House with suspicion. They have feared that centralized control by the president's press secretary could lead to censorship in a rigidly governed government propaganda operation. A typical exchange took place in correspondence between Eugene S. Pulliam, Jr., publisher of the Indianapolis *News*, and Salinger which was published in *Editor and Publisher* in April 1961. Pulliam asked nine questions of Salinger, one of which was: "What is the purpose of your weekly meetings with the principal government information chiefs? Is it for 'coordination'?" Salinger replied that the sessions "are designed principally to keep each of us informed about what is going on in the huge Federal establishment." He agreed that "it is logically possible to impute censorship motives to such meetings; it is also possible to impute positive moves such as a desire to get more information out and in better detail." Despite Salinger's justification of the sessions on the ground of improved information, and despite the press's confidence in Klein personally, the possibilities of censorship are regarded by some newsmen as inherently dangerous. The way in which the wartime Office of War Information dealt with the problem and certain other aspects of the press-governmental relationship will be considered in later chapters.

17. Enter Radio, Television, and Magazines

Until 1920 newspapers were the only effective means by which Americans got news. Correspondents had organized themselves and made arrangements at the Capitol, the White House, the Supreme Court, and the executive departments on that assumption. Popular weekly and monthly magazines developed rapidly after 1890 and some gave space to public matters in their columns. Capital news writers contributed to them but regarded them as a sideline. By 1930 radio was invading the newspaper's monopoly as a news distributing agent. Led by *Time*, which was founded in 1923, a new type of news magazine was appearing, accompanied by spiraling circulations. Specialized journals which found subscribers among certain business, professional, or labor interests were expanding and demanding expert coverage of Washington.

In radio's first years, after 1922, it was an entertainment medium, broadcasting music, speeches, and sports. News coverage and transmission is expensive and requires an elaborate organization and experienced workers. It took newspapers more than half a century to develop adequate agencies to do that work. If radio was to go into news coverage it must secure the cooperation of the existing newspaper arrangements or build up its own system of reporting and transmitting. Eventually it did both. By 1924 it was technically possible to broadcast over nationwide chains the national conventions of both political parties. James D. Preston, superintendent of the Senate Press Gallery and chief of press arrangements for both party conclaves, had also to provide for reporters for the new medium. On the eve of the election the following November, Coolidge, running for a full term in the office which he had held since Harding's death, broadcast a speech from the White House which was carried over twenty-seven stations from Boston to San Francisco. His inaugural address on March 4, 1925, was likewise broadcast.

The national conventions, returns, and inaugural addresses were broadcast in 1928 and 1932. Presidential radio speeches became routine. Meanwhile both the United Press and the International News Service were experimenting with sale of news for use over the air although the Associated Press held back. The National Broadcasting Company and the Columbia Broadcasting System were expanding. The American Newspaper Publishers Association, fearing that radio would cut newspaper circulations, tried to throw up a roadblock. Therefore Paul W. White, formerly with the United Press, began to build a newsgathering system for CBS. In November 1933 the Columbia News Gathering System, Inc., applied for admission to the congressional press galleries. The Standing Committee's records contain ninety-eight letters and forty-one telegrams from newspapermen who were practically unanimous in opposing the application. Some of the critics argued that since stations were licensed by the Federal Radio Commission they could not operate on the same basis as did the newspaper, with its constitutionally-protected freedom. The application was rejected.

David Lawrence, publisher of the *United States Daily*, began broadcasting over NBC in 1928. He gave way to H. R. Baukhage, one of his staff, in 1934. Other Washington newspapermen now became interested in radio. Publishers found that radio news not only did not cut newspaper circulation but in some circumstances actually stimulated it. The years between 1934 and 1939 saw more and more newspapermen become radio reporters and saw the chains and individual stations draw from the ranks of those with newspaper experience to build their own newsgathering and news broadcasting staffs. The same years saw some journals which owned broadcasting stations order their Washington correspondents to record vocal discussions of capital news and rush the records home to go over the air. And the Transradio Press Service, Inc., appeared. Its promoters planned for it to provide news coverage for radio stations like that which the telegraphic press services offered the newspapers. It died eventually, the victim of competition as the existing strong press services went in for radio news.

Some radio reporters, such as Earl Godwin of NBC, kept their press connections and were therefore admitted to the press galleries at the Capitol and to the White House press room and press conferences. Others, Fred Morrison of Transradio Press, for instance, had no such claim. He and others like him were forced to report Congress from the public galleries and enjoyed none of the arrangements whereby accredited newspapermen could call members off the floor for interviews or sit at press tables in committee hearings. Seats in the public galleries subjected them to rules which forbade visitors to write. Appearance of a pencil and paper to take notes brought stern words from the doorkeeper and possible expulsion.[1]

Fulton Lewis, Jr., became a reporter on the Washington *Herald* in 1924. He began to broadcast fishing and hunting news over Station WCAP in the capital a year later. In 1928 he joined the staff of the International News Service and in 1937 he went to the Mutual Broadcasting System as a reporter. In 1938 he applied to the Standing Committee of Correspondents for admission to the press galleries and was turned down. He determined to break down the barriers.

He wrote to Senator Matthew M. Neely of West Virginia, chairman of the Senate Rules Committee, and to every member of the House Rules Committee arguing that printing processes should not have a perpetual monopoly on reporting news. Representative John J. Dempsey of New Mexico, a Democrat and a majority member of the House Rules Committee, ran into Lewis at a local hotel a few days later. He promised to support the move. The two planned strategy.

Lewis's original plan had been to go over the heads of the Standing Committee and to try to bring about an amendment of the rules to admit radio men to the existing press galleries. Now he decided to seek separate facilities and a separate rule.[2] On February 13, 1939, the Standing Committee debated a letter from Speaker William B. Bankhead asking the committee's views on applications by radio and magazine reporters. The chairman appointed a special committee to discuss the matter with him.

The minutes do not record the results of their conference with the Speaker.

Meanwhile Senators Guy M. Gillette, an Iowa Democrat, and W. Warren Barbour, Republican, of New Jersey, formed a bipartisan group within the Senate Rules Committee to support Lewis and the radio newsgatherers. Although no resolution was offered immediately, a Rules subcommittee consisting of those two held a hearing on February 24. Lewis was the principal witness supporting a change. He argued that his function was the same as that of any reporter covering the Senate. He expressed doubt that more than six would apply and said that they would not want broadcasting facilities at the Capitol. They sought the right to attend proceedings in a gallery reserved for them and typewriters and a place to write. Neville Miller, president of the National Association of Broadcasters, and Kenneth Berkeley, general manager of Stations WRC and WMAL in Washington, also appeared.

Alfred F. Flynn of the *Wall Street Journal,* chairman of the Standing Committee, spoke for that group. Conceding that there was merit in the radio reporters' plea, he argued that the press gallery was already too crowded. Admission of the broadcasters, he said, would open the way for other groups "who have been unable to qualify under the high standards established by Congress for membership in the gallery," and he pointed out that the Standing Committee had found it necessary to impose "Special Card Days," limiting attendance when news of peculiarly great interest developed. On those occasions, he said, more than four-fifths of the gallery membership were barred.[3]

For half a century Senate rules had provided for a press gallery, had limited admission to newspaper reporters, and had directed the Standing Committee, acting under the supervision of the Rules Committee, to govern it. Before radio reporters could be admitted it would be necessary to amend the Senate rule. Barbour and Gillette introduced the necessary resolution on April 6.[4] They would rewrite the last sentence of Rule 24. That was the sentence which, when it was drawn in 1884, confined the use of the press gallery to reporters for daily newspapers. As they drew it, the rule would also admit "bona fide reporters for daily news dissemination through radio, wire, wireless and similar media of transmission." The Senate adopted it on April 25.[5]

Meanwhile the House of Representatives moved in the same direction. Dempsey introduced a resolution on April 18 to add a paragraph to Rule 34.[6] That was the rule which had been originally drawn in 1857, was extensively rewritten under Randall in 1880, and amended several times since in minor details. It set aside the press gallery and authorized the Speaker, acting through the Standing Committee, to control it. Dempsey reported the additional paragraph out of the Rules Committee and it was adopted without debate on the 20th. It established a separate gallery for "reporters of news to be disseminated by radio, wireless and similar means of transmission," and placed control in the "Standing Committee of Radio Reporters, subject to the direction and control of the Speaker." [7]

One privilege extended to some newspapermen was overlooked by this paragraph. It did not admit to the floor the radio counterparts of the press associations, as did the rule governing the press galleries. In spite of the fact that the reporters of the telegraphic press associations did not invoke the privilege and that the original reason for granting it had long since been forgotten, the radiomen asked for the same treatment. On May 30, 1940, the House added the following clause to the rule: "and the Speaker may admit to the floor, under such regulations as he may prescribe, one representative of the National Broadcasting Company, one of the Columbia Broadcasting System, one of the Mutual Broadcasting System, and one of the Transradio Press Service." [8] In actual practice no seats on the floor have been assigned them.[9]

The radio reporters now had the same authority in the rules that the newspapermen had won after 1877. They prepared to go the rest of the way along the trail that the journalists had blazed. First, they set up an association to govern the radio galleries in the way the Standing Committee governed the press galleries. Then they approached the Senate Rules Committee and the Speaker. Lewis submitted a proposed set of regulations which were adapted from those which Randall had worked out with the Standing Committee after 1877. Lewis's draft was accepted by the governing authority in each house and was printed in the

Congressional Directory. In place of the Standing Committee of Correspondents, the Executive Committee of the Radio Correspondents' Association was placed in control. In the second paragraph the sentence which required certification in writing for admission was made to read: "It shall be prerequisite to membership that the radio station, system, or news-gathering agency which the applicant represents shall certify in writing to the Radio Correspondents' Association that the applicant conforms to the regulations of Paragraph 1." Other necessary points were also amended to conform.

Speaker Bankhead accepted the changes. The Senate Rules Committee also did so, although in writing a clause to be added to the *Regulations Governing the Senate Wing of the United States Capitol* it preceded them with a sentence reading "A section of the gallery heretofore set aside for the Ladies Gallery shall be set apart for the use of the radio correspondents."

For that was the next step. Now space was needed. In each House the radio reporters were given the front row of seats in the gallery which adjoined the press gallery and ran from the press gallery rail to the east corner of the chamber. A rail was installed behind that row to separate the reporters from the visitors in the seats farther to the rear. Entrance was gained from the corridor to the east. In addition to a gallery from which to observe and report floor proceedings, space was needed in which to write, telephone, receive messages, file records, and rest. Newspapermen had long been provided with such space. The Speaker and the Architect of the Capitol agreed to build a small room on the gallery floor in the broad corridor to the east of the House chamber. From here the radio reporters walked about forty feet to the seats reserved for them in the legislative hall itself. A simple ceremony officially opened the facilities on May 20, 1939. Robert M. Menaugh, a former page who had continued in the employ of the House, was selected by the executive committee and appointed by the Speaker as superintendent.

The Senate moved a little more slowly. In the summer of 1939 carpenters moved a wooden partition which had set off a part of the gallery floor corridor to the east of the Senate Chamber to add that area to the press gallery. Here new partitions gave space for the Senate radio gallery a few feet from the entrance to the seats reserved for radio reporters overlooking the chamber itself. It was incomplete when Congress adjourned. In September Germany invaded Poland and President Roosevelt called Congress into special session. Since no Senate radio gallery superintendent had been named, Menaugh took over nominal direction and arranged to have furniture installed. The following January, D. Harold McGrath was placed in charge. He had worked on newspapers in Colorado and in Walla Walla, Washington, and had come to the capital as secretary to Senator Lewis B. Schwellenbach of that state.

Acceptance by Congress cleared the way to the rest of Washington's news facilities. Stephen S. Early decided that since doors at the Capitol had been opened to them, radio news reporters should have the right to attend presidential press conferences. A move was started to refer to the former "press conferences" held by Roosevelt and by cabinet officers as "news conferences." Radio reporters were admitted to the press rooms in the executive departments. When King George VI and Queen Elizabeth of Great Britain came in June, credentials to some of the events of the visit were issued to radio reporters on the same basis as those issued to newspapermen. And social recognition was extended when they and their wives were invited to White House receptions, as newspaper correspondents and their wives had been for many years.

Radio newsmen worked with these facilities through World War II. Afterwards, with television about to appear and with the need for broadcast booths apparent (in spite of Lewis's testimony to the contrary in 1939), they asked more space. In the back wall of the Senate radio gallery was an old door which had been locked. It opened into an office which could be reached through a different entrance and which was then occupied by the Secretary to the Majority. In 1945 the Rules Committee found other space for him and added that room to the radio gallery. Booths were installed from which senators and correspondents could make live broadcasts and greater space was made available for typewriters, records, and a lounge. A booth was assigned to each of the four major chains. The room was partially ready in time for broadcasts to be made from there on V-E Day. Meanwhile, Vice-President Truman had promised McGrath that he would dedicate it when it was complete. Although he moved on to the White House before that time came he kept his promise.

On November 7, 1945, the president took scissors and cut a ribbon which had been stretched across the door. The new Senate radio gallery was open.

The House of Representatives, too, provided a larger area. On the gallery floor on the west side of the House wing was an old storeroom adjoining the Foreign Affairs Committee room. By passing through, one reached a steep, narrow stairway to similar quarters on a lower level. This space on both floors was turned over to the radio reporters and broadcast booths installed. At the same time the allotted gallery seats in the legislative hall were moved from the southeast corner to the southwest, a few feet from the door to the new workrooms. The new radio quarters were occupied on January 1, 1946.[10]

At about the same time the White House took steps to improve contacts with the four major radio chains. Whenever the president wished to make a "fireside chat" or arrange for radio or television coverage of any other occasion it was necessary for his press secretary to consult a responsible officer of each chain separately and arrange time and details to conform. Late in 1945 Charles G. Ross asked the chains to set up a committee so that he could deal with a single individual to arrange details of presidential broadcasts. Each of the four, therefore, named from its Washington news staff a member and an alternate of a "White House Liaison Group." One member becomes the spokesman at the White House for all of the chains. The spokesman changes every three months. The liaison group has continued to cooperate with presidential press secretaries.[11]

After 1945 it became customary for radio reporters to use the radio galleries not only to write their newscasts. They invited senators and representatives to visit them to be interviewed in live broadcasts or on tape. Then television came. It brought with it plans for studios where members of the two houses could go on the air before the cameras or where films could be made of them. In 1947 three NBC reporters, Earl Godwin, Richard Harkness, and Robert McCormick went on the air in a televised panel discussion, the first to be broadcast direct from the Senate radio gallery. On October 5 of that year Truman initiated presidential telecasts from the White House by appearing before the cameras in a speech opening a food conservation program. One of the broadcast booths in the Senate radio gallery was turned into a small television studio, but it made possible a picture only of the head of a senator as he spoke before the camera.

Neither house of Congress allows its floor proceedings to be photographed or telecast except on a very few special occasions. Senate committees may do so, but the Speaker refuses to permit House committees to. In 1969 broadcast journalists hoped that Speaker McCormack would change his mind eventually on that point. But the joint sessions of the two houses to hear the president deliver his annual message on the state of the Union have been presented on the country's television screens every year since 1947. Is this the last step in news transmission—from the galloping horsemen of 1833 to video?

By 1953 the Senate radio gallery that had been rebuilt eight years earlier was definitely inadequate. Willard F. Schadel of CBS-Radio, chairman of a special committee of the Radio and Television Correspondents' Association (the word "television" was added to the organization's name that year) went before the legislative subcommittee of the Senate Appropriations Committee on July 26, 1953, to urge funds to remodel the gallery. When the then-existing Senate facilities were provided in 1945, he said, they serviced four major networks and twenty-five individual stations, while there were no television networks. In 1953, he said, there were one hundred and fifty-five correspondents representing four major radio networks, four major television networks, three major television film agencies and thirty-five individual radio stations or special news services.[12] Congress appropriated $33,000. During the recess workmen invaded the gallery. By the time the lawmakers returned in January 1954, reconstruction was complete. The room was remodeled to provide four booths for broadcast or recording. In addition, there are two television studios, each ten by fifteen feet. Films or live telecasts can be made in them simultaneously. A folding acoustical door between them can be opened to provide a single studio, twenty by fifteen feet. This is large enough to make possible a variety of shots on a panel program. Office space and typewriters are found along one side of the area and in a balcony over the booths. Nevertheless, by 1969 the radio and television reporters found these facilities inadequate and asked the Senate for money for reconstruction. The necessary appropriations have not been made, however.

The advent of television and the planned construction of the Rayburn Office Building and the extended east front of the Capitol led the radio and television reporters to seek more space. Menaugh wrote to this author on March 23, 1968, that as early as 1947 he and the officers of the Radio and Television Correspondents' Association asked Speaker Martin to assign them the Foreign Affairs Committee rooms when that committee was given new quarters. Those rooms were on the southwest corner of the gallery floor, adjoining the House radio and television gallery and opposite the entrance to the press gallery. Plans for the Rayburn Building included a new subway to that structure which would end at the Capitol at a point where new elevators and a new elevator lobby would be needed. The new elevators have been installed on the west side of the building and reach the gallery floor at the point where the House radio and television gallery used to be. Construction, of course, forced the reporters to move.

Menaugh and officers of the association called on Speaker Rayburn on August 19, 1960, and on June 29, 1961, to ask that the Foreign Affairs Committee rooms be assigned to them. On the latter date the Speaker promised to accede to their request as soon as the committee moved to its new quarters. After his death Speaker McCormack confirmed the arrangements. Meanwhile, while elevator construction was going on the reporters were given temporary space in part of their new quarters. Remodeling cost about $130,000. The new rooms, which included broadcast booths and enlarged space for writing, were occupied in April 1966.

Three rooms were also provided in the Rayburn Office Building. One is a work room, with typewriters, telephones, and booths for radio broadcasting and for feeding audio lines. A smaller room was originally intended for controls but has been adapted as a general workroom. The third is a studio, thirty feet by thirty feet, which contains furniture similar to that in a congressional office. There, members may be filmed for televised statements in surroundings that appear to be their own offices. At the Rayburn Building there is also a place assigned to park a large mobile television unit.

Additional space was also provided in the new Senate Office Building. A studio equipped with the furniture of an office, similar to that in the Rayburn Building, was included. There are also darkrooms for news photographers. In the Capitol a former committee room in the gallery floor opposite the west entrance to the press gallery was made available as the photographers' press gallery. The radio and television reporters' success in securing special congressional recognition and facilities separate from the press gallery reacted not only to their benefit. It established a precedent which enabled magazine writers to secure the same advantages.

Time was established in 1923. The "trade press," each journal of which is devoted to articles dealing with a particular business or profession, appeared as a result of the country's enormous industrial expansion after the Civil War and it grew rapidly after World War I. With the government from 1920 on exercising an increasing control over business and offering it increasing service, trade paper editors required more and more material from the capital. In 1933 David Lawrence changed his *United States Daily*, with its newspaper format, to the weekly *United States News*, a slick-paper magazine. It was soon followed by *Newsweek*, which became a competitor of *Time*.

Therefore, the decade after 1930 saw many newspapermen in Washington looking to magazines, first as a supplementary field of writing and income, and later as a new and better-paying full-time employment field. But if a newspaper correspondent severed his connections with the daily press, or if a news magazine or trade journal brought in a reporter who lacked a newspaper tieup, he had to report from the public galleries and be subject to the same disadvantages that the early radio reporters faced.

At the beginning, *Time* relied on newspaper writers in Washington. They corresponded for the magazine on a part-time basis. The first was Henry Cabot Lodge, then a member of the Washington staff of the New York *Herald-Tribune*, later a United States senator from Massachusetts, ambassador to the United Nations, and ambassador to Vietnam. Later Harold Horan became the first full-time correspondent. In 1935 its real expansion started when two more correspondents were added. Two years later *Time* correspondents applied for admission to the press galleries. Under the regulations limiting membership to those filing daily newspaper telegraphic material, they were barred. In 1939 the activities of the radio correspondents raised the question again. Minutes of the Standing Committee of Correspondents show that on April 29 of that year Horan of *Time* and Don Kirkley of the Oil News Bureau applied and were rejected. At the same meeting the correspondents discussed the arrangements being made for separate radio galleries.

After the two houses of Congress amended their rules to make possible facilities for the broadcasters, the magazine writers tried again. The rule changes which the radio reporters had secured made it possible for the Speaker and the Senate Rules Committee to provide for the periodical writers on the authority which they already possessed, without calling up action on the floor again. Appeals were made to the responsible authorities in each house. As a result, it was agreed in 1941 to recognize the periodical press galleries and to give them a listing in the *Congressional Directory*. Official recognition meant that they had the privilege of the press tables at committee hearings and certain other rights at the Capitol. Furthermore, congressional recognition and *Congressional Directory* listing opened the doors to presidential and cabinet news conferences and press rooms.

As had been done in the case of the radio reporters, regulations similar to the time-honored press gallery provisions adapted in phraseology at the necessary points, were sanctioned by the Speaker and the Senate Rules Committee. The governing body was the Executive Committee of the Periodical Correspondents' Association. The regulations appeared for the first time in the *Congressional Directory* issued in May 1941. Names of forty-five writers were listed. Of those, twelve worked for *Time* and six for *Newsweek*.

Meanwhile the periodical staff men worked under makeshift arrangements. Frank McNaughton, who became a congressional correspondent of *Time* in 1941, wrote to this author in June 1954:

> *The magazine reporters were recognized by the House and Senate as legitimate newsgatherers, but they were without any facilities for work; no telephones, no access to releases (other than friendly association with the Press Galleries, which could not be abused), no typewriters, no room in which to work or hang a hat. The Speaker's Office (Mr. Sam Rayburn of Texas) did allow the periodicals men use of a telephone in a washstand booth and a place to hang hats. Mr. Rayburn always gave all news media full cooperation, as did Mr. Bankhead before him.*

In 1946 McNaughton, then chairman of the Executive Committee of the Periodical Correspondents' Association, lobbied for more space. When the radio correspondents moved to their new quarters in the House in 1946, the periodical writers were given their former gallery, both the seats overlooking the legislative hall from the southeast corner and the small room on the gallery floor to the east. In January 1947, with the Republicans in control of both houses, McNaughton approached Senator Wayland Brooks of Illinois, chairman of the Rules Committee. The committee acted quickly.

In February the chamber on the gallery floor on the west side of the Senate wing which had been the Minority Conference Room was turned over to the periodical press writers. At the same time they were given the front row of seats in the public gallery in the northwest corner of the Chamber itself, extending from the press gallery to the corner on the west. Access was gained from a door opening into a corridor almost directly opposite the periodical press gallery workroom. William M. Perry was named superintendent.[13] Thus the periodical press reporters had recognition and working facilities comparable to those of the newspaper and radio and television staff men.

18. The Press and Twentieth-Century War

During the Civil War Lincoln kept a sharp eye on public opinion. But he made no effort to direct it. Steps even to inform the country as to the administration's goals consisted of little more than the messages to Congress and other rare public utterances. Lincoln led the Union to success through four years of bloodshed in spite of cool support from divided public opinion and in spite of harsh press opposition. As the United States went into World War I and demanded the public backing which modern warfare demands, Wilson, too, faced divided public opinion and widespread opposition.

In 1861 the president had no precedent to guide him in providing machinery to publicize his aims. In 1917, however, the limited experience with government information services, the development of the public relations field and the precedent of those foreign powers which had used active propaganda as a weapon during three years of fighting showed the way. The result was the Committee on Public Information. George Creel, its chairman, said the committee did not disseminate "propaganda" in the widely accepted and critical sense of that word. Furthermore, as he saw it, it was not an agency of censorship. In three books which he published since the war he held that the Committee on Public Information limited itself to telling the truth regarding America's war participation and aims.[1]

Creel had no earlier organization to which he could look for experience or guidance. But in his case that was an advantage.

Possessed of imagination and impulsive self-confidence and enjoying the president's support, he leaped into innovations with little or no restraint from government agencies which might react with jealousy. Many congressmen were suspicious, some Washington correspondents quarreled with him, and editorials criticized him. Nevertheless, he was able to write later that the committee had achieved most of its aims. The disinterested authors of a separate study reached the same conclusion.[2]

The committee was created to meet two problems which the administration faced when Congress declared war on April 6, 1917. First, antiwar sentiment was strong. The previous November Wilson had been reelected largely because thousands of voters credited him with having kept us out of the European struggle. Now, less than six months later, the president asked that we join the fight against the Central Powers. Reasons for the administration's switch had to be made clear. Secondly, the Civil War experience with newspaper revelation of military secrets and British and French experience with newspaper censorship caused discussion of how best to restrain the press. The system that was worked out, a voluntary censorship which the country's journals were asked to accept as a patriotic duty, was carried out under Creel's watchful eye.

On April 13, 1917, a joint letter to the president over the signatures of the secretaries of state, war, and navy discussed the problem and said that the two functions, censorship and publicity, could be joined in one agency. The chairman, they wrote, "should be a civilian, preferably some writer of proved courage, ability and vision, able to gain the understanding cooperation of the press and at the same time rally the authors of the country to a work of service." The next day Wilson issued an executive order instructing the three secretaries and Creel to comprise the committee.[3]

Creel was born in Missouri, the son of a Virginian who had served in the Confederate army. He spent his early years editing a magazine in Kansas City and later engaged in journalism and in fighting for municipal reforms in Denver. He became imbued with Wilson's form of liberalism and took active part in the presidential campaigns of 1912 and 1916, supporting the man who became his wartime chief.

The committee was created while Congress debated the

Espionage Act, a measure designed to prevent or punish active interference with mobilization. Although the press censorship sections which were considered in early drafts were deleted before the act was passed, to many of the country's newspapermen Creel's agency became, in critical editorials, the government's "censorship bureau."[4] But Creel pointed out proudly that no compulsion was used. Censorship was voluntary and was carried out by having a card printed which listed eighteen types of news relating to troop or ship movements and developments of secret military devices which newspapers were asked not to print if the facts came into their possession. Copies of the card, designed for bulletin boards, were given to each newspaper. Furthermore they were notified that the Division of News of the Committee on Public Information would be open around the clock and could be called at any time for advice on questionable items. Creel wrote that there were violations "as a matter of course," but that as the press came to realize the need for restraint "the voluntary censorship grew in strength and certainty."[5]

At least that was Creel's public attitude in 1920. Twenty years later he looked back at his experience and saw the matter differently. In 1941 he wrote that voluntary censorship had been a failure and that the press had unpatriotically published much information that should have been withheld. He vigorously opposed reinstituting it if war were to come again. Any information that became available to the press, he wrote in a magazine article which was published a few months before the Japanese attack on Pearl Harbor, also became available to enemy agents. In place of newspaper censorship he urged very rigorous control of communications at the nation's borders in order to intercept messages from enemy spies.[6]

But the Division of News was in operation more to disseminate information than to censor it. Creel moved early to establish contact with the press corps. The minutes of the Standing Committee of Correspondents describe a special meeting in the Navy Department library, the first temporary office of the Committee on Public Information, on the evening of April 20, 1917. "The committee met informally with George Creel, newly appointed chief of the publicity bureau for the State, War, Navy and other departments," the secretary recorded. "Mr. Creel outlined briefly his plans for publicity to the committee." On May 9

Creel laid his voluntary censorship plan before another meeting with the Standing Committee, this time in his new office at 10 Jackson Place. The minutes still describe him as "chief of the publicity bureau" and said, "Mr. Creel, after preliminary remarks, presented press regulations as formulated by the committee on public information. General discussion followed. Opinions were that the spirit of the regulations was reasonable and fair although objection was raised to some of the provisions." The Standing Committee debated calling a meeting of all of the correspondents, but the minutes do not show whether or not it was held.

As the war progressed the Division of News became the official channel for issuing mimeographed releases for all government agencies. Reporters maintained their own contacts at the War and Navy Departments, nevertheless, and covered the press conferences held by the secretaries. Creel reported that he cooperated closely with the heads of the two military departments but that Secretary of State Robert Lansing remained distant.[7] The Committee on Public Information issued mimeographed summaries of the press conferences, published a small-format newspaper, and made other announcements bearing on the war program. It gave out daily casualty lists.[8]

The Division of News and the dissemination of official information to the press constituted only part of the committee's work. The "Four Minute Men" worked under its guidance telling the country of war needs in short speeches in motion picture theaters and the lecture platform. Another division mobilized the nation's artists to plaster the billboards with posters intended to arouse patriotic spirit. A Division of Films put out motion pictures, while other branches told the story through labor and women's organizations and by advertising. A large Foreign Press Section, which maintained offices in New York and San Francisco, distributed material to the newspapers in the allied and neutral countries while various devices delivered the story of this country's side of the dispute behind the enemy's lines.

By the time the threat of active part in a world war cast its shadow across the country for the second time in this century, the government had had extensive experience with public information. On the other hand, in some respects it found that very experience, providing many viewpoints as to detail, confusing. The emergency programs of the New Deal had seen agencies multiply rapidly as the administration changed its approach to its complicated problems. Now the question of public information as the military effort sped up and as the extensive propaganda circulated by the Axis powers had to be counteracted saw new, temporary organizations created, recreated and multiplied. Each new agency had its own public information branch.

In World War I the lack of experience had caused the whole matter to be left to Creel's committee, and he prepared his program with little interference from the outside. World War II, however, saw not only a rapid expansion of the existing departmental information services but it also saw new temporary agencies divide between them the various tasks which the Committee on Public Information had carried out alone. They also took on themselves some jobs which Creel had not attempted.

After the attack on Poland and before that on Pearl Harbor several agencies were established which dealt with public information and defense. There was the Office of Government Reports. Its duties were changed from time to time, but its principal function was to act as a channel between the government and the public and the state governments. It also handled certain relations with the motion picture industry. Then there came the Coordinator of Inter-American Affairs, which carried on a program after August 16, 1940, under the direction of Nelson Rockefeller. It was followed by the Coordinator of Information, which directed its attention toward the rest of the world other than Latin America. In October 1941 the president established the Office of Facts and Figures under Archibald MacLeish, a poet and, at the time, librarian of Congress. It was ordered to lay down an information policy. It also provided information to public officials themselves, but it did not have direct contact with newspaper and radio correspondents.[9] The OFF, however, lacked authority to coordinate the information activities of other government news officials. Therefore, on February 20, 1942, MacLeish wrote to the Director of the Budget recommending that his body be replaced by another with stronger authority to enforce coordination. All four of these agencies in addition to the expanding public relations and current information branches of the State, War, and Navy Departments were in operation when the Japanese bombs fell on Pearl Harbor. Their very number meant overlapping, confusion, and contradictions.

As the country buried its Pearl Harbor dead and flexed its muscles to strike back, however, its first thought, as far as the press was concerned, was not directed toward the release of war program news. Its first thought was directed toward stopping the channels through which enemy intelligence agents might reach their home offices and toward drying up possible leaks to them through the newspapers and radio. The Office of Censorship was established by executive order, invoking the statutory power of the First War Powers Act, on December 19, 1941. In spite of the forebodings which the experienced Creel expressed in print seven months earlier, voluntary censorship worked this time, with few slipups and with general praise from editorial voices throughout the country.

The confidence that the press had in the man in charge was no doubt largely responsible for that. Byron Price, whom Roosevelt named to head the office, had lived in the capital for twenty-two years, first as a staff member and later as chief of the Washington bureau of the Associated Press. Four years before war broke out he had become Executive News Editor of that service with his offices in New York. These tasks had given him not only an intimate knowledge of the federal government but extensive contact with press and radio executives throughout the country and familiarity with telegraphic and cable communications. And in building his staff so soon after the entrance of this country into the war, he was able to take his pick of those press leaders who offered their patriotic services.

Since the obvious first step was to draw codes of wartime practices for the press and radio, Price and his assistants took Creel's plan as a base and conferred with Army and Navy officials as well as with those of other affected agencies. When the new draft was ready it contained eight general headings. It asked that news not be printed or broadcast if it should become known to the newspaper or radio station and if it dealt with troop movements, ships, planes, fortifications, war production, weather, photographs and maps, and certain other matters. The code was revised four times, usually in favor of greater liberality as the military situation improved.

Manned by newspapermen and backed by positive policy statements which called for the widest possible freedom of news consistent with security, the Press and Radio Divisions of the

Office of Censorship operated on a twenty-four-hours-a-day, seven-days-a-week basis to advise news executives on borderline cases. Accepting long-distance telephone calls and telegrams from throughout the country, examiners tried to give on-the-spot decisions. On one occasion a newspaper facing a deadline had a staff member read a questionable story over the telephone and a censor gave line-by-line clearance as the copy was taken to the composing room. Washington correspondents, of course, sought and usually were given quick advice on possibly questionable stories received from sources other than the public relations bureaus of the War and Navy Departments.

Its aid to newspapers and radio stations in exercising patriotic restraint was actually a secondary duty of the Office of Censorship. Its agents examined every letter, telegram or cable, and listened in to every telephone conversation that crossed the nation's borders in an effort to stop the channels by which enemy agents might send material to their home offices. The number of personnel engaged in this duty was larger than that of the Press and Radio Divisions. Cooperating with the Federal Bureau of Investigation and with intelligence officers of the armed services, Office of Censorship agents helped to intercept and identify some spies.[10]

In World War I the Committee on Public Information both administered the voluntary press censorship and acted as a channel for the distribution of war information. In World War II the Office of Censorship handled only the restrictive side of the dual problem. Distribution was attacked by agencies which were kept carefully separate.

The enormous task of mobilizing the nation's industry, recruiting and reorganizing the armed services for active warfare, taking strategic action on the fighting fronts, and explaining our war aims to the rest of the world brought unavoidable differences of opinion among the various Washington offices attacking the problems. Since these offices, unlike the situation as we went into World War I, possessed public relations branches, each now laid its own view before the country. The situation was further complicated by the fact that the expanding defense movement after 1939 had seen five information offices set up while the existing public relations branches of the defense departments and the State Department expanded. Washington correspondents, therefore, found themselves receiving statements which bore official sanction but which were not always consistent. To some extent the releases reflected interdepartmental jealousy. Demands appeared for a central clearing agency with power to coordinate information conflicts and thereby present before the public a uniform policy.

Describing the confusion and the demand, Elmer Davis, who eventually undertook the task of resolving that confusion, wrote eight years later that his work was complicated by some newspapermen and others who protested that coordination of these efforts and a uniform policy suppressed legitimate differences of opinion and set up centralized censorship. Or, Davis said, correspondents, who sometimes feed on internecine quarrels, protested that he was suppressing good stories. "I don't know the answer to that one," he wrote. "You can have either clearance and coordination or conflict and confusion; one makes a better war effort, the other makes better headlines. Take your choice." [11] The government's choice was the better war effort. But it took months to decide how it should be done.

In December 1941 and January 1942 Milton S. Eisenhower, former director of the Department of Agriculture Office of Information, surveyed the problem for the Budget Bureau and recommended that an office be created with power to bring about closer cooperation.[12] On March 7 the Budget Bureau drew up a proposed executive order to create an Office of War Information that was essentially that which Eisenhower had suggested. Roosevelt, however, delayed because of differences of opinion over the handling of information sent to foreign countries.

Not until June 13 did the president sign Executive Order 9182. Creating the Office of War Information, it combined therein the OFF, the OGR, the Division of Information of the Office of Emergency Management, and the foreign information branches of the COI. It carefully left in the hands of the CIAA the responsibility to operate in Latin America independently of the OWI. Likewise such constituent agencies of the OEM as the War Production Board and the Office of Price Administration were allowed to operate their own information services. And the order did not interfere with existing public relations branches of the armed services or the State Department's Division of Current Information.[13]

Although the older department press services continued in operation, the order directed the OWI to "Coordinate the war informational activities of all Federal departments and agencies for the purpose of assuring an accurate and consistent flow of war information to the public and the world at large." It also directed the new organization of "Review, clear and approve" all proposed radio and motion picture programs sponsored by Federal departments. The director was authorized to "establish by regulation the types and classes of informational programs and releases which shall require clearance and approval by his office prior to dissemination," and "to require curtailment or elimination of any Federal information service, program or release he deems to be wasteful and not directly related to the prosecution of the war effort."

Elmer Davis was named director. He was a native of Indiana, a former editorial writer for the New York *Times* and the author of a history of that paper. Later he became nationally known as a radio commentator. As associate director the president named Milton S. Eisenhower. Several of those who were already working in the constituent branches were added to the new organization, bringing their own people and methods. The circumstances surrounding the creation of the OWI made its job of coordination difficult. Davis's report which was submitted to President Truman in September 1945 said that its chances of success would have been greater if it had been established three months earlier.

The OWI faced the same congressional and press suspicion that the Committee on Public Information had faced in World War I. That is, Congress and the press watched warily any centralized government information service, fearing that the administration might set up a powerful propaganda ministry. Furthermore, although the executive order directed departmental information services dealing with war information to cooperate, those agencies remained separate, responsible to their own cabinet chiefs and in a position to cooperate grudgingly rather than willingly with such an upstart temporary organization.

Davis early proposed to the War and Navy Departments that the release of military news be determined in conference, and that trusted officers bring him a complete report of all operations every day. The other departments agreed. They sent, however, representatives of their own public relations bureaus who did not have authority to make binding decisions and who displayed their superiors' concern with security. "I did not then realize the strong disinclination of the armed services to compromise or agree on any issue, especially if they could construe it as affecting security," his report said. The report had much to say about his difficulties with the armed services and their imperfect cooperation. As the war progressed, however, relations improved as the military situation improved. Davis arranged to have releases from the armed services' information offices submitted to the OWI to check for consistency in policy, although actual release was made by the department that originated the material. This occasionally brought protests over delay, but the director regarded that as inevitable and a condition which did not void the need for a careful policy check. For a while Davis held press conferences. They were discontinued, however, when he found them unsatisfactory as far as relationships with correspondents were concerned.

The OWI's function as a coordinator of war news and as an agency for the release of news was actually only a small part of its total activity. The Domestic Branch also arranged for radio time for government departments asking it, supervised contacts with the motion picture industry, produced documentary films, provided assistance to magazine and book writers and cooperated with the advertising industry in the conduct of government campaigns promoting various forms of home-front activity. The Overseas Branch was larger than the Domestic Branch. Leasing short-wave radio stations and sending its agents to neutral countries and to the parts of enemy countries which were occupied by our armed forces, it sought to make clear America's war aims. Just before V-E Day the Overseas Branch employed more than 8,400, about half of whom were citizens of foreign countries employed in their own lands.[14]

The OWI came to an end by executive order on September 15, 1945. During the actions in Korea and Vietnam there has been discussion of the desirability of establishing offices similar to the Office of Censorship or the OWI. In neither case, however, has there been a formal declaration of war, which would bring with it extension of the president's legal powers and the broader moral and political justification for the work of such agencies. As we have already seen, however, the president's press secretary tries to bring about some coordination of government information policy in a manner similar to that attempted by the OWI. And the Nixon administration, in establishing a new office, that of Coordinator of Information, has gone a step farther in this direction than has been attempted in the past. A move at the time of the Cuban Missile Crisis of 1962 to lay down a self-censorship code similar to the one administered by the Office of Censorship will be discussed in chapter 21.

19. The Columnists

For the nonjournalists among the readers of this book it seems desirable at this point to give a definition. In the parlance of today's newspaperman a "syndicate" is a commercial enterprise which sells a wide range of reader fare to newspapers. Some are operated by enterprising journals which get back part of their own newsgathering costs by reselling distinctive material to noncompeting presses. Some are operated in conjunction with and as part of the service of the Associated Press or the United Press International. Some are separate commercial enterprises. They sell to newspapers comic strips, pictures, cartoons, fiction, special reader material of various types—and "columns."

The syndicate is descended from operations which appeared in the Middle West soon after the Civil War and in New York after 1880. The "yellow journalism" of New York after 1895 interested the country's press in some of the innovations which that spectacular circulation race developed. The newspapers which introduced the features began selling some of those novel features to others outside the city. The period between World War I and about 1932 was one in which syndicate expansion was especially marked. The Associated Press added a feature service and a photo service before 1926. Other telegraphic press associations started syndicate services about the same time. Their salesmen traveled the country to persuade editors to lay before the public new material ranging from crossword puzzles to recipes and prepared editorials. It was at this time that newspapers started using full pages of comic strips.

Meanwhile newspaper writing, including Washington correspondence, was changing. The fading of direct party influence and the growth of the telegraph press services, which served newspapers of all political hues, led to the principle that reporting should be nonpartisan and objective. By 1920 the idea that opinion should be limited to the editorial page was generally accepted in most newspaper ranks. Whereas the nineteenth-century correspondent had trumpeted support of his political party position, after the turn of the century his heir on the capital journalistic scene became a less-biased observer. Good newspaper writing was characterized by brevity, evaluation of the facts to place the important and interesting in the opening paragraphs, and rigid adherence to timeliness. Interpretation, explanation and discussion of related events which took place more than one day from the day of publication were minimized. Where the nineteenth-century correspondent bluntly put forth his fact and opinion without qualification, the twentieth-century news writer carefully quoted some responsible source for practically every statement which he wrote. He sometimes, it is true, named "an informed source," "a spokesman who declined to permit the use of his name," or "sources close to. . . ." Although there was room for well-written description or narrative, the growth of these principles had brought about a sterility and uniformity of literary style and news story structure by 1925 which was far from the individuality of the vigorous offerings of a hundred years ago.

One result was *Time,* a magazine that developed a very large circulation due to the broader time element in its news stories and the novelty of its literary style. Another result—and this was part of the growth of the newspaper syndicate—was the Washington columnist. Around 1930 there mushroomed a group of Washington writers each of whom built a personal reputation based on the peculiar quality of his literary output. Syndicate salesmen pushed the products of those who showed promise. Frankly opinionated, they brought back some of the flavor of nineteenth-century Washington correspondence. Each writer of a century ago, however, was limited to one or two papers and maintained a theoretical anonymity behind a signed pseudonym. He worked closely within his paper's political party associations. The twen-

tieth-century columnist has his writings delivered to a large number of papers by the syndicate which employs him and makes his
name a valuable asset. He develops a following which makes the
subscribing newspaper value him for the circulation which he
brings even though he may differ with the stand of the paper's
editorial page. Although opinionated, he is seldom actively associated with one of the two major political parties. But he does back
certain consistent views of his own regarding public policy.

The earliest work similar to what became the syndicated
Washington column was to be found in the writings of David
Lawrence. Born in Philadelphia and brought up in Buffalo, he
entered Princeton University in 1906. There he covered campus
activities for the Associated Press and became a supporter of
Woodrow Wilson while Wilson was president of the university.
Graduating in 1910, Lawrence joined the Washington staff of the
Associated Press. He was assigned to the White House when
Wilson became president and was one of the founders of the
White House Correspondents' Association.

He transferred to the New York *Evening Post* in 1916. Here
he could broaden the subject matter of his daily writings. Three
years later he incorporated under his own name to offer his work
to several newspapers. He organized the Consolidated Press in
1920 to distribute his writings as well as other news features
through a nationwide telegraph system. He has continued his
column although his syndicate connection and system of distribution had undergone changes. As a young man he supported
Wilson's political liberalism. After 1921 he leaned toward the
conservative position of the Republican Party. He has been a
consistent critic of the Democratic Administrations.

The next writer to help build the groundwork for what was
to become a popular feature was Mark Sullivan. He, like Lawrence, was one of the supporters of Harding and his successors
and was a critic of Roosevelt and Truman. Born on a southeastern
Pennsylvania farm, he graduated from West Chester State Teach-
ers College, worked on some small newspapers in his home state,
and took a law degree at Harvard. During the elder Roosevelt's
administration he supported progressive policies, writing in the
Ladies' Home Journal and later in *Collier's*. He remained with the
latter until 1917. He moved to Washington in 1919 as correspondent for the New York *Evening Post*. After 1924 he wrote for the

New York *Herald-Tribune*, which was already syndicating some of its features. Its syndicate now distributed Sullivan's writings. When Hoover entered the White House, Sullivan became personally close to him. The writer was one of the group who exercised by playing medicine ball with the president. When Roosevelt became chief executive, Sullivan was a mainstay of the journalistic opposition. He wrote his last column on the day before he died, on August 13, 1952.

Lawrence's Consolidated Press and Sullivan's distribution by the Herald-Tribune syndicate helped spread the idea of a signed political column. Paul Mallon has been described as the first true columnist of the later pattern. He exploited his by-line in a large number of papers and popularized his work by revealing extensive background and otherwise unpublished Washington gossip and fact without attributing his material to a responsible source as more cautious reporters did. His columns were marked by strong opinion. He, too, was a conservative critic of the New Deal. The column capitalized on the reputation which came to him after he broke the secret Senate roll calls in 1929. A native of Mattoon, Illinois, he was educated at Notre Dame University and worked on the South Bend *News-Times* and the Louisville *Courier-Journal.* He joined the United Press staff in New York in 1920 and was transferred to Washington a few years later. When he started his column in 1932 it was an almost instant success. He retired in 1945 and died on July 30, 1950.

Then Drew Pearson and Robert S. Allen appeared. Their success completed the build-up of the Washington column into widespread acceptance. They have been followed by many other writers who capitalized on their experience and Washington contacts and who, publicized by their syndicates, have developed personal reader followings. By 1935 the average circulation manager regarded one or more of the well-known Washington columns as necessary.

Pearson was born in Evanston, Illinois. He graduated from Swarthmore College in 1919, traveled through the Balkans with the British Red Cross, and returned to teach geography at the University of Pennsylvania. He joined the staff of David Lawrence's *United States Daily* in 1926. Three years later he went to work for the Baltimore *Sun* Washington bureau. Allen is a Kentuckian whose varied early life included work on the Louisville

Courier-Journal and the *Capital Times* and *Wisconsin State Journal* in Madison. He studied at the Universities of Kentucky and Wisconsin and saw army service on the Mexican border and in World War I. He went to Washington in 1925 with the *Christian Science Monitor.*

He and Pearson collaborated in 1931 on an anonymous book, *The Washington Merry-Go-Round.* It ranged over the whole Washington scene. It sometimes displayed venom, sometimes satire, sometimes sarcasm. But it praised hardly any one in government except Senator George Norris of Nebraska. The House of Representatives was "The Monkey House." The Supreme Court justices were "Nine Old Men." The press corps came in for a raking although publishers were more damned than the correspondents. The book hit the city like a tornado and speculation as to the authorship raged. Their identity soon came out. The *Monitor* fired Allen. Pearson remained with the *Sun* but after a second book, *More Merry-Go-Round,* he, too, was unemployed.

Late in 1932 the two persuaded a syndicate to bring out their idea of a column bearing the name of their first book. Its readership grew fast. The column was much like the book. It specialized in revealing the unrevealed "inside" which more cautious reporters did not attempt sometimes for lack of verification and sometimes for lack of an authoritative source to be quoted. It took a liberal, generally pro-Democratic point of view which it has maintained to the present day, although not always without some criticism of those in Democratic administrations. As their reputation grew Pearson and Allen were able to capitalize on tips which were furnished them secretly, and they exploited the inevitable internecine differences of opinion that develop within government. The accuracy of their stories has often been questioned by other Washington writers, but events have shown them more often correct than in error.

Allen was commissioned a lieutenant colonel in World War II and went overseas on General George H. Patton's staff leaving Pearson to conduct the column alone. Allen lost an arm in a jeep accident in Germany. After the war he went into other journalistic work in the capital, leaving his former collaborator in sole charge of the column. Pearson came in for a dubious distinction when the angry President Truman described him in a news conference as an "s.o.b." Assisted by Jack Anderson, he continued the column until his death on September 1, 1969, along lines similar to those which it had followed for more than thirty-five years.

Anderson was described in material issued from Pearson's office as his heir apparent. His by-line often appeared alone in place of that of his older colleague, or often the two names appeared jointly. He has developed a reputation in Washington for persistent legwork, impelled by a moral consciousness which has produced evidence that courts as well as committees of both houses have had to consider. The cooperation between Pearson and Anderson on articles which led to the Senate censure of Senator Thomas Dodd of Connecticut is only one of several examples of similar action arising out of his investigations.

Anderson was born in Long Beach, California, and was brought up in Salt Lake City as a Mormon. As a boy he worked on a suburban weekly newspaper and by the time he was eighteen he held a job on the Salt Lake *Tribune*. He served as a Mormon missionary in 1942 and 1943. Drafted while working as a civilian war correspondent and inducted in China in World War II, he was assigned to the Shanghai edition of the *Stars and Stripes*. He joined Pearson's staff after his return to the United States in 1947.

And there was Walter Lippmann. In a strict sense of the word Lippmann was not a Washington columnist. He was a commentator on national and world affairs who traveled very extensively and who, before 1967 when he shifted his base to New York, had made Washington his headquarters for many years. He was born in New York on September 25, 1889, the son of well-to-do cultured parents. He finished the requirements for an undergraduate degree, with a major in philosophy, in three years at Harvard and stayed on for a fourth year as an assistant to William James. He associated himself with the Socialist party and for a short time assisted the newly elected Socialist mayor of Schenectady, New York. In 1914 he was one of the original board of editors of the *New Republic*. During World War I he was an intelligence officer and afterwards was one of the aides to the American delegation to the Versailles peace conference. After the war he became an editorial writer on the New York *World* and he was named editor of the editorial page when Frank I. Cobb died in 1923.

With the death of the *World* in 1931, this liberal editor of a liberal journal, to the astonishment of many associates and admirers, transferred to the Republican New York *Herald-Tribune*. Critics have accused him of trimming his sails to the change of his new employer. And they have pointed out, as evidence in support of their criticism, that he opposed Franklin D. Roosevelt's election in 1932 and supported Alfred M. Landon, the Republican nominee, in 1936. Admirers deny that he was inconsistent or false. He doubted that Roosevelt had a true philosophy of public affairs and felt that the New Deal had taken undesirable turns. He has been a consistent critic of this country's Vietnam policy.

When he reached the age of seventy, in 1959, the National Press Club put on a special program to honor him. At that time, in addition, Marquis Childs and James Reston edited a volume, *Walter Lippmann and His Times*, containing a dozen chapters, each by a different author and each viewing a different aspect of Lippmann's career and writings. The writers included Frank Moraes, former editor of the *Indian Express* of Bombay and author of several books about Indian and Asian problems; Raymond Aron, writer for *Le Figaro* of Paris; Childs and Reston, and eight other American journalists or academicians. So much for individuals among the Washington columnists.

During the nineteenth century, and as we have particularly noted during the Civil War, political leaders sought the cooperation of the newspaper correspondents to push careers and to secure the flattery that many men in public life want. A somewhat similar personal relationship sometimes develops between some of the syndicated columnists and officeholders. The writers exploit such relationships to secure the inside information on which their reputations are based. The columnists, moreover, are the principal beneficiaries of a practice which has developed since World War II for the purpose of keeping writers informed even though they are asked not to publish what they learn or are asked not to give the source of their information. Particularly in the Departments of State and Defense, newsmen, with special attention given to the influential columnists, are given background secrets in order to assure greater accuracy in their writing and to use them as channels while at the same time some diplomatic, military or political necessities are respected. In such cases the writers respect what has become known as the "Lindley Rule."

The rule was named for Ernest K. Lindley, formerly of *Newsweek* and later with the State Department. Lindley wrote to this author on December 5, 1967: "Presumably it was named for me because of my role in organizing the meetings of leading opinion writers with Secretaries of State, and other important persons, and as President of Overseas Writers shortly after the Second World War, when we found it necessary to have a stringent rule in order to permit responsible officials to talk freely, especially about delicate or dangerous international problems." Under the rule writers are not to quote the source of their information. Lindley wrote, however, that it was not intended for the transmission of "hard news."

The columnists insist that although they benefit from contacts with government officials they keep their freedom to comment and to criticize. Nevertheless, in view of the fact that they write with a strong dose of opinion and frankly eschew the objectivity of the bulk of news writing, they tend to make their associations in government with those of congenial outlook. Thus they become peculiarly important in providing information and in acting as contacts between government and the public.

20. Washington Correspondents Are Sociable

A Washington correspondent, as do those who follow almost any profession or business, likes to meet with his fellows in clubrooms where they can discuss their mutual problems and exchange fact, gossip, and humor. Dining rooms, a bar, and lounge and meeting rooms are essential. The capital newsmen have established several social groups. Those in existence today are the heirs of earlier bodies which faltered and died before more permanent bases could be worked out. The first, the Washington Correspondents' Club, was founded and a tentative constitution and by-laws considered on February 26, 1867. The members met again on March 6 in the *Tribune* rooms to amend and approve the basic documents. It gave a dinner on the 13th.

L. A. Gobright was the first president. Its constitution and by-laws were amended again on September 26, 1868. They were printed in 1870 and a copy deposited in the Library of Congress. At that time Ben: Perley Poore was president. Twenty-nine active members were listed. Among them was Samuel L. Clemens, clerk to Senator William M. Stewart of Nevada. He had not yet made famous the pen name "Mark Twain." No paper was given beside his name in the membership list. There were seven honorary members. They included Vice-President Schuyler Colfax, who had edited a newspaper in Indiana, and Speaker James G. Blaine, who had been at the helm of an Augusta, Maine, newspaper before going into politics.

The preamble of the constitution said the club's purpose was "to secure the advantages of organization and for the cultivation of fraternal sentiments." Applicants could be elected to membership by a three-fourths vote. Honorary membership "may be bestowed upon such persons as have been or may be professionally connected with Journalism, and who have achieved eminence in that profession or in other public position." The annual membership fee was set at five dollars, with monthly dues one dollar. The club met the last Saturday of each month, with the annual business session and election of officers on the third Saturday in December. This club either remained an exclusive group of selected membership or received only cool support, for its rolls comprised barely a fourth of the eligible capital reporters. It soon disappeared.

With the Washington Correspondents' Club limited to those who wrote for journals outside the city, staff members of the Washington papers soon countered with their own organization. The *National Intelligencer* of September 19, 1867, described the establishment of a Press Club with a membership list drawn from that group. But except for the initial notice of organization and of the election of John C. Proctor of the *National Intelligencer* as president little has been left to describe its activities. Neither of the 1867 clubs apparently tried to maintain clubrooms. Both were short-lived.

The next move in this direction did not take place until 1883. The Washington Press Club which was founded in that year included both correspondents and local staff men and it provided clubrooms on Pennsylvania Avenue above Fourteenth Street, around the corner from Newspaper Row. They adjoined the offices of the Baltimore *American,* and Frank H. Truesdell of that paper seems to have been one of its most active members. The *Evening Star* of January 7, 1884, described "the Washington Press Club's first reception, at their rooms, No. 1420 Pennsylvania avenue." The members enjoyed a "handsome lunch," heard songs from the club's "quartette," and listened to speeches from many of the city's newspapermen. This club, too, died at an unrecorded date.

At least one other short-lived group tried to maintain such social and professional conveniences as a clubroom, bar, and dining room. On an upper floor of a building on E Street, two doors east of the corner at Fourteenth, there was a gambling establishment known as the Congressional Club. Its assets included a kitchen and elaborate dishes and silver. The National Capital Press Club was organized in February 1891. It rented this property and bought the equipment. It must have been gay. All accounts agree that sociability accompanied by food and drink reigned and that credit was extended liberally to members. That was fatal. Deficits mounted. Members' bills remained unpaid. Various efforts were made to meet costs. On one occasion the club realized seven thousand dollars from a benefit in which a theatrical troupe from New York performed. The Pennsylvania Railroad brought the cast to Washington and returned them without charge. In spite of such efforts, however, in the spring of 1895 the equipment was sold at auction to meet debts and the club was dissolved.[1]

The Gridiron Club, which has become a nationally famous institution to whose dinners invitations are eagerly sought, was the first social group to outlast the original growing pains. It preceded the National Capital Press Club and is still active. Its dinners, attended by the president and by invited politicians in addition to a guest list of others who have been extended the desired privilege of attendance, are imitated in state capitals and by college journalism student groups throughout the country.

Ben: Perley Poore was the first president of this club, too. The idea arose when Mr. R. F. Crowell of Washington gave a dinner for a group of correspondents. At that time the opinion was voiced that the newspapermen should continue such gatherings but should conduct them themselves.[2] The first of the famous functions was held in a restaurant on May 23, 1885. The first president to accept an invitation and to speak was Benjamin Harrison. He was present in January 1892. Cleveland was the only chief executive who refused every invitation. Since then it has been customary for each president to attend all dinners held in his administration unless illness or some other unavoidable cause prevents it.

The club holds a dinner once a year, and more than once in some years, at which it presents humorous skits in which the members of the club take part. They poke fun at the serious problems of the political leaders and diplomats among the guests. Originally it limited its membership to forty men selected from the ranks of the correspondents and the staffs of the Washington papers. That number has since been raised to fifty. In addition a few associate members are taken in because they possess special skills which they can apply to the preparation of the skits.

Some of the guests are invited to speak after the skits are finished. During the first few years the fun was derived by interrupting and heckling the guests although the members avoided treating the chief executive with disrespect. After 1890, however, that type of heckling and horseplay was abandoned in favor of the satire present in the skits. A tradition that "no reporters are present" has applied to speeches made there, so they have not normally been reported in the press. Some presidents, however, have themselves released for newspaper publication their Gridiron Club addresses.

On a few occasions dramatic incidents have taken place which could not be suppressed. The most famous such had Theodore Roosevelt as the principal actor. It was at one of these dinners that he used the word "muckrakers" to apply to the magazine writers, who had been exposing evils in the country's political and business life. The word has since become generally accepted as applying to that group. But the one that went down as the most dramatic occurrence in Gridiron annals was the Roosevelt-Foraker incident.

The president and Senator Joseph B. Foraker of Ohio had been close political and personal friends. More recently they had differed on several policy matters and the senator had been in the forefront of certain of the president's quarrels with Congress. The immediate incident grew out of disorder involving Negro troops at Brownsville, Texas. Roosevelt had ordered the soldiers discharged, but Foraker had headed a Senate investigation which reached conclusions other than those of the president. Both were Gridiron guests in January 1907. Called on to speak, the president turned toward the senator and, in bitter words which were entirely out of the spirit of the good-natured fun which had prevailed, went into a harsh exposition of his side of the Brownsville incident. The senator then rose and gave back as good as he had received. The room was tense, and the excited discussion of the incident which circulated in street gossip during the next several days got into newspaper accounts in spite of the club's rules.

The Gridiron Club does not meet the demand for clubrooms and a bar. Unfortunate experience showed, however, that too loose organization and too liberal credit ended in disaster. Not until 1908 was a new attempt made. Then it was built to sail around the reefs which had wrecked the predecessor group. The National Press Club, which was formed in that year, has lasted. On March 12, 1908, thirty-two men met in the Washington Chamber of Commerce and agreed to try again. One of the features of the meeting was a speech by John Russell Young of the Washington *Star* on the weaknesses of the earlier attempts. The name was accepted at a second meeting on the 17th. On the 29th, two hundred correspondents gathered in the Gridiron Room of the Willard Hotel, pledged their membership and accepted a constitution. The new organization would promote social enjoyment among the members, cultivate literary taste, encourage friendly intercourse among newspapermen and those with whom they are thrown in contact in the pursuit of their vocation and foster the ethical standards of the profession.

The first clubrooms were occupied on May 2. Located in an apartment over a jewelry store at 1205 F Street, they were equipped with secondhand furniture, including the necessary bar and card tables. A no-credit rule was established from the start. Among the guests at the formal housewarming on May 18 were the British and Japanese ambassadors, William F. ("Buffalo Bill") Cody, and actor James K. Hackett. Visits by the great and near-great have featured the club throughout its life. It has grown steadily. There have been periods of financial stringency but they have never threatened the club's existence. The need for expanded quarters has caused several moves. In March 1909 the club rented rooms at Fifteenth and F Streets over a drugstore. By 1913 that space would accommodate only two-thirds of the members at a meeting. On March 20, 1914, therefore, the club took rooms on the top floor of a building on G Street just off Fifteenth. The structure also housed Keith's Theatre. Quarters over the city's leading vaudeville theatre had certain advantages. The country's best-known performers were invited up for after-the-show visits. They sang for their supper, of course—for the benefit of the membership.

Not only vaudeville stars found their way to the clubrooms. Every president since Taft has been a visitor. Harding, a publisher, was a member and on one occasion startled the club waiters by appearing in answer to a casually delivered invitation to play hearts with a group of the reporters who had covered his campaign. Truman was still vice-president when he was photographed playing a piano in the clubrooms with actress Lauren Bacall seated on the instrument.

Taft, who entered the Fifteenth Street clubrooms for the first time on January 31, 1910, was the first to suggest that the organization build its own quarters. Fifteen more years passed, however, before active steps were taken in that direction. In January 1925, when Henry L. Sweinhart of the Havas News Agency was president of the club, he appointed a building committee. As chairman he named James William Bryan, a former newspaperman, printer, and publisher who had more recently been engaged in financial promotion. Bryan's work was characteristic of the speculative twenties. The account of his negotiations and the club's activities during the next several years, as described in its sponsored book, reads like a combination get-rich-quick scheme and a fiction-writer's dream of an international spy story. It had everything except murder.

There were negotiations with New York financiers, Detroit real estate trustees and Hollywood producers. There were first, second, and third mortgages, complicated refinancing, corporate reorganization and stock issues. There was active lobbying by club members to get through Congress special legislation from which the club and its building corporation might benefit. There was a crucial bottle of bootleg Scotch whiskey delivered at the right time and an attorney who played his player piano at the wrong time. While he did so interested visitors read a signed document which he had not intended that they see. The Press Building Corporation claims the distinction of being the first to seek corporate reorganization after Congress amended the bankruptcy laws to make that possible as a relief measure in 1933. Its petition was filed within minutes after President Roosevelt signed the act.

Out of it all the National Press Club reached this position: It controls, through trustees, about 77 percent of the common stock of the Press Building Corporation, which owns a fourteen-story office building. It enjoys at a very low rental the use of the clubrooms, which occupy most of the thirteenth and all of the fourteenth floors. Although it pays almost literally no rent it contributes to the building's real estate taxes.[3] In the clubrooms are attractive and comfortably furnished dining rooms, a bar, lounges, library, offices, an auditorium, private dining rooms, and club offices. Although it was built with bonds bearing a high interest rate and although it operated at a loss during its early years and went through bankruptcy proceedings, the building is now meeting its debt charges.

The National Press Building stands on the southeast corner of Fourteenth and F Streets, the north end of the block which became Newspaper Row after 1865. To clear the ground it was necessary to tear down the old Ebbitt Hotel, where Poore died. Located across the street from the Willard Hotel, on the ground occupied by the *Tribune*'s Civil War office, two blocks from the White House, the Press Building is approached from every direction by streets which are haunted by the ghosts of the last century's reporters.

Demolition of the buildings on the site started on January 6, 1926. On April 8 President Coolidge laid a cornerstone, although because of construction difficulties it was not *the* cornerstone. Instead, it was a block set on a temporary brick structure placed on the sidewalk for the occasion and later removed. Months later, when construction had advanced far enough, the present stone, with its inscription saying that it was laid by President Coolidge, was put in place. The first tenants moved in on August 25, 1927. The theatre which occupied a part of the structure opened on September 19. That theatre has since been closed and offices and stores built into that area. In December, making a procession of it, the members brought the club's trophies from the old quarters.

In 1948 the organization celebrated its fortieth anniversary by publishing a book containing eighteen articles, some serious and some facetious, written by twenty-two different authors selected from the club's membership. Issued under the title *Dateline: Washington,* it was produced under the editorship of Cabell Phillips of the New York *Times.* It discussed not only the history and activities of the club but certain other aspects of capital journalism and has been the major source for this chapter.

Louis Lautier, who opened the way for Negro members in the congressional press galleries, was the first of his race, too, to be admitted to the National Press Club. He became a member in 1955.

The club's best known activities are its periodic luncheons

which are addressed by statesmen. Speeches made by American and world governmental leaders are covered by radio and television and are reported in the world's press as authoritative statements on public matters. Practically every leading world figure, including Nikita Khrushchev, who has visited Washington has appeared, to speak in English or in his native language with simultaneous translation.

Until 1971 women were not admitted to membership in the National Press Club. Even members' wives were not allowed in the bar at all and in the dining room only under certain restrictions. Wives and lady guests were restricted to a separate cocktail lounge. The Gridiron Club still bars them. Women correspondents suffered such restrictions in spite of the fact that for nearly a century they have been important members of the press corps.

Jane Grey Swisshelm's claim that her one day's appearance in the Senate press gallery made her the first woman Washington correspondent was discussed in chapter 9. She returned during the Civil War to write again for the *Tribune* and for the St. Cloud, Minnesota, *Democrat*. At least two other women corresponded during the war. Sara Jane Lippincott, writing over the pseudonym "Grace Greenwood," contributed to both the *Times* and the *Tribune*. Laura Catherine Redden wrote as "Howard Glyndon" for the *Missouri Republican*.[4] In 1867 Mrs. Harriet Elizabeth Prescott Spofford wrote for the New York *World*.[5] Her work was done secretly while she was in Washington with her lawyer-husband during the winter months. Later, writing at her home in Newburyport, Massachusetts, she developed a modest literary reputation for magazine fiction and essays.

Between 1870 and 1880 the *Congressional Directory* each year listed about a half dozen women, although there was a good deal of turnover among them. The most famous in this period were Mrs. Emily Edson Briggs, who became well known for her Philadelphia *Press* letters signed "Olivia," and Mrs. Mary Clemmer Ames who, like Mrs. Spofford, later developed a substantial literary reputation. Miss Austine Snead, whom Richardson erroneously credited with being the first woman correspondent, was listed as with the *World*. Richardson said that Miss Snead and her mother came to Washington in the late 1860s and that she worked in the face of some opposition.[6]

Of the women correspondents during this period, Mrs. Briggs

was the best known and the most highly admired by her contemporaries. She did not, however, develop the literary reputation that has attached to Mrs. Spofford or Mrs. Ames. She was listed in the *Congressional Directory* as a press gallery member until 1879, when the Standing Committee ruled that each paper could include only three names to cover Congress. Although no longer allowed to cover "the hill," she remained active until 1882. In 1906 a collection of her letters was published in book form. Although women disappeared from the *Congressional Directory* they remained on the scene, devoting their attention particularly to society reporting. Various writers on the capital scene refer to them. They did not return to the press gallery until after 1900.[7]

Mrs. E. N. Chapin published a little book under the title, *American Court Gossip, or Life at the National Capital* at Marshalltown, Iowa, in 1887. The preface says: "These Washington sketches were mostly published in the Iowa State Register and were written in a hasty manner. . . . As an ex-secretary of the Ladies Press Association at Washington, I beg the indulgence of the Guild everywhere." This Ladies Press Association at Washington left few other indications that it ever existed. Mrs. Edna M. Coleman's book on White House gossip refers to Mrs. Mary Lockwood as a member of the National Press Association. In 1890 Mrs. Lockwood wrote a series of sketches of Washington scenes and descriptions of some of the old houses and she was influential in establishing the Daughters of the American Revolution. These ladies' press organizations, or this organization, for the two references may apply to the same group, must have been like the early men's press clubs; they lived out brief existences and passed, leaving little to reveal to the later student of press history. The first women's organization to last did not appear until 1919.

Mrs. Florence Brewer Boeckel started the discussions which brought about the establishment of the Women's National Press Club. A former newspaperwoman she was at that time a partner in a publicity firm. After preliminary discussions she persuaded four others to join her and issue a call for an organization meeting. The call, dated September 23, 1919, said that "it might be both pleasant and profitable for the newspaper and magazine women in Washington to have some means of getting together in informal and regular fashion." Among the purposes of an organization, it said, would be to "give us an opportunity to hear more intimately than we otherwise could, prominent men and women who come to Washington." In addition to Mrs. Boeckel, the call was signed by Eleanor Taylor Marsh, Mrs. Boeckel's publicity partner, Carol Rigby of the *Christian Science Monitor*, Elizabeth M. King of the New York *Evening Post* and Caroline Vance Bell of the Newspaper Enterprise Association. The first meeting was held on the evening of September 27 in the office of Mrs. Boeckel's and Mrs. Marsh's publicity firm. The first official luncheon meeting took place on November 6 and Lily Lykes Rowe was elected president. Miss Rigby was named honorary president and Mrs. Marsh secretary-treasurer. A constitution was drawn up in 1926.[8]

Membership in the Women's National Press Club is limited to those who are actively engaged in newspaper or related work, although that is interpreted to include publicity and other forms of writing. It has not tried to maintain clubrooms, although it keeps an office and secretary in the National Press Building. Its principal activity is a weekly luncheon, to which outstanding personalities are frequently invited. Most of the major figures in Washington's governmental and diplomatic life have met with the women reporters on these occasions. In addition, the club from time to time holds social gatherings or professional programs jointly with the National Press Club. In 1927 it started an annual Stunt Dinner Party, a feminine counterpart of the Gridiron Dinner, at which were presented lampoons which compare with those of the men's groups. Mrs. Franklin D. Roosevelt attended that affair in March 1933 to become the first president's wife to do so. For the next several years presidents as well as their wives were often present, the only social function among press organizations in Washington which was so honored.

The Stunt Party was abandoned after 1963. The club, however, continues its other activities, principal among which is its presentation of the Eleanor Roosevelt Golden Candlestick Award. The award, consisting, as the name points out, of a golden candlestick, was established after Mrs. Roosevelt's death to be presented each year to that woman who, in the membership's opinion, best embodied the ideals of the former first lady. Mrs. Lyndon B. Johnson received it in 1968. The club also holds an annual congressional dinner for legislators during the first week of each session and a spring dinner in conjunction with the annual April meeting of the American Society of Newspaper Editors. In 1970 the club celebrated its fiftieth anniversary by publishing a history of women correspondents and of itself.

From time to time there have been conversations about possible merger of the National Press Club and the Women's National Press Club. Margaret A. Kilgore, president of the women's group in 1969, wrote to this author that "it will probably happen eventually, but not yet." Nevertheless, in 1970 and 1971 steps were taken which could be moves in that direction although actual merger is not in immediate prospect. In October 1970 a proposal to admit women members was voted on by the men's organization. A majority approved, but the Board of Directors ruled that under the constitution the plan had to be laid before the annual meeting in January 1971 for further consideration. At that time admission of women was again approved. In turn, the women's club voted to admit men and, according to press accounts, eight applications were promptly received.

The fair sex of the Washington press have also formed a second organization. Fifteen from the staffs of the Washington papers met on April 4, 1932, to break ground for the American Newspaper Women's Club, Inc. Organization was completed at a second meeting on May 2 when the original fifteen were joined by ten others who thus became listed as "other charter members." Among the latter group were five correspondents for outside newspapers as well as additional representatives from the Washington journals' staffs. Kate Scott Brooks of the Washington *Post* was elected president to serve, as have her successors, for two years.

Active members of the American Newspaper Women's Club, like those of the Women's National Press Club, are drawn from the ranks of those actively engaged in newspaper work, publicity, or other literary activity. Unlike the older organization it admits as associate members those whom it invites from among the city's social leaders or women leaders in business and the professions. Thus its activities are shared by the wives of practically all of the cabinet members, sometimes by the president's family, and by those representing the feminine side of Congress, the diplomatic corps and the city's business life.[9] The club's aims have been described as "maintaining headquarters for its members, aiding civic, cultural and philanthropic endeavors as well as helping its own members in financial distress." Founded during the depression, it established at the beginning a Fellowship Fund to help newspaperwomen who had money problems. It has also endowed a bed at Children's Hospital and has given to war and disaster relief funds and the Milk Fund for undernourished children. Unlike the Women's National Press Club, it maintains its own clubrooms, at 1604 Twentieth Street, N.W.[10]

The Overseas Writers Club was organized in 1920 by reporters who had covered the Peace Conference at Versailles and who, on their return to Washington, wished to continue the professional association found in their common task abroad. Since then reporters who have been foreign correspondents and who have later joined the capital press corps have been eligible.[11] The Overseas Writers hold regular luncheons to which are invited speakers who appear frequently in the foreign news. For many years it was a custom to have the secretary of state as a guest once a year. But it has not always been possible to keep that up.

And there is one more professional group among the Washington newsmen. The State Department Correspondents' Association was started in 1930 to carry out professional duties which it was felt at the time were needed although its function has become primarily social. At the beginning it set qualifications for admission to the secretary's press conferences and tried to limit them and the use of the State Department press room to legitimate correspondents. More recently, however, press gallery lists or admission to the White House news conferences have been accepted as criteria at the State Department. "Purposes now are merely to promote the general welfare of the correspondents, keeping a check on information policies, serving as agency for protests and the like, giving parties on appropriate occasions, notably just before Christmas with the Secretary present," Edward E. Bomar of the Associated Press wrote to this author in June 1953.

21. Washington Correspondence and Correspondents at Midcentury

Mark Ethridge, former executive editor of the Louisville *Courier-Journal*, once wrote: "My greatest apprehension on the news and editing side has been whether newspapers, which are evanescent in their very nature, are accepting the awful responsibility devolved upon all of them by what Alistair Cook called 'America's vaulting into the saddle of power.'"[1]

When World War II broke out the press clung to a traditional truculence toward and suspicion of government. Developments since then have brought new conflicts to which no peaceful solution seems to be in sight. On the one hand the rapid extension of governmental authority over more and more sides of American life has brought a growing bureaucracy which shows little understanding of the mores which motivate the reporter. On the other, the country's projection onto the world's diplomatic and military stage leads government to call on the press for backing of a type which the press gives grudgingly.

James Reston of the New York *Times* pointed out, in lectures which were published under the title, *The Artillery of the Press*, that the president is gaining broader control over information which reaches the news media in spite of a rearguard action on the part of the latter. There are many indications that his statement may be broadened. The executive is gaining control at the expense of Congress and in so doing is winning greater direction of the information which reaches the reporters as well as the public and the legislators.

Recent developments, if they are considered in the perspective of the history of the press-government relationship, must be thought about, moreover, in relation to the developing governmental initiative in giving out news. From the time the official journal disappeared until well into the twentieth century the initiative lay with the correspondent. He made his contacts with government officials, asked the questions, and tried to persuade the official to give him exclusive information. In turn, he sometimes did certain journalistic-political favors for the official.

But more and more in recent years government has become the originator. This is to be seen in the development of departmental information services. It is to be seen in the addition of a press secretary to the White House staff. It is to be seen in the addition to the staffs of many members of both houses of Congress of an aide who is actively or in effect a press secretary. It is to be seen in the practice of members of both houses of Congress of having statements taped or filmed for broadcast in their home districts and having printed newsletters sent to a mailing list of constituents, newspapers, and broadcasting stations. It is to be seen in the way congressional committee proceedings in some cases are carried on more for the publicity to be thus derived than for the need for such proceedings as part of the legislative process.

While government has undertaken more and more to take the lead in offering information to the press and public, that development has been looked on with reservations by the press. And insofar as that initiative has been exercised by the White House and the executive departments, it has been looked on with reservations by Congress. Congress and the press have protested that the executive has sought to extend its power through publicity. As far as the press is concerned, too, this has come coincidentally with charges that government suppresses that information which officeholders would find it inconvenient to allow to become known. And whereas a few officials have been frank to say that at times, in dealing with foreign and defense problems, government is justified in using the press and public information as a weapon, newsmen have countered angrily, denying that such calculated employment is justified.

Government, on the other hand, has protested that the press is irresponsible. In particular, government has found itself embarrassed and its diplomatic and military position made difficult by publication of what officials felt should have been kept secret or should not have been published from the point of view and with the emphasis which was given it in the media. The press, however, refuses to respect any need for secrecy or to withhold what it finds out unless there is an actual declaration of war.

The difficulty of amicable relations between government and the press was illustrated forcibly in November 1969. Attacks by Vice-President Spiro Agnew on television news and on newspapers in two speeches which followed close on one another gave voice to criticism of the type which the newsman has come to expect from some government officials. Never before, however, had so aggressive an onslaught come from so highly placed an official. Two somewhat related incidents occurred in 1971. On February 23 and again on March 23, the Columbia Broadcasting System aired a program, "The Selling of the Pentagon," which criticized the Defense Department public information machinery. A congressional committee demanded the "out-takes" and reporters' notes which were used in its preparation. But CBS officials refused to provide them, even under threat of a sentence for contempt. Three months later the New York *Times* and other papers published classified material relating to the Vietnam War. After the first documents appeared, a government effort to prevent publication of the rest was overturned in the courts.

Such phrases as "paper curtain," "credibility gap," "freedom of information," "the right to know," "cover-up," and "news management" have come into common use in capital press circles.[2] And both the press and members of Congress protest that the president has greatly expanded "executive privilege" in denying the right either of the press, the citizenry at large, or of congressional committees to White House or departmental files.

The House of Representatives started a special study of the problem in 1955. Representative William L. Dawson of Illinois, chairman of the House Committee on Government Operations, established a special subcommittee on government information. As chairman he named Representative John E. Moss of California. The Moss subcommittee has published thirty reports which require nearly three feet of shelf space. There are hundreds of pages of the testimony of press spokesmen and of administrators dealing with the information practices of various government departments. There are hundreds of pages of correspondence between the subcommittee staff and government officials. There are hundreds of pages devoted to papers written by the subcommittee's competent and hard-working staff. There are hundreds of pages in which are printed such documents as letters from presidents to cabinet chiefs advising them on information policies. There are hundreds of pages devoted to copies of executive orders or directives.

These publications show the extreme complexity of the problem. The subcommittee's researches have not only delved into the question of what executive information should be available to the public at large—and this, of course, includes reporters. The legal questions represented by the thorny matter of the right possessed by Congress itself to demand information or documents from executive departments has also occupied the attention of the subcommittee staff.

The testimony of many department officials showed that they felt no responsibility to allow public scrutiny of their activities. It showed that in many cases it simply did not occur to them that the theory of democratic government gave the public a certain right to information, and they felt it more convenient, when the question arose, not to be bothered with strangers asking questions and going into their files. Under subcommittee prodding many have changed their policies to permit wider access. Some members of the staff have felt that this, as much as legislation, has been one of their principal achievements.

And the subcommittee has put through Congress two statutes designed to clarify the matter. The first was intended to place a new interpretation on an old measure. In 1789, as part of the task of setting up the new government, Congress passed a law directing department heads to maintain records and to make regulations governing their protection and filing. During President Grant's administration a legal question was raised as to whether or not a citizen could require that he be allowed to see certain documents. The attorney general advised that the 1789 statute gave the department head the right to refuse. In 1958, as a result of a study by the Moss subcommittee, a statute was passed by both houses and signed by President Eisenhower which simply says that the 1789 statute is not to be so interpreted.

That legislation did not, however, give positive orders that such documents were to be made available to a citizen on demand. In a press release issued in 1964, Representative Moss said that his staff had been studying for ten years the difficult problem of a "freedom of information" statute which would order department officials to release information while at the same time defining the necessary limitations on such orders. A bill to that effect was passed by both houses in 1966 and was signed by President Johnson on July 4, to take effect a year later. While making it mandatory that department officials allow the public to examine documents in their possession, the statute recognized the need for exceptions. Therefore it included eight clauses setting up categories of sensitive information of which publicity was not to be required. Those eight, of course, included secret diplomatic and defense information and information which dealt with criminal investigations. Furthermore, they exempted certain confidential business information and statements which had been filed with government officials and which reflected on personal character.

In 1963 a reorganization made the Moss subcommittee permanent and merged it with the subcommittee on foreign operations. With the enactment of the two statutes and the publication of the testimony which it had gathered, which caused many government officials to ease their earlier restraints, the work of the subcommittee's staff has slowed down. It continues to receive complaints and to investigate.

The problem of the relationship between the government and the newsman at a time of tense foreign relations was especially highlighted by three events which came in rapid succession in 1960, 1961, 1962, and by the Vietnam war. The struggle in Asia, however, although it has brought a normal amount of friction over the release of news, has not resulted in the violent blowup over government announcements and over press coverage as did the U-2 affair, the Bay of Pigs, and the Cuban Missile Crisis.

In a lecture before the Council on Foreign Relations Reston said: "I knew for over a year that the United States was flying high-altitude planes (the U-2) over the Soviet Union from a base in Pakistan to photograph military and particularly missile activities and bases, but *The New York Times* did not publish this fact until one of the planes was shot down in 1960." He went on to ask the question as to whether or not this was a correct judgment, and answered: "I think it was, but in other circumstances, the press is criticized for not printing intelligence and even military information." [3] Gordon Eliot White, Washington correspondent of *Chicago's American,* the *Deseret News* of Salt Lake City, and some other western papers, tried at the Pentagon to follow up some leads about the U-2. An Air Force colonel in the office of the secretary of defense called him aside and asked him to lay off. He did.[4]

If Reston knew that the U-2 was flying from bases in Pakistan over the Soviet Union, he was one of very few who possessed that knowledge. Even within the National Aeronautics and Space Administration, the Central Intelligence Agency and the State Department as well as among the responsible officials of the Lockheed Aircraft Corporation, the number of persons in on the secret had been kept to a minimum. Hagerty and other information officers were in the dark. Reston does not make clear in his published lecture whether or not he knew that the plane was capable of flying at eighty thousand feet and of continuing for long distances. The sketchy information that had been allowed to reach aviation publications had given its ceiling as fifty-five thousand feet and indicated that it was fairly slow and could remain in the air for only four hours. The plane, such stories said, was used for weather research.

Francis Gary Powers took off from an air base at Peshawar, Pakistan, early on Sunday, May 1, 1960, to fly across the Soviet Union to Bodo, Norway, taking pictures with the plane's sophisticated photographic equipment. As the earth's rotation brought Sunday to Washington some hours later, Hugh S. Cumming, Jr., chief of intelligence and research in the State Department, received a cryptic telephone call at his home. "Our boy isn't back yet," his caller said.[5] For the next four days the country's press was dominated by stories of Princess Margaret's marriage and, with lower play, the meeting of the Supreme Soviet in Moscow and riots in Turkey. Tuesday's papers carried, with very secondary emphasis, a small story from Turkey that a weather plane was missing. But behind the scenes in Washington and in Moscow things were boiling.

The few in Washington who were in on the secret were aware only that the plane had not arrived in Norway. Not knowing whether the pilot was alive or dead, or whether or not he was being questioned, and not knowing whether or not the Russians were examining the plane's secrets, they proceeded in the dark according to imperfect previously arranged plans. They ordered released in Turkey an announcement that a weather plane, which was adapted for meteorological research and which flew out of the American base near Adana, was missing in the Lake Van area and was being sought. An enterprising Turkish journalist at Adana sent the story to his paper in Istanbul and the United Press International moved it on to this country.

The day was well advanced in Moscow on the following Thursday, although it was only 3:00 A.M. in Washington, when Khrushchev dramatically and angrily told the Supreme Soviet that the United States had sent a spy plane into Soviet airspace and that a Soviet missile had shot it down. He left American experts wondering about the pilot and the plane. The press wires had the information in Washington before eight o'clock and Washington correspondents began calling officials.

During the next few days the Russians skilfully doled out the information which they possessed in such a way as to keep Americans guessing how much they knew. Some Washington officials were unreachable at crucial moments, and the information officers in the affected branches of government tripped over each other. Secretary of State Christian Herter was in Athens and the president and some other officials went on Thursday for a practice in security to the planned secret hideaway in Maryland which had been built for them in case Washington were bombed. The plan for the exercise had been made some weeks earlier. Shortly after noon Hagerty said that the president had ordered an investigation and that further information would come from the State Department and from the National Aeronautics and Space Administration. Reporters hurried to those offices. At 12:45 Lincoln White, State Department press spokesman, clung to the story of a weather plane. He said that further investigations were being made and that it was possible that the pilot had lost consciousness due to oxygen failure near the border between the Soviet Union and Turkey. In that case, he said, the plane might have continued automatically over the Soviet Union. Even a day later White insisted: "There was absolutely no—NO—no deliberate attempt to violate Soviet air space."

On Thursday, after the statements from Hagerty and from White, which came within less than an hour of one another, reporters hurried to NASA. There they found the information officers uninstructed. After a telephone call to Hagerty, those officers said they would prepare a statement. They hurriedly put one together, still sticking to the story of a weather plane which was supposed to fly only over Turkish territory. The statement speculated on the possibility of an oxygen failure.[6]

On Saturday morning, again before the sun reached Washington but in time for the press wires to get the news there as the city awakened, Khrushchev went before the Supreme Soviet for a second time. In an angry, derisive speech, he revealed that the Russians had the pilot and the wreckage of the plane and that Powers had told them that he was on an intelligence mission. It was a frantic day in Washington. While correspondents harassed information officers demanding statements, the information officers, in turn, pressed officials. These remained closeted at the State Department trying to decide what kind of a statement to make. The president was in Gettysburg but was in touch by telephone with those in the State Department meeting.

At 6:00 P.M. White, who had told the newsmen twenty-nine hours earlier that there was no deliberate attempt to violate Soviet airspace, appeared again before the correspondents in the State Department press room. Now his statement admitted that "a flight over Soviet territory was probably undertaken by an unarmed civilian U-2 plane." It justified the flight on the grounds of defense needs and Soviet rejection of Eisenhower's "open skies" proposal. "For the first time in its 184-year history," wrote the authors of a book about the flight, "the government of the United States had conceded publicly that it had deliberately lied, that it had committed espionage, and violated the territory of another country." [7]

There was much angry reaction in the following weeks over the fact that the government had been caught in an embarrassing lie. Typically, a year later the New York *Times*, in an editorial, agreed that defense secrets are necessary. "But the government had a duty also," it said. "Neither prudence nor ethics can justify any administration in telling the public things that are not so. . . . What some leaders of our Government stated . . . did not square with the facts. If they could not reveal the facts, they would have done better to remain silent. A democracy—our democracy—cannot be lied to."

Seven months after Powers's flight, on a very cold January day, Eisenhower turned over his duties to his young successor.

At the time of his television debates with Nixon during the campaign Kennedy had not known that, with Eisenhower's approval, the Central Intelligence Agency was secretly recruiting Cubans among the anti-Castro colony in this country for an armed force intended to overthrow the bearded dictator. Kennedy was informed of the fact some weeks before he took office but carefully said nothing in his inaugural address nor later.

Although the plan was secret, it was a poorly kept secret. Of course it was impossible to prevent from leaking out the fact that a considerable body of men was training in the Guatemalan highlands and was receiving arms that obviously came from the United States. Cubans in Florida were being recruited. And the fact of an imminent invasion was talked about among the exile colony. Castro's frenetic speeches repeatedly said that the United States was planning an invasion and he called on his people to resist to the death.

On November 19, 1961, the *Nation* published an editorial that made it known that there were training camps in Guatemala. Its information came from Ronald Hilton, director of the Institute of Hispano-American and Luso-Brazilian Studies at Stanford University. Few newspapers followed it up. On January 10, ten days before Kennedy was inaugurated, Paul P. Kennedy, the New York *Times* correspondent in Mexico and Central America, sent a story under a Retalhuleu, Guatemala, dateline which said that men were being trained on a coffee plantation there for Guatemala's "almost inevitable clash with Cuba." The story did not say that the camp was being financed and supplied by the United States nor that training was being carried on under the direction of American military leaders. Nor did it say that the trainees planned to invade Cuba. President Miguel Ydígoras Fuentes ordered Kennedy expelled from Guatemala after this story appeared, but his own press secretary later persuaded him to reverse the order.

In the recriminations which followed, several critics said that the American press should have taken the lead in attacking the movement as illegal and morally wrong and should have tried to persuade Kennedy to drop the plan.[8] Some of the postmortems also said that a few correspondents got leads on the invasion plans but refused to publish their information as a patriotic duty. Pierre Salinger wrote later, however, that "it is fair to say that some of the press went after the story as if it were a scandal at city hall or a kidnaping—not a military operation whose entire success might depend on the elements of surprise and secrecy." [9] He also wrote that his own official information of the proposed invasion came with a telephone call from the president as the Cubans were about to land. And the president at that time gave him no information. "[J]ust say that you know only what you've read in the newspapers," he was ordered.[10]

The plans worked out by the Central Intelligence Agency called for the destruction of the Cuban Air Force on Saturday, April 15. Bombers took off from Puerto Cabezas, Nicaragua, that day and bombed the airfields. But they did not destroy Castro's aviation, nor seriously damage it, and two of the aircraft, riddled with bullets, landed in Florida. One came down at Key West and one at Miami. Their pilots were rushed into seclusion, and American officials announced that they were defecting Castroite flyers. That was not true.

The following night ships carrying the invasion force of eager Cubans, armed and trained by American experts, approached the Bahia de Cochinos on the south coast of the island. From the beginning, plans miscarried. Ships carrying their reserve ammunition and water and much of their food were either sunk or they fled from the attacks of Castro's planes. Once ashore, the invaders fought bravely and well with the ammunition they had, hoping that United States armed forces would back them, that underground guerrillas within Cuba would cooperate to relieve the pressure on them, or that, at least, Castro's planes that controlled the air and harassed them would be destroyed by the active intervention of air cover from the great military power to the north. None of these things took place. By Thursday the survivors were scattered and were trying to escape either by sea or by fleeing through the swamps.

This happened just as the country's newspaper executives were gathering for their annual meetings. It has long been customary for the American Society of Newspaper Editors to meet in Washington during the third week of April each year. The next week the editors go on to New York for the annual members meeting of the Associated Press and the annual meeting of the American Newspaper Publishers Association. The president normally addresses them in Washington. And Kennedy had also accepted an invitation to address the Bureau of Advertising of the ANPA in New York a week later.

The executive, who had argued that the invasion was a Cuban affair and therefore had refused to commit American armed forces, faced the two journalistic groups while still crushed by the failure and by the recriminations, some of which blamed him personally. Before the Washington meeting he made a dramatic speech in which he promised that we would not abandon Cuba. Between then and his next address he thought at length about the proper place of the press in a national crisis. In this emotional atmosphere there was a great deal said about the part which the press played in the fiasco. Some writers argued that the information media should have brought pressure on the administration to drop the ill-starred adventure. Others condemned the few news stories which were carried about the plans and the Guatemalan camps prior to the invasion as revelations of secrets which helped Castro. The press was criticized for giving untruthful and misleading optimistic statements which were issued by a New York public relations firm during the first day of the attack. After it was all over reporters probed for more information about the background of the attempt.

Salinger described the events of April 12. On that day the president announced, on meeting his news conference, that "I do not think that any useful purpose would be served by my going into the Cuban question this morning." In spite of his attempt to head off probing in this area one reporter insisted on asking whether or not Secretary Rusk and Under Secretary of State Chester Bowles had opposed the Cuban venture. The president answered only that "the facts will come out in due time." [11] Back in his office Kennedy burst out: "What the hell do they want me to do—give them the roll call vote? I can't do that without compromising everybody involved and they ought to know that. If I'm going to knock some heads together, now isn't the time to do it with everybody looking down the barrel at us." It was then that Salinger made a suggestion which he would later regret. And Arthur M. Schlesinger, Jr., in a later book, has said that the president's next speech was a mistake.[12] Salinger suggested that the president "lay it on the line" before the ANPA.

Kennedy faced the publishers on the evening of April 27. He said in part:

The very word "secrecy" is repugnant in a free and open society; and we are as a people inherently and historically opposed to secret societies, to secret oaths, and to secret proceedings. . . . No official of my administration, whether his rank is high or low, civilian or military, should interpret my words here tonight as an excuse to censor the news, to stifle dissent, to cover up our mistakes, or to withhold from the press and the public the facts they deserve to know.

But I do ask every publisher, every editor, and every newsman in the nation to re-examine his own standards, and to recognize the nature of our country's peril. In time of war, the government and the press have customarily joined in an effort, based largely on self-discipline, to prevent unauthorized disclosures to the enemy. In time of "clear and present danger," the courts have held that even the privileged rights of the First Amendment must yield to the public's need for national security.

If the press is awaiting a declaration of war before it imposes the self-discipline of combat conditions, then I can only say that no war ever posed a greater threat to our security. If you are awaiting a finding of "clear and present danger," then I can only say that the danger has never been more clear and its presence has never been more imminent.

The press, he said, had made available to our enemies many details of our armed strength that should have been kept secret. He offered to cooperate if the press would consider "the voluntary assumption of specific new steps or machinery."

The speech did not pin the problem specifically to the Bay of Pigs failure. Newspaper editorials across the country, however, criticized the timing of the president's remarks, so soon after the Cuban venture, and saw a connection between them. And a meeting was scheduled with the president for May 7. On that date seven men headed by Mark Ferree, president of the ANPA and assistant general manager of the Scripps-Howard newspaper chain, and Felix McKnight, president of the ASNE and executive editor of the Dallas *Times-Herald*, met with Kennedy in the White House. (In 1969, as he puts these lines on paper, the writer wonders what the gods were thinking as they brought together Kennedy and a Dallas editor.) Others in the group included Turner Catledge, executive editor of the New York *Times* and a former member of that paper's Washington staff, and Benjamin H.

McKelway, president of the Associated Press and editor of the Washington *Evening Star*. There were no other members of the current or former corps of Washington correspondents. The president and the newspaper bosses failed to find any common ground on which they could agree. The statement that was issued after the meeting said that "it was agreed that the government and the press group would continue to review this subject and meet again in several months." No further conversations were held, however.

It was Cuba, again, which brought the third explosion over governmental secrecy and news release at a time of a difficult diplomatic and military confrontation. The press might have quarreled less with the government over its handling of the missile crisis of October 1962 if the assistant secretary of defense for public affairs had not at that time claimed that government had a right to use the news as a weapon. He may have used the word "lie," arguing that it was permissible under these circumstances. That he used that word is disputed.

There was a good deal of evidence that autumn that led American intelligence officials to believe that Cuba required their particularly close attention. On Sunday, October 14, photographs taken by two U-2 planes found indications that Soviet intermediate-range and medium-range ballistic missiles were being installed there. Officials quickly decided that those missiles could not be allowed to be finished. Officials quickly decided that they must not permit the Russians to install them in a position to launch nuclear warheads against cities in the United States and Latin America. How best to meet the dangerous situation was debated for the next week by the leaders in the White House, the State Department, the Defense Department, and the Central Intelligence Agency.[13]

Kennedy attended many of the meetings of the relatively small group which met for long hours in deepest secrecy that week. On the other hand, he engaged in carefully calculated activities intended to conceal his preoccupation and that of the others. He met the usual groups of visitors and made his scheduled speeches to support Democratic candidates in the congressional race which was then going on. Meanwhile Pierre Salinger and other information officers were carefully kept in the dark.

By the end of the week it was decided to impose a blockade to stop Soviet vessels which were carrying missiles to Cuba. And if that failed to bring about the removal of the weapons, the next step was to be either an air strike on the missile bases or an invasion. Ships, planes, and troops began to move. On Saturday morning, the 20th, Kennedy was in Chicago to make a campaign speech. It was there that a telephone call from Washington reached him which caused him to cancel the rest of his engagements and to return to the White House. Trying to conceal from the country—and from the Cubans and Russians—that steps were being taken to counter an extremely dangerous situation the president told Salinger to announce that he had a cold. His health was good. The story of the cold was only one of several concealments to which the administration resorted in the next two days. Movements of ships and troops are hard to cover up. It was given out that these were routine maneuvers.

On Monday evening Kennedy delivered a televised address which told the whole story and told of the government's decisions. During the tense week that followed, of diplomatic notes back and forth between Washington and Moscow, of personal notes between Kennedy and Khrushchev, and of action in the United Nations and the Organization of American States, the press gave intensive coverage. A Washington correspondent, John Scali of the American Broadcasting Company, was used by the Soviets as a channel for one of its approaches to the State Department. On other occasions both Moscow and Washington communicated with each other by public announcements which were transmitted rapidly by press wires instead of the slower diplomatic channels. By the end of the week agreement had been reached whereby the United States bound itself not to invade Cuba in return for Russian promises to remove the missiles.

During that tense week Salinger worked closely with Arthur Sylvester, assistant secretary of defense for public affairs, and Robert J. Manning, assistant secretary of state for public affairs. On October 23, the day after the president's speech, Salinger called to the White House some leaders of the nation's news, radio, and television industries. One of the group was Hagerty, Salinger's predecessor as press secretary, who was now head of the news staff of the American Broadcasting Company. Salinger discussed with them possible guidelines for the release of news during the tense period.

The next day he issued a statement setting forth twelve

points. "During the current tense international situation," the statement said, "the White House feels that the publication of such information is contrary to the public interest. We ask public information media of all types to exercise caution and discretion in the publication of such information." The twelve points dealt with various aspects of troop movements and the activity and readiness of the Air Force and the Navy. The statement said that a twenty-four-hour, seven-days-a-week watch would be set up in the Department of Defense and asked papers to seek advice if a question arose.[14]

Although editorials during World War II had in general supported Byron Price's Office of Censorship, this request that the press act in a similar manner when there had been no declaration of war was received coolly. Furthermore, there was criticism of the untruth which had been announced about Kennedy's cold and his return from Chicago and of the incorrect announcements made about movements of the fighting forces toward Cuba. The Moss subcommittee looked into the matter and criticized Salinger.

At the time that he announced the twelve-point program Salinger also said that orders had been handed down in both the State and Defense Departments that any official in either who talked to a newsman must either have present during the interview a staff member from the Department of Public Affairs or must report the fact of such a conversation to the information officers. Newsmen were angered by these orders and sought to contact cooperative officials without that surveillance. The order was soon rescinded in the State Department and, later, in the Defense Department by Secretary of Defense McNamara on June 30, 1967.

Further fuel was poured on the flames by two statements made by Sylvester. On October 30, in an interview, he said: "News generated by actions of the government as to content and timing are part of the arsenal of weaponry that a President has in application of military force and related forces to the solution of public problems, or to the application of international political pressure." [15] In December, speaking to the New York Deadline Club, he said, according to press accounts: "It would seem to be basic, all through history, that a government's right—and by government I mean people—that it is inherent in the government's right, if necessary, to lie to save itself when it's going up into a nuclear war. This seems to me basic." [16] He later denied that he used the word "lie." Of course such remarks brought angry howls from the editorial wolves.

There is discernible a certain movement through these three occurrences. The U-2 incident caused the government to lie in making its public announcements, and later to concede that it had done so. The Bay of Pigs again saw the government carefully withholding information. The president then got into a discussion with the press which only highlighted the essential conflict between the two. The press leaders refused to retreat a step or to give the government the cooperation which Kennedy asked. The Cuban missile crisis saw the government again using untruths to conceal its moves in an extremely tense international situation. And this time a government official justified lying as part of the government's "weaponry." Press leaders denied that lying was justified.

And the two incidents of 1971 carried the government-press conflict one step farther. For the first time in the history of the two institutions, government threatened the press with court action. The move of a congressional committee to demand private material related to the CBS documentary, "The Selling of the Pentagon," and the Department of Justice effort to restrain the publication of the secret Pentagon papers were regarded by newsmen as steps by congressional and administration chiefs to intimidate the information media.

Conflict, therefore, was the significant mark of the relationship between the press and the government as the country approached the end of its second century of independence.

NOTES / INDEX

1 News in Washington

[1] This correspondence is in the Jonathan Bayard Smith Collection, Manuscript Division, Library of Congress.

[2] Douglass Cater, *The Fourth Branch of Government* (Boston, 1959), chapter 3.

2 Parliament and Congress

[1] Fred Siebert, *The History of Freedom of the Press in England, 1476–1776* (Urbana, Ill., 1952); Francis Williams, *Dangerous Estate* (London, 1957); Harold Herd, *The March of Journalism* (London, 1952); Joseph George Muddiman [J. B. Williams, pseud.], *A History of English Journalism to the Foundation of the Gazette* (London and New York, 1908); Laurence Hanson, *Government and the Press, 1695–1763* (London, 1936); R. W. Postgate, *That Devil Wilkes* (London, 1956); Georges Jacques Weill, *Le journal: origines, évolution et rôle de la presse périodique* (Paris, 1934). The last of these books has never been published in English. It has been translated into Spanish and two editions brought out in Mexico City.

[2] Elizabeth Gregory McPherson, "Reports of the Debates of the House of Representatives During the First Congress," *Quarterly Journal of Speech*, February 1944, p. 69.

[3] Elizabeth Gregory McPherson, "Reporting the Debates of Congress," *Quarterly Journal of Speech*, April 1942, p. 142.

[4] Elizabeth Gregory McPherson, "The Southern States and the Reporting of Senate Debates," *Journal of Southern History*, May 1940, pp. 223–27.

[5] U.S., Congress, House, *Journal*, 6th Cong., 2d sess., 1800, p. 734.

[6] Ibid., pp. 735–37.

[7] U.S., Congress, House, *Annals of Congress*, 7th Cong., 1st sess., 1802, p. 407.

[8] Senate, *Annals of Congress*, 7th Cong., 1st sess., 1801, p. 22; U.S., Congress, Senate, *Journal*, 7th Cong., 1st sess., 1801, pp. 38, 41.

[9] U.S., Congress, House, Committee on Rules, *Report of the Committee on Rules*, 12th Cong., 1st sess., December 2, 1811.

[10] House, *Journal*, 13th Cong., 1st sess., 1813, p. 29.

[11] House, *Journal,* 14th Cong., 1st sess., 1815, pp. 44, 50.

[12] Asher Crosby Hinds, *Precedents of the House of Representatives of the United States Congress,* 5 vols. (Washington, 1907), vol. 2, pp. 1052–56; Senate, *Journal,* 6th Cong., 1st sess., pp. 45, 51–54, 98.

[13] House, *Journal,* 12th Cong., 1st sess., 1812, *Supplemental Journal,* pp. 438, 445–46. House, *Annals of Congress,* 12th Cong., 1st sess., 1812, pp. 1255–57, 1263–66, 1271–74.

[14] U.S., Congress, *Biographical Directory of the American Congress* (Washington, 1927), p. 940; New York *Gazette and General Advertiser,* December 19, 1809.

3 Correspondents Appear at the Capital

[1] Ben: Perley Poore, "Washington News." *Harper's New Monthly Magazine,* January 1874, pp. 225–36.

[2] Joseph Tinker Buckingham, *Personal Memoirs and Recollections of Editorial Life,* 2 vols. (Boston, 1852), vol. 2, p. 17.

[3] Oliver Carlson, *The Man Who Made News: James Gordon Bennett* (New York, 1942), p. 80.

[4] Frederic Hudson, *Journalism in the United States* (New York, 1873), p. 286.

[5] Providence *Journal,* June 20, 1883.

[6] William Horatio Barnes, *The Fortieth Congress of the United States: Historical and Biographical,* 2 vols. (New York, 1869), vol. 1, p. 185. I have not included Robert Walsh, editor of the *National Gazette* of Philadelphia, among these pioneers because he was not a Washington correspondent although through a curious set of circumstances he has been listed as one. Bennett once wrote in his *Herald* that Walsh sat in his Philadelphia office writing "stupid letters" to himself, thereby gaining a reputation as a Washington correspondent. That line was reprinted by Frederic Hudson in his *Journalism in the United States.* Therefore Frank Luther Mott in his *American Journalism* (New York, 1941), p. 198, listed Walsh as a Washington pioneer. The *National Gazette* files, however, show that Walsh not only had no Washington correspondence but that he did not write to himself any such letters as Bennett describes.

[7] John Quincy Adams, *Memoirs of John Quincy Adams Comprising Portions of His Diary From 1795 to 1848,* 12 vols. (Philadelphia, 1876), vol. 6, p. 61.

4 Jacksonian Democracy and the Press

[1] There is much literature on Blair. In particular see William Ernest Smith, *The Francis Preston Blair Family in Politics,* 2 vols. (New York, 1933). Also see the same author's "Francis P. Blair, Pen-Executive of Andrew Jackson," *Mississippi Valley Historical Review,* March 1931, pp. 543–56.

[2] U.S., Congress, House, *Congressional Globe*, 25th Cong., 2d sess., 1838, pp. 173–79.

[3] U.S., Congress, House, Select Committee, *Death of Mr. Cilley—Duel*, 25th Cong., 2d sess., April 21, 1838, H. Rept. 825.

[4] Senate, *Congressional Globe*, 25th Cong., 2d sess., 1838, pp. 186, 194, 302–3; U.S., Congress, Senate, *Report of the Select Committee*, 25th Cong., 2d sess., April 12, 1838, S. Doc. 337.

[5] Arthur M. Schlesinger, Jr., *The Age of Jackson* (Boston, 1945), p. 290.

5 *The New York* Herald

[1] U.S., Congress, Senate, *Register of Debates*, 20th Cong., 1st sess., 1827, p. 8.

[2] U.S., Congress, Senate, *Journal*, 23d Cong., 2d sess., 1835, pp. 198, 238; Senate, *Journal*, 24th Cong., 1st sess., 1835, p. 5.

[3] U.S., Congress, House, *Journal*, 25th Cong., 2d sess., 1838, p. 510.

[4] Senate, *Journal*, 25th Cong., 2d sess., 1838, pp. 311, 318, 376; U.S., Congress, Senate, *Congressional Globe*, 25th Cong., 2d sess., 1838, p. 506.

[5] Senate, *Congressional Globe*, 25th Cong., 3d sess., 1838, p. 61.

[6] Senate, *Congressional Globe*, 25th Cong., 3d sess., 1839, pp. 100–103.

[7] Senate, *Journal*, 27th Cong., 1st sess., 1841, p. 73; Senate, *Congressional Globe*, 27th Cong., 1st sess., 1841, p. 145.

[8] Senate, *Journal*, 27th Cong., 1st sess., 1841, p. 78.

[9] Southard's order was not given in such official or semiofficial Senate records as the *Journal*, the *Congressional Globe*, or the then-current official compilation known informally as *Jefferson's Manual*. It was recorded, however, in a privately printed competitor for that manual. See *Manual of Parliamentary Practice, compiled originally for the Senate of the United States by Thomas Jefferson. The Constitution of the United States, and the Rules for Conducting Business in Both Houses of Congress. With all the Amendments, Erasures and Additions down to the year 1848.* (Columbus, Ohio, 1848), pp. 192–94.

[10] Nathan Sargent, *Public Men and Events from the Commencement of Mr. Monroe's Administration, in 1817, to the Close of Mr. Fillmore's Administration, in 1853*, 2 vols. (Philadelphia, 1875), vol. 2, pp. 135–36.

[11] John Quincy Adams, *Memoirs of John Quincy Adams Comprising Portions of His Diary From 1795 to 1848*, 12 vols. (Philadelphia, 1876), vol. 11, p. 250.

[12] James E. Pollard, *The Presidents and the Press* (New York, 1947), p. 218.

[13] When I wrote my doctoral dissertation I was unable to identify Parmelee. Both Professors Arthur M. Schlesinger and his son, Arthur M. Schlesinger, Jr., author of *The Age of Jackson* and other books and later an aide to President Kennedy, were on the committee which administered my final oral examination. At that time the younger Professor Schlesinger told me that he believed that the T. N. Parmelee, who wrote the "Recollections

of an Old Stager," *Harper's New Monthly Magazine,* serially, August 1872 to June 1874, was probably the *Herald* correspondent to whom Adams and Hone referred. The articles were published anonymously but Schlesinger said that the name was handwritten in the magazine's files in the Harvard College Library.

6 Democrats and Whigs

[1] Charles Henry Ambler, *Thomas Ritchie, a Study in Virginia Politics* (Richmond, 1913), pp. 240–60; Nathan Sargent, *Public Men and Events from the Commencement of Mr. Monroe's Administration, in 1817, to the Close of Mr. Fillmore's Administration, in 1853,* 2 vols. (Philadelphia, 1875), vol. 2, pp. 266–68; William Ernest Smith, *The Francis Preston Blair Family in Politics,* 2 vols. (New York, 1933), vol. 1, chapter 4; Thomas Hart Benton, *Thirty Years View,* 2 vols. (New York and London, 1856), vol. 2, pp. 650–52; James E. Pollard, *The Presidents and the Press* (New York, 1947), pp. 233–39.

[2] Ambler, *Thomas Ritchie, a Study in Virginia Politics,* p. 264; U.S., Congress, House, Senate, *Congressional Globe,* 29th Cong., 1st sess., 1845–46, pp. 14–19, 66–67, 176–79, 1129–30, 1167–70.

[3] Ambler, *Thomas Ritchie, a Study in Virginia Politics,* p. 266; U.S., Congress, Senate, *Congressional Globe,* 29th Cong., 2d sess., 1847, pp. 366, 416; U.S., Congress, Senate, *Journal,* 29th Cong., 2d sess., 1847, p. 320.

[4] Pollard, *Presidents and the Press,* discusses them. Buchanan's troubles with the *Union* and the *Constitution* are told in Roy F. Nichols, *The Disruption of American Democracy* (New York, 1948).

[5] Nicolay Papers, Manuscript Division, Library of Congress.

[6] Cincinnati *Gazette,* October 2, 1867; Ben: Perley Poore, *Perley's Reminiscences of Sixty Years in the National Metropolis,* 2 vols. (Philadelphia, 1886), vol. 2, p. 20.

[7] House, *Congressional Globe,* 29th Cong., 1st sess., 1846, p. 457.

[8] L. A. Gobright, *Recollection of Men and Things at Washington During the Third of a Century* (Philadelphia, 1869), pp. 76–77.

[9] New York *Tribune,* December 6, 1846.

7 The Telegraph

[1] Robert Luther Thompson, *Wiring a Continent* (Princeton, 1947), p. 47.

[2] Ibid., pp. 221–22; Alexander Jones, *Historical Sketch of the Electric Telegraph* (New York, 1852), pp. 132–37.

[3] Oliver Gramling, *AP: The Story of News* (New York, 1940), pp. 19–21.

[4] Victor Rosewater, *The History of Cooperative Newsgathering* (New York, 1930), p. 66.

[5] Ibid., pp. 381–85.

[6] L. A. Gobright, *Recollection of Men and Things at Washington During the Third of a Century* (Philadelphia, 1869), pp. 171–73.

[7] *The Congressional Directory for the Second Session of the Thirty-Second Congress* (Washington, Alfred Hunter, publisher, 1853), p. 47.

[8] New York *Herald*, November 26, 1850.

[9] New York *Tribune*, November 30, 1852.

[10] Associated Press dispatch in papers of December 1, 1856.

[11] New York *Herald*, December 3, 1860.

[12] Gobright, *Recollection of Men and Things at Washington During the Third of a Century*, pp. 228–29.

[13] Nicolay Papers, Manuscript Division, Library of Congress.

8 The Arrest of John Nugent

[1] U.S., Congress, Senate, *Journal*, 30th Cong., 1st sess., 1848, p. 353.

[2] *Nugent vs. Beale*, 18 Fed. Cas. 471.

[3] Grund to Edmund Burke, April 17, 1849, and August 17, 1853, Burke Papers, Manuscript Division, Library of Congress; Grund to William L. Marcy, April 9, 1853, Marcy Papers, Manuscript Division, Library of Congress.

[4] For the Nugent proceedings, see Senate, *Journal*, 30th Cong., 1st sess., 1848, pp. 353–403.

9 The Press as Disunion Neared

[1] Jane Grey Swisshelm, *Half a Century* (Chicago, 1880).

[2] Ibid., p. 130.

[3] U.S., Congress, House, *Congressional Globe*, 32d Cong., 2d sess., 1852, p. 52.

[4] House, *Congressional Globe*, 34th Cong., 3d sess., 1857, pp. 274–77.

[5] U.S., Congress, House, Select Committee, *Alleged Corrupt Combinations of Congress*, 34th Cong., 3d sess., March 3, 1857, H. Rept. 243.

[6] House, *Congressional Globe*, 34th Cong., 3d sess., 1857, pp. 404–5, 411–12, 426–45, 630.

[7] Glenn Brown, *History of the United States Capitol*, 2 vols. (Washington, 1902), vol. 2, pp. 124–27.

[8] House, *Congressional Globe*, 35th Cong., 1st sess., 1857, p. 32.

[9] Ibid., pp. 59, 170.

[10] U.S., Congress, Senate, *Journal*, 35th Cong., 1st sess., 1858, pp. 62, 96, 110.

[11] U.S., Congress, Senate, *Congressional Globe*, 35th Cong., 2d sess., 1859, p. 304; Senate, *Journal*, 35th Cong., 2d sess., 1859, p. 119.

[12] Senate, *Congressional Globe*, 35th Cong., 2d sess., 1859, p. 304; Senate, *Journal*, 35th Cong., 2d sess., 1859, p. 119.

10 The Civil War—1

[1] "Documents: Federal Generals and a Good Press," *American Historical Review*, January 1934, p. 284.

2 *The Proper Relationship Between the Army and the Press in War*, Army War College Document 528 (Washington, 1916). Other aspects of the problem are discussed in James G. Randall, *Constitutional Problems Under Lincoln* (New York, 1926), chapter 19; the same author's "The Newspaper Problem in its Bearing Upon Military Secrecy During the Civil War," *American Historical Review*, January 1918, pp. 303–23; Bernard A. Weisberger, *Reporters for the Union* (Boston, 1953), chapter 1.

3 Henry Villard, *Memoirs of Henry Villard, Journalist and Financier*, 2 vols. (Boston and New York, 1904), vol. 1, p. 173.

4 Louis M. Starr, *Bohemian Brigade* (New York, 1954), p. 68.

5 Ibid., pp. 70–71; J. Cutler Andrews, *The North Reports the Civil War* (Pittsburgh, 1955), p. 116; Villard, *Memoirs of Henry Villard, Journalist and Financier*, vol. 1, pp. 209–10.

6 Starr, *Bohemian Brigade*, pp. 72–73.

7 Lincoln's letter is in John G. Nicolay and John Hay, *Complete Works of Abraham Lincoln*, 12 vols. (New York, 1909), vol. 11, pp. 120–22. The incident is discussed in Ralph Ray Fahrney, *Horace Greeley and the Tribune in the Civil War* (Cedar Rapids, Iowa, 1936), pp. 92–95, and in Harlan Hoyt Horner, *Lincoln and Greeley* (Urbana, Ill., 1953), pp. 246–47. Horner implies that Lincoln may not have written the letter of November 21.

8 Starr, *Bohemian Brigade*, p. 77, quoting the New York *Tribune* of March 12, 1862.

9 Ives to Bennett, January 29, 1862. James Gordon Bennett Papers, Manuscript Division, Library of Congress.

10 Villard, *Memoirs of Henry Villard, Journalist and Financier*, vol. 1, p. 156.

11 Ben: Perley Poore, *Perley's Reminiscences of Sixty Years in the National Metropolis*, 2 vols. (Philadelphia, 1886), vol. 2, pp. 62–63.

12 Both letters are in the James Gordon Bennett Papers, Manuscript Division, Library of Congress.

13 Andrews, *The North Reports the Civil War*, pp. 615–18.

11   The Civil War—2

1 L. A. Gobright, *Recollection of Men and Things at Washington During the Third of a Century* (Philadelphia, 1869), p. 334.

2 Ibid., p. 319.

3 Ibid., pp. 335–36.

4 Ibid., p. 334.

5 Henry Villard, *Memoirs of Henry Villard, Journalist and Financier*, 2 vols. (Boston and New York, 1904), vol. 1, pp. 171–73.

6 Ibid., p. 173; R. S. West, Jr., "The Navy and the Press During the Civil War," *United States Naval Institute Proceedings*, January 1937, p. 38.

7 Villard, *Memoirs of Henry Villard, Journalist and Financier*, vol. 1, p. 339.

8 James Gordon Bennett Papers, Manuscript Division, Library of Congress.

9 U.S., Congress, House, Committee on the Judiciary, *Telegraphic Censorship*, 37th Cong., 2d sess., March 20, 1862, H. Rept. 84, p. 1.

10 Gobright tells of several clashes with the censor. Also see Whiteley to Bennett, September 10, 1862, James Gordon Bennett Papers.

11 House, Committee on the Judiciary, *Telegraphic Censorship*, pp. 2–3.

12 Ibid., passim.

13 The orders governing the telegraph which were issued from August 1861 to February 25, 1862, are to be found in *The War of the Rebellion: A Compilation of the Official Records of the Union and Confederate Armies* (Washington: published under the direction of the secretary of war, 1880–1901), series 2, vol. 1, p. 899; series 2, vol. 2, pp. 40, 246; series 3, vol. 1, pp. 324, 390.

14 Suspensions of newspapers and arrests of editors are discussed in Robert S. Harper, *Lincoln and the Press* (New York, 1951).

15 Gideon Welles, *The Diary of Gideon Welles*, 3 vols. (Boston and New York, 1911), vol. 1, p. 357.

16 Frank Abiel Flower, *Edwin McMasters Stanton, the Autocrat of Rebellion, Emancipation and Reconstruction* (Akron, 1905), pp. 214–15.

17 James E. Pollard, *The Presidents and the Press* (New York, 1947), p. 366.

18 Gobright, *Recollection of Men and Things at Washington During the Third of a Century*, pp. 348–57.

12   Washington Correspondents and Correspondence

1 Ben: Perley Poore, *Perley's Reminiscences of Sixty Years in the National Metropolis*, 2 vols. (Philadelphia, 1886), vol. 2, p. 525.

2 U.S., Congress, House, *Congressional Globe*, 39th Cong., 1st sess., 1866, p. 1032.

3 U.S., Congress, Senate, *Congressional Record*, 43d Cong., special session of the Senate, 1873, p. 48.

4 Senate, *Congressional Record*, 51st Cong., 1st sess., 1890, pp. 1794–96.

5 Francis A. Richardson, "Recollections of a Washington Correspondent," *Records of the Columbia Historical Society*, 1903, pp. 24–42.

6 George Rothwell Brown, *Washington, a Not Too Serious History* (Baltimore, 1930), p. 344.

7 For descriptions of Newspaper Row, see Brown, *Washington, A Not Too Serious History*, pp. 331–35; Ralph M. MacKenzie, *Directory of Washington Correspondents* (Washington, 1903), pp. 12–13; and Fred A. Emery, "Washington Newspaper Correspondents." *Records of the Columbia Historical Society*, 1935, pp. 248–88.

13   The Press at the Capitol

1 U.S., Congress, House, *Congressional Globe*, 41st Cong., 2d sess., 1870, pp. 4314–16, 4318–22, 4692; U.S., Congress, House, Select Commit-

tee, *W. Scott Smith*, 41st Cong., 2d sess., June 22, 1870, H. Rept. 104.

[2] U.S., Congress, Senate, *Journal*, 42d Cong., special session of the Senate, 1871, p. 162.

[3] U.S., Congress, Senate, Select Committee, *Publication of the Treaty of Washington*, 42d Cong., special session of the Senate, May 25, 1871, S. Rept. 5.

[4] Harry W. Baehr, *The New York Tribune Since the Civil War* (New York, 1936), pp. 96–97.

[5] U.S., Congress, Senate, *Congressional Globe*, 42d Cong., special session of the Senate, 1871, pp. 846–931; Senate, *Journal*, 42d Cong., special session of the Senate, 1871, pp. 164–65.

[6] U.S., Congress, House, *Congressional Record*, 43d Cong., 2d sess., 1875, p. 2232; U.S., Congress, House, Committee on Ways and Means, *China Mail Service*, 43d Cong., 2d sess., February 27, 1875, H. Rept. 268.

[7] The Washington *Post, A History of the City of Washington: Its Men and Institutions* (Washington, 1903), pp. 138–39.

[8] House, *Congressional Record*, 47th Cong., 2d sess., 1883, p. 3747.

[9] The meeting is described in the *Evening Star* of March 6 and in U.S., Congress, House, Select Committee, *Charges against H. V. Boynton*, 48th Cong., 1st sess., April 1, 1884, H. Rept. 1112.

[10] Cincinnati *Commercial Gazette*, May 8, 1883.

[11] The correspondence is in House, Select Committee, *Charges against H. V. Boynton*, pp. 247–56.

[12] House, *Congressional Record*, 48th Cong., 1st sess., 1884, p. 741.

[13] House, Select Committee, *Charges against H. V. Boynton*, p. vi.

[14] House, *Congressional Record*, 48th Cong., 1st sess., 1884, p. 2871.

14 The Press at the Capitol

[1] U.S., Congress, Senate, Committee on Rules, *Use of Reporters' Galleries in the Senate*, 76th Cong., 1st sess., April 21, 1931, S. Rept. 317, p. 3.

[2] Samuel J. Randall Papers, University of Pennsylvania Library.

[3] Checks in the Library of Congress, the National Archives, the office of Speaker Samuel Rayburn, and the Clerk of the House failed to produce the original of Randall's order. In 1953 Mrs. Henry Bacon of Goshen, N.Y., Speaker Randall's daughter, turned over her father's papers to the University of Pennsylvania Library. A search through those papers for parts of 1877, 1879, and 1880 revealed the Adams letter quoted here. There were parts of the collection including correspondence in 1877 and 1878 which this writer found it impossible to examine but which may contain the sought-after correspondence. The secret of the Standing Committee's origin may still be in that collection.

[4] *Standing Rules for Conducting Business in the Senate of the United States*, reported by the Committee on Rules, January 11, 1884 (Washington, 1884).

[5] *Rules for the Regulation of the Senate Wing of the United States*

Capitol, adopted by the Committee on Rules, March 15, 1884 (Washington, 1884).

[6] U.S., Congress, House, *Congressional Record,* 60th Cong., 2d sess., 1909, pp. 2649–50. See also House, *Congressional Record,* 62d Cong., 1st sess., 1911, p. 20.

[7] House, *Congressional Record,* 64th Cong., 1st sess., 1916, p. 1214. See also House, *Congressional Record,* 64th Cong., 2d sess., 1916, p. 277.

[8] New York *Times,* January 24, 1929.

[9] "Mallon 'Upsets' Senate," *Editor and Publisher,* January 25, 1929, p. 1.

[10] U.S., Congress, Senate, *Congressional Record,* 71st Cong., 1st sess., 1929, p. 259.

[11] Ibid., pp. 1597–98, 1618–24.

[12] George H. Manning, "Secret Vote Leak Arouses U.S. Senate," *Editor and Publisher,* May 25, 1929, p. 64.

[13] Senate, *Congressional Record,* 71st Cong., 1st sess., 1929, pp. 1726–30; New York *Times,* May 23, 1929.

[14] George H. Manning, "Press Forces Senate to Alter Rules," *Editor and Publisher,* June 1, 1929, pp. 9, 56.

[15] The Mallon debate is in scattered parts of Senate, *Congressional Record,* 71st Cong., 1st sess., 1929, pp. 1597–3054 passim.

[16] The author has private information on this point.

15   *The Press at the White House*

[1] Ben: Perley Poore, "Washington News," *Harper's New Monthly Magazine,* January 1874, pp. 225–36, does not identify MACK although the article includes a drawing of the president talking to the reporter. Francis A. Richardson, "Recollections of a Washington Correspondent," *Records of the Columbia Historical Society,* 1903, pp. 24–42, says MACK was McCullagh.

[2] James E. Pollard, *The Presidents and the Press* (New York, 1947), pp. 413–28.

[3] Those who wish more detail on the press relationships of these presidents are referred to Dr. Pollard's excellent study. It has been relied on heavily in the preparation of this chapter.

[4] Personal interview with James D. Preston.

[5] Letter from Fred A. Emery to the author in September of 1953.

[6] Interview with James D. Preston.

[7] David S. Barry, *Forty Years in Washington* (Boston, 1924), pp. 267–69.

[8] Delbert Clark, *Washington Dateline* (New York, 1941), pp. 55–56.

[9] Oswald Garrison Villard, "Press and Presidents." *Century,* December 1925, pp. 193–200.

[10] Pollard, *The Presidents and the Press,* pp. 604–5.

[11] Arthur Wallace Dunn, *From Harrison to Harding: A Personal Narrative Covering a Third of a Century,* 2 vols. (New York, 1922), vol. 1, p. 201.

[12] J. Fred Essary, *Covering Washington* (New York, 1927), p. 98.

13 Ray Stannard Baker, *Life and Letters of Woodrow Wilson,* 8 vols. (New York, 1927–39), vol. 4, p. 230.

14 *Editor and Publisher,* April 4, 1914, p. 834.

15 Clark, *Washington Dateline,* p. 61; Essary, *Covering Washington,* p. 90.

16 Frank R. Kent, "Mr. Coolidge," *American Mercury,* August 1924, pp. 305–90; Villard, "Press and Presidents."

17 Pollard, *The Presidents and the Press,* p. 741.

18 Ibid., pp. 737–70.

19 Samuel I. Rosenman, comp., *The Public Papers and Addresses of Franklin D. Roosevelt,* 13 vols. (New York, 1938–50), vol. 2, pp. 30–31.

20 Ibid.

21 Clark, Washington Dateline, pp. 74–76; Rosenman, *The Public Papers and Addresses of Franklin D. Roosevelt,* vol. 2, p. 38.

22 Clark, *Washington Dateline,* pp. 74–76.

23 Personal letter to the author from John Russell Young, White House reporter for the *Evening Star* of Washington for many years, written in January 1954. This author, as a member of the Associated Press staff in Washington from 1933 to 1937, was a frequent visitor to the White House press room and attended many of Roosevelt's press conferences.

24 Anthony Leviero, "Press and President; No Holds Barred." *New York Times Magazine,* August 21, 1949, p. 10.

25 W. H. Lawrence, "Mr. President, What Do You Think of ———." *New York Times Magazine,* December 27, 1953, p. 33.

26 George E. Reedy, *The Twilight of the Presidency* (New York, 1970), p. 163.

27 Arthur Krock, "Mr. Kennedy's Management of the News," *Fortune,* March 1963, p. 82.

28 For instance, see Richard Rovere, "Letter from Washington," *New Yorker,* March 30, 1963, pp. 163–70.

29 See the account of arrangements for this interview in Fred Friendly, *Due to Circumstances Beyond Our Control* (New York, 1967), pp. 146–51. This account of Kennedy's news conferences depends on the author's own observation and to some extent on private contacts. Some book sources include: Pierre Salinger, *With Kennedy* (New York, 1966); Fred Friendly's book, cited above; Douglass Cater, *Power in Washington* (New York, 1964); and James Reston, *The Artillery of the Press* (New York, 1967). Magazine sources include the articles of Krock and Rovere cited above and Tom Wicker, "Q's and A's About the Press Conference," *New York Times Magazine,* September 8, 1963, pp. 24–25, 120; and James E. Pollard, "The Kennedy Administration and the Press," *Journalism Quarterly,* winter 1964, pp. 3–14.

30 Reston, *The Artillery of the Press,* p. 53.

31 This statement is based on private and personal statements to the author by some correspondents.

32 William S. White, *The Professional: Lyndon B. Johnson* (Boston, 1964), pp. 70–72.

16 The Press in the Departments

[1] J. A. R. Pimlott, *Public Relations and American Democracy* (Princeton, 1951), p. 85.

[2] T. Swann Harding, "Genesis of one 'Government Propaganda Mill,'" *Public Opinion Quarterly*, summer 1947, pp. 227–35.

[3] *First Report of the Secretary of Agriculture* (Washington, 1889), pp. 10–11.

[4] *Report of the Secretary of Agriculture for 1910*, p. 263.

[5] U.S., Congress, House, *Congressional Record*, 60th Cong., 2d sess., 1908, pp. 4137–40.

[6] House, *Congressional Record*, 61st Cong., 2d sess., 1910, p. 664; U.S., Congress, House, Committee on the Census, *Press Bureau*, 61st Cong., 2d sess., January 24, 1910, H. Rept. 296.

[7] House, *Congressional Record*, 62d Cong., 2d sess., 1912, p. 6851.

[8] U.S., Congress, House, Committee on Rules, *Department Press Agents: Hearing on H. Res. 545*, 62d Cong., 2d sess., May 21, 1912.

[9] House, *Congressional Record*, 63d Cong., 1st sess., 1913, pp. 4409–10.

[10] Bruce Catton, "Handouts," in *Dateline: Washington*, edited by Cabell Phillips et al. (Garden City, N.Y., 1949), p. 165.

[11] Scott Hart, "From Such a Bond," in *Dateline: Washington*, pp. 30–31.

[12] Harding, "Genesis of one 'Government Propaganda Mill,'" p. 231.

[13] Ibid., p. 232.

[14] Department of the Army, *Special Regulations No. 10–70–1* (Washington, February 25, 1952), p. 2.

[15] Lieutenant Heyward E. Canney, Jr., "The History of Army Public Information." Typewritten monograph prepared in the Public Information Division, Department of the Army, in 1950 and made available to this writer by Lieutenant Colonel Frederick Blanchard, administrative officer of the division, in August 1952.

[16] Unless otherwise cited all War Department information herein presented is from Canney's monograph.

[17] Sketch provided by the Office of Information.

[18] Interview with Michael J. McDermott in August 1952.

[19] Interview with Miss Helene Philibert who worked for many years in the Navy Information section.

[20] Interview with McDermott.

[21] Bureau of the Budget, *The United States at War* (Washington, 1946), p. 211; Material given the writer by the Office of Information, Department of the Navy.

[22] *The United States at War*, pp. 217–19; all other State Department material, unless otherwise cited, is derived from an interview with McDermott.

[23] In addition to the letter here referred to, I had an interview with Robert J. McCloskey on September 11, 1967.

[24] Copies of orders and memoranda dealing with the organization of 1948 and 1949 were given to the writer in 1952.

[25] Information given by William E. Odom, special assistant to the assistant secretary of defense for public affairs and by other officials of the Department of Defense during interviews on September 12, 1967. Odom supplied further information in letters on October 5, 1967, and March 7, 1969.

[26] *Wall Street Journal,* March 21, 1969.

17 Enter Radio, Television, and Magazines

[1] Interview with Fred Morrison in June 1954.

[2] Interview with Fulton Lewis, Jr., in June 1954.

[3] This discussion is based on records of the Standing Committee.

[4] U.S., Congress, Senate, *Congressional Record,* 76th Cong., 1st sess., 1939, p. 3875. See also U.S., Congress, Senate, Committee on Rules, *Use of Reporters Galleries in Senate,* 76th Cong., 1st sess., April 21, 1939, S. Rept. 317.

[5] Senate, *Congressional Record,* 76th Cong., 1st sess., 1939, pp. 4720–21.

[6] U.S., Congress, House, *Congressional Record,* 76th Cong., 1st sess., 1939, p. 4422.

[7] Ibid., p. 4561.

[8] House, *Congressional Record,* 76th Cong., 3d sess., 1940, p. 7208.

[9] Letter to the author from Speaker Joseph W. Martin, Jr., on June 25, 1954.

[10] This account is based on minutes of the Radio Correspondents' Association and on interviews with Robert M. Menaugh and D. Harold McGrath.

[11] Interviews with Bryson Rash of ABC and Lewis B. Shollenberger of CBS, members of the group for their respective chains in 1954. Rash was on the original one in 1946.

[12] U.S., Congress, Senate, Subcommittee of the Committee on Appropriations, *Legislative-Judiciary Appropriation, 1954: Hearings on H.R. 5805,* 83d Cong., 1st sess., 1953, pp. 49–50.

[13] This account of the periodical press is based largely on a personal interview with William M. Perry in the Senate periodical press gallery in 1954 and on personal letters from Frank McNaughton and from George Cullen, president of the Periodical Correspondents' Association in 1954.

18 The Press and Twentieth-Century War

[1] Creel wrote *How We Advertised America,* a book which was devoted entirely to the Committee on Public Information, in 1920 and *Rebel at Large,* an autobiography, in 1947. His third book is *Complete Report of the Chairman of the Committee on Public Information* (Washington, 1920).

[2] James R. Mock and Cedric Larson, *Words that Won the War: The Story of the Committee on Public Information, 1917–1919.* (Princeton, 1949).

[3] Ibid., pp. 50–51.

[4] George Creel, *How We Advertised America: The First Telling of the Amazing Story of the Committee on Public Information that Carried the Gospel of Americanism to Every Corner of the Globe* (New York and London, 1920), chapter 2.

[5] George Creel, *Complete Report of the Chairman of the Committee on Public Information* (Washington, 1920), p. 13.

[6] George Creel, "The Plight of the Last Censor," *Collier's,* May 24, 1941, p. 13.

[7] George Creel, *Rebel at Large: Recollections of Fifty Crowded Years* (New York, 1947), p. 159.

[8] Creel, *Complete Report of the Chairman of the Committee on Public Information,* pp. 13–14; Delbert Clark, *Washington Dateline* (New York, 1941), chapter 15.

[9] Bureau of the Budget, *The United States at War* (Washington, 1946), chapter 8.

[10] This discussion of the Office of Censorship relies almost entirely on Theodore F. Koop, *Weapon of Silence* (Chicago, 1946).

[11] Cabell Phillips et al., ed., *Dateline: Washington* (Garden City, N.Y., 1949), p. 223.

[12] Unless otherwise cited the discussion of the OWI which follows is based on the report which Elmer Davis wrote for the president in 1945. Both Mr. Davis and Dr. Milton Eisenhower read an earlier draft of this chapter and Dr. Eisenhower made suggestions which have been incorporated in it.

[13] *The United States at War,* pp. 220–26.

[14] Ibid., p. 230.

19 The Columnists

Notes were not used in this chapter. It derives from the author's own contacts and from various biographical reference sources. Some literary references are: Elmo Scott Watson, *A History of Newspaper Syndicates in the United States, 1865–1935* (Chicago, 1936); Charles Fisher, *The Columnists* (New York, 1944); and Cabell Phillips, "Autocrats of the Breakfast Table," in *Dateline: Washington,* edited by Cabell Phillips et al. (Garden City, N.Y., 1949), pp. 171–82.

20 Washington Correspondents Are Sociable

[1] In addition to the newspaper references cited in the text, on the early clubs, see Arthur J. Dodge, *A Short History of Newspapers, Newspapermen, and Newspapermen's Clubs in the Life of the National Capital* (Washington, 1942); Duncan Aikman, "Prehistory," in *Dateline: Washington,* edited by

Cabell Phillips et al. (Garden City, N.Y., 1949), pp. 21–25; Fred A. Emery, "Washington Newspaper Correspondents," *Records of the Columbia Historical Society*, 1935, p. 265; George Rothwell Brown, *Washington: A Not Too Serious History* (Baltimore, 1930), p. 338.

2 Arthur Wallace Dunn, *Gridiron Nights* (New York, 1915), p. 3.

3 Letter from Theodore F. Koop, president of the club in 1953.

4 J. Cutler Andrews, *The North Reports the Civil War* (Pittsburgh, 1955), p. 48.

5 Mrs. Harriet Elizabeth Prescott Spofford to Manton Marble, January 17 and 27 and February 6, 1867. Marble Papers, Manuscript Division, Library of Congress. In her letters to Marble, Mrs. Spofford referred to her letters which were written over the signature of "Rustic" and "Personal" or "Percival." Her handwriting was not clear. Files of the *World* reveal nothing over those signatures although her letters to Marble refer to the fact of their having been published.

6 Francis A. Richardson, "Recollections of a Washington Correspondent," *Records of the Columbia Historical Society*, 1903, p. 36.

7 Theron C. Crawford, "The Special Correspondents at Washington," *Cosmopolitan*, January 1892, p. 356; Edna M. Colman, *White House Gossip from Andrew Johnson to Calvin Coolidge* (Garden City, 1927), pp. 195–97; Ben: Perley Poore, *Perley's Reminiscences of Sixty Years in the National Metropolis*, 2 vols. (Philadelphia, 1886), vol. 2, p. 309.

8 From a typewritten history of the club written in 1934 by Winifred Mallon and made available to the author by Miss Marie Sauer of the Washington *Post*, president of the club in 1952.

9 Letter to the author from Elisabeth May Craig, former Washington correspondent for several Maine newspapers.

10 This sketch is based on booklets, menus, and programs given to the author by Miss Katherine Brooks of the *Evening Star* in 1952.

11 Interview with Paul Wooton.

21 *Washington Correspondence and Correspondents at Midcentury*

1 Mark Ethridge, "Fateful Crisis of the Newspaper," *Nieman Reports*, October 1960, pp. 14–19.

2 Some sources on the freedom of information controversies are: James Russell Wiggins, *Freedom or Secrecy* (New York, 1956); Kent Cooper, *The Right to Know* (New York, 1956); Francis E. Rourke, *Secrecy and Publicity; Dilemmas of Democracy* (Baltimore, 1961); Clark Mollenhoff, *Washington Cover-Up* (New York, 1962); and Harold L. Cross, *The People's Right to Know* (New York, 1953); as well as James Reston, *The Artillery of the Press* (New York, 1967); and Douglass Cater, *The Fourth Branch of Government* (Boston, 1959), and *Power in Washington* (New York, 1964)—both of which latter books have been cited previously. See also the annual reports of the Freedom of Information Committees of the American Society of Newspaper Editors and Sigma Delta Chi.

[3] James Reston, *Sketches in the Sand* (New York, 1967), p. 182.

[4] Gordon Eliot White, "The Story's Out," *Editor and Publisher*, May 14, 1960, p. 15.

[5] Unless otherwise cited, this discussion is drawn from David Wise and Thomas B. Ross, *The U-2 Affair* (New York, 1962).

[6] Ibid., p. 84.

[7] Ibid., p. 108.

[8] Neal D. Houghton, "The Cuban Invasion of 1961 and the U.S. Press, in Retrospect," *Journalism Quarterly*, summer 1965, pp. 422–32; Dom Bonafede, "The Press in the Cuban Fiasco," *Nieman Reports*, July 1961, pp. 5–6.

[9] Pierre Salinger, *With Kennedy* (New York, 1966), p. 146.

[10] Ibid., p. 145.

[11] Ibid., p. 154.

[12] Ibid., p. 155. Arthur M. Schlesinger, Jr., *The Thousand Days* (Boston, 1965), p. 296.

[13] Elie Abel, *The Missile Crisis* (Philadelphia and New York, 1966); Salinger, *With Kennedy*; Schlesinger, *The Thousand Days*; also various contemporary newspaper and magazine articles.

[14] Salinger, *With Kennedy*, pp. 290–91.

[15] The text of Sylvester's remarks as given here was taken from Cater's *Power in Washington*, p. 13, which was in turn taken from the New York *Herald-Tribune* of November 1, 1962. The wording given in Salinger, *With Kennedy*, and some other sources differs slightly although all agree that he used the words *weapon* and *weaponry*.

[16] *Aviation Week and Space Technology*, December 17, 1962.